Motorhomes:
The Complete Guide

Motorhomes:
The Complete Guide

David and Fiona Batten-Hill

ROBERT HALE · LONDON

© David and Fiona Batten-Hill
First published in Great Britain 2009

ISBN 978-0-7090-8405-1

Robert Hale Limited
Clerkenwell House
Clerkenwell Green
London EC1R 0HT

www.halebooks.com

The right of David and Fiona Batten-Hill to be identified as
authors of this work has been asserted by them in accordance
with the Copyright, Designs and Patents Act 1988

A catalogue record for this book is available from the British Library

2 4 6 8 10 9 7 5 3 1

Printed by Kyodo Nation Printing Services Co. Ltd, Thailand

Contents

List of Illustrations

Some campsite pitches are sought after for the view, as here by Derwentwater

Introduction

Since you are reading this, you are clearly wondering about motorhomes. Whether you are thinking of hiring one, buying one or simply extracting the maximum from the one you have, you will find out everything you need to know within these pages. But before plunging headlong into the fascinating world of motorhoming, you should know at least the basics, in order to give your reading a foundation.

So what is motorhoming all about? That is what this book sets out to explain. Any writer has to work from experience, and Fiona's and mine has been gained from using motorhomes day in, day out over many years and many more miles. My wife and I have lived, cooked, eaten and slept in motorhomes, in England, Scotland, Wales, Ireland, Jersey, France, Germany, Holland and Spain. We have carried out tests for monthly magazines, on brand-new motorhomes, on as-new yearlings and on much loved, ten-year-old examples. We have photographed and written about them all, from tiny camper vans to huge American models. We have assessed products, campsites, ferries, tourist attractions and much, much more. And we have undertaken all the associated, nitty-gritty tasks, finding out about on-board systems, legal requirements at home and abroad, insurance, laws, travelling needs, summer use, winter storage and servicing. We have found the short cuts, survived the pitfalls and emerged smiling! Our groundwork is the core of your education and offers a foundation on which you can build your own experience.

Here are answers to some questions you probably did not even know you had. But do you need to become a motorhome expert to enjoy the hobby? No. All you need is the ability to enjoy the freedom that is of your own making. No suit-cases, flights or train trips. No 'Breakfast is served at 8.30 a.m. – not a minute later!', no 'Vacate the room by 11 a.m.'; no early call of 'Housekeeping' – no worries. Instead, your home is not what you make it but where you take it. You will have a different outlook each time you drive on. A tempting sort of nutshell? Read further and you will realize that this scarcely touches the surface, let alone scratching it. Please accept the warmest of welcomes, to the on-ramp of the road to freedom.

1 First Steps

What is motorhoming all about? Is it a hobby? A relaxation? An adventure? To many, it is all three – and more. And it is safe to say that to most people who engage in it, using a motorhome is the key to a kind of freedom few holiday-makers enjoy. To go hiking or mountaineering you need the right terrain, to go boating the waters must be suitable, to go gliding or flying you need the right conditions, an aircraft and the runway. A motorhome can take you to the right places and to an infinity of destinations. Motorhomers' activities are wide-ranging: at one end of the scale, they simply enjoy weekends away at a nearby campsite. At the other end, they embark on long-range tours, at home and abroad. In between are climbers, hikers, flying enthusiasts, motorcyclists, dog breeders, boat owners, balloonists and all manner of others who share a common denominator – their motorhome is their multi-role companion. Place of residence, kitchen, washroom, living room, bedroom, office, luggage carrier and retreat: all are there, rolled into one.

Given the right kind of motorhome, anyone can have this kind of freedom and many are seizing the chance eagerly. While a motorhome is often a retirement investment, more and more young families are discovering what it can offer them. Some couples and families use a small motorhome that can be taken into town or parked outside a shopping centre; the vehicle becomes practically a second, or even a first, car. Others use a larger motorhome frequently all year round – it becomes a haven nearly every weekend. Still others choose the biggest motorhome, for long-term tours. Some even live in a motorhome full time. It is all about choice. There are some rules that need to be applied but they are there for your own safety and convenience, rather than being applied by petty individuals for ill-conceived, irrelevant reasons.

To get the most from a motorhome you need to understand motorhomes. This is a question of balance. Bar-room 'experts' might dismiss motorhomes as Ford Transits with carpets, but there is obviously more to them than this. On the other hand, there are those who will swamp you with detail, much of it extraneous. Understanding what you are dealing with involves taking a middle course, to achieve a working knowledge of the vehicle and its on-board hardware. So let us start with the basic part, the base vehicle.

Beginner's Look

All motorhomes, from the smallest to the largest, have one thing in common: they are based on commercial vehicles. Some are conversions based on recognizable goods vehicles, others hide their commercial underpinnings behind bespoke bodywork. We will examine the conversion part in detail in a later chapter but for now, knowing the kind of vehicles involved will enhance your understanding.

The smaller conversions are based on the archetypal light van, which is itself often a derivative of a production car. So if you see a Peugeot Partner with a motorhome bodyshell, windows, curtains and cheerful exterior graphics, you are looking at a Micro motorhome. These conversions often squeeze a quart into a pint pot remarkably effectively, as their proud owners will verify.

Next up the scale is the panel-van conversion. In this case, a larger van is the starting point. A Ford Transit, Renault Trafic, Fiat Ducato or something similar becomes the recipient of motorhome furniture and fittings. It acquires double glazed, acrylic windows, roof ventilators, a water filler, a mains electricity socket and, inside, furniture, beds and carpets. Like Micro motorhomes, panel-van conversions are unbelievably space efficient; they include more than the unenlightened believe possible. But there is a disadvantage that can be expressed in a single word – headroom. A standard medium to large van cannot offer full standing headroom. Some motorhomers are quite happy with this but those who are not can choose one of two available options.

The first is a conversion with an elevating roof. In this the fixed roof is cut away and replaced by one that can be raised. Such roofs are sourced externally, or made by the motorhome manufacturer and give the best of both worlds. When closed, the roof hardly affects the vehicle's wind resistance and allows it to negotiate such obstacles as overhanging branches and some car-park height barriers. Elevated, the roof gives full standing headroom.

The next option is still a panel-van conversion but one with a high roof. Used for the transport of all manner of goods, from parcels to hanging garments, tall vans can be seen daily on Europe's highways. With a motorhome conversion, such a van gives standing headroom and can have tall units inside, as well as fixed head-level lockers. Unsurprisingly, conversions of this kind are among the most popular, particularly with couples. Such a vehicle, in motorhome terminology, is called a 'high top'.

The Trigano Tribute 550 is a modern panel-van conversion, the Fiat Ducato X/250

Coach Class

We now come to the kind of vehicle most people associate with the word 'motorhome', although some still mistakenly call it a camper van. It has a recognizable commercial vehicle cab, with an extension over its roof and a body made of flat panels punctuated by an entry door, windows and service mouldings; it is a coachbuilt motorhome, and comes in two kinds. The sort with a large section over the cab is simply called a coachbuilt. This section, called the luton, contains a high-level bed; whether the name stems from Luton's fame as a hat-making centre since the seventeenth century or from the commercial vehicle maker Bedford's plant there remains unclear. Motorhoming families often favour such a conversion.

This type of motorhome's sibling is the low profile. Built in basically the same way as a coachbuilt, it still has an overcab section but this does not contain a bed. Instead, the section is given over to storage space, usually incorporating lockers, cubbies or both. In some instances, a low-profile conversion is nearly as tall is its coachbuilt counterpart but some are noticeably lower.

Both coachbuilts and low profiles are built on a chassis cab. This, as its name implies, is a chassis with a recognizable cab section. The naked chassis is clad with specially made bodywork by the convertor. Often, components are shared across a number of models within a range, just the length of the vehicles differs, at least externally. Inside, the differently sized conversions have different layouts, as will become clear later. And in many conversions, the same or similar construction techniques, materials and fittings to those used in caravans are employed.

Coachbuilts, low profiles and some of the other kinds of conversion sometimes share a refinement to the base chassis. This comes from a German manufacturer. The Al-Ko chassis is a replacement of all but the leading 2 metres or so of the standard chassis. Made of galvanized steel and bolted to special extensions just behind the cab, the Al-Ko chassis is lighter and lower than the standard one, partly because of the use of torsion bar rear springs instead of leaf springs. This makes the conversion noticeably less tall as well as improving the vehicle's on-road dynamic abilities and its load-carrying capacity.

You may have noticed motorhomes with a further development of this chassis. Six-wheeled models are often called twin-axle motorhomes. More correctly, they are tag-axle motorhomes. A few vehicles, twin-wheeled motorhomes, have a back-to-back pair of rear wheels and therefore have six tyres. These are built on vehicle makers' heavy-duty twin-wheeled chassis cabs. But the tag-axle Al-Ko chassis invariably follows a front-wheel-drive chassis cab. This is why you will not encounter rear-wheel drive Ford Transit conversions or any Mercedes-

A tag-axle Al-Ko chassis conversion on Fiat Ducato, ready to receive its floor panel and bodywork. The six bolts – immediately behind the cab – mark the join with the shortened original chassis rails

Benz conversions with an Al-Ko chassis. And the reason for using six wheels is not to improve the vehicle's tail end grip or its looks. The additional axle, whether it is twin or tag, increases the conversion's load-carrying capacity.

A-Team

Look around, on the road or at a campsite or motorhome show, and you will see the kind of conversion that comes next in the line-up. This breed of motorhomes hides its base vehicle under a bushel, or rather under its bodywork. It does not have a recognizable commercial vehicle's 'face'. The rear bodywork will be much the same as that of a coachbuilt or low-profile model but the cab, windscreen, doors and all points forward of the main body are built by the motorhome manufacturer. With this special, wide cab, which is always finished in the same colour as the rear bodywork, it resembles a luxury coach. This is an A-Class motorhome.

A-Class motorhomes are often regarded as the upper echelon of the available models. This is often the case but some manufacturers have recently introduced more affordable A-Class models. And smaller models, some little larger than a big panel-van conversion, are appearing in the A-Class ranges. These, aimed at the younger end of the market, are often very stylish and, importantly to some, carry no obvious association with commercial vehicles.

Behind and beneath the bodywork, A-Class motorhomes have the same base vehicles as coachbuilts and low profiles. The chassis of Fiat, Peugeot, Mercedes Benz and Ford lie beneath A-Class motorhomes and there is a small but significant difference that permits the use of tailored cab panels. Rather than using a chassis cab, A-Class motorhomes use a chassis cowl. This is essentially a chassis cab with no external panels. The floor is there, as are the bulkhead between the driver and the engine, the dash panel, the seats, the steering wheel and the pedals. However, the bonnet, front wings, grille panel, doors, windscreen and roof are absent, for obvious reasons.

Some A-Class models have an Al-Ko chassis, though this is not necessarily used to reduce the vehicle's overall height. The chassis's lower rails allow the inclusion of a double floor, which allows some service items to be positioned between the floor panels. This practice is also used in some coachbuilt models. Apart from effectively lowering the vehicle's centre of gravity, this arrangement offers easier routing of service conduits such as wiring and water pipes, as well as giving a lot of conveniently accessible storage space.

Wide Boys

The final breed of motorhome is considered top-of-the-range but not necessarily for any reason other than their size. American roads are generally big, so the overall size of US-built motorhomes should come as no surprise.

In fact, American motorhomes come in a variety of shapes and sizes. There are equivalents to European panel-van conversions, coachbuilts and A-Class models but it is the last that are most commonly seen in this country. With a few exceptions, American motorhomes can be considered as large A-Class models, but there are radical differences between their base vehicles and their construction methods and those used in Europe.

American A-Class motorhomes, rather than having a chassis cowl, have a purpose-built chassis. This often has twin rear wheels. The power unit is far more likely to burn petrol rather than diesel fuel, which reflects the relative prices, and taxation levels, of the two fuels on either side of the Atlantic. The largest of the American motorhomes are 'pusher' models, with a rear-mounted engine driving the rear wheels.

Generally speaking, American motorhomes' construction methods, though similar to European ones, pay relatively little attention to overall weight. The result is that the bodywork, furniture and fittings are extremely sturdy, if heavy.

Electrically extended side or tail sections, called slide-outs, make these big vehicles' interiors bigger still. These, and the kind of build quality associated with American motorhomes, can make them immensely luxurious.

Driving Ambitions

It is important to know which kind of vehicle can be legally driven by whom. This involves examining the Driver and Vehicle Licensing Agency's (DVLA's) tortuous regulations, but when expressed carefully, they are clear enough.

A driving test pass before 1 January 1997 carries a bonus. With such a pass, you automatically received Category C1 + E entitlement. Your Category B car licence permits you to drive vehicles up to a maximum authorized mass (MAM) of 3,500 kg, or 3.5 tonnes. However, a Category C1 licence permits you to drive vehicles up to 7,500 kg and tow a trailer up to 750 kg in weight. If you want to tow a heavier trailer, you need your Category C1 + E. This lets you tow a trailer over 750 kg, provided the gross train weight – the combined weight of the towing vehicle, the trailer and its load – is no more than 8.25 tonnes. Motorhome manufacturers offer a large number of sub-3.5-tonne models, so Category B licence holders have a range of vehicles to choose from.

If you passed your driving test after 1 January 1997 you have no automatic C1 entitlement. So, you can drive a motorhome weighing up to 3.5 tonnes and tow a trailer weighing up to 750 kg laden. To drive a heavier vehicle (and tow a heavier trailer), you must pass the appropriate Driving Standards Agency (DSA) test and meet the European Council Directive's medical standards. You have to renew your licence every five years after you reach forty-five years of age and annually after sixty-five. All renewals need supporting medical evidence.

When you reach the age of 70, your C1 entitlement is removed. You can apply to renew it by obtaining a medical examination report form D4, available from the DVLA, via its website or from one of its local offices. Having examined you, your GP has to complete the form. There is a fee for this. The DVLA does not pay this fee but will pay for any subsequent medical examinations, should they prove necessary.

With a Category B licence you can drive a 3.5-tonne vehicle but nothing heavier. You can also tow a trailer weighing up to 750 kg laden, provided that the motorhome and trailer together weigh less than 3.5 tonnes and that the trailer weighs less than the motorhome. While you could add a '+E' category to your existing licence so that you can tow something heavier, this seems rather restrictive. With Category B + E, you can tow a trailer weighing over 750 kg with a 3.5 tonne motorhome, whereas if you were to upgrade to a

An Adria Twin tries to out-illuminate the Norwich Union York Wheel

Category C1 + E licence you could tow a trailer over 750 kg with a motorhome up to 7.5 tonnes, provided the combination of the two weights is less than 12 tonnes.

Enhancing your driving licence obviously entails going back to driving school, along with people who need the higher categories to legally drive professionally. The information that follows is correct at the time of writing and it contains current fees and timescales based on an average pupil's progress.

The first part is common to all licence categories beyond Category B. You need provisional status for the category or categories you require. To acquire this, you must have two documents, completed and ready to send to the DVLA. The first is the D4 medical examination report form referred to; your GP must examine you and fill in the relevant parts of the form. The second is an application form D2, which you fill in and send to the DVLA.

Once you have a provisional licence for the relevant category or categories, you can approach a DSA-approved school that offers training for these categories. There are two theoretical tests, which you must pass before the practical training begins. One is the Theory Test, which consists of sixty multiple-choice questions – you have to get fifty-one of them right to pass. The second is the Hazard Perception Test. This is rather like a computer game, in which you must react correctly to the virtual hazards contained in nineteen film clips. The test is scored not only on how many of the hazards you spot but on how quickly you react to them; to pass, you must score at least fifty out of seventy-five.

A Category C1 licence lets you drive a vehicle weighing up to 7.5 tonnes, and tow a 750-kg trailer, load included. For any category, the driving school is likely to give you a pre-training assessment in the relevant kind of vehicle. For Category C1 training, this might be a non-articulated lorry weighing around 8 tonnes. The assessment lasts for an hour and costs £40.00 + VAT. After the assessment comes the training. This takes three days on average and the DSA C1 driving test is on the third day. The training costs £596.00 + VAT and the test costs £89.00 inclusive.

Should you want to tow a loaded trailer weighing more than 750 kg, you need an addition to your Category C1 licence. To achieve C1 + E status, which lets you tow a 'rig' – motorhome, trailer and load – weighing up to 12 tonnes, you need further training and another driving test. If you have your Category C1, this training takes only two days and you would not need another pre-assessment. This training costs £480 + VAT and there is a further test fee of £89.00. Your Category C1 + E licence places you in the same position as a driver who passed a car test before 1 January 1997 but with a 12-tonne weight limit.

The next category is a heavy goods vehicle (HGV) licence. With this you can drive a vehicle weighing 3.5 tonnes or more. There is no general upper weight limit because this is dictated by the load ratings of the vehicle's axles. So the top limit of an eight-wheeled vehicle is around 30 tonnes. This is the kind of licence you need to drive a large American motorhome. No matter what your previous licence is, obtaining Category C status entails the same form-filling as above. You need a D4 medical examination report form and a D2 application form to have provisional Category C added to your existing licence. You also have to pass the Theory and Hazard Perception tests, after which comes the training. A pre-assessment in a larger vehicle is also required at most training schools.

This vehicle, in which you will also be taught to drive, must weigh more than 10 tonnes and have at least eight forward gears. If you start with a Category B licence, you will need an average of five days' training, with a Category C driving test on the fifth day. The training will cost £240 + VAT per day, which is a total of £1,200.00 + VAT. If you pass the £89.00 Category C driving test – and 75 per cent do so at the first attempt – you are free to drive an American motorhome weighing more than 7.5 tonnes.

If you want to tow a trailer with a car on it, behind your American model, you will need one more category to go on your Category C licence. Category C + E licences allow you to drive articulated vehicles up to 42 tonnes in weight. Your '+E' training and test can be undertaken using either a trailer with a draw-bar or an articulated lorry. On average, a Category C pupil needs two to three days' training to pass a trailer test. This costs £260.00 + VAT per day, and there is another DSA test, at £89.00 inclusive.

Finally, there is the question of the size of vehicle you may drive. In the UK, your motorhome can be up to 2.55 metres – a little over 8 ft 4 in – wide, not counting its mirrors. Lengthwise, it can be up to 12 metres – 39 ft 5 in. Driving a bigger vehicle requires you to have an HGV licence, regardless of weight.

Full Supporting Programme

There are some motorhomes that do not fall into the categories outlined here. First, there is the vehicle that everyone thinks of as a camper van. The VW Combi is the best-known motorhome base van. Using a VW Beetle floor pan, with the air-cooled flat four engine that was at its heart, Combis have covered many a mile in the hands of happy campers. Now, from the early 'split screen' model to the later 'bay window' variety, they are classics. In fact you can still buy a Combi-based camper new; they have been built in Brazil since 1948, and now they are only built there. The sole remaining Combi conversions, the Rio and the Diamond, are available from Danbury Motorcaravans of Yate, near Bristol. Later, VW went on to include a water-cooled engine and there is now a new version, the Californian.

The world of kit cars has spawned a motorhome or two. These, using donor parts from common production cars, could be assembled by anyone with a

The 'split screen' VW camper enjoys classic status these days. This one was spotted on Jersey

knowledge of mechanical procedures. One of the two best-known is the Rickman Rancher, which uses Ford Escort mechanical parts attached to a steel ladder chassis carrying a GRP body. Offered by a company known for producing modified motorcycles and associated accessories, the Rancher was a small, two-berth coachbuilt motorhome.

The Starcraft was a rival that used Ford Cortina parts, even down to the leading section of the body. Also a two-berth coachbuilt motorhome, it was unusual in that some examples had six wheels. This configuration used the Cortina's original driven live rear axle, attached with the original Ford trailing arms to the Starcraft's chassis. Where an extra pair of wheels was included, they were carried on Indespension units, the kind used on trailers. The system was arranged so that the trailing pair of wheels was lightly laden. When the vehicle took corners, the trailing wheels would reduce body roll as well as increasing the total load carrying capacity. Builders of these kits frequently used caravan or motorhome parts and practices and the results were often more than adequate.

Two motorhomes that are out of the ordinary come from outside Europe. They are American answers to the archetypal motorhome, and each involves the marriage of a 'domestic' body to a light commercial vehicle. The first is the dismountable which lives up to its name, being a roughly coachbuilt-style body that sits on a pick-up truck. In fact, these conversions are often called 'pick-ups'

A British-built fifth-wheeler that's typical of the breed. The 'caravan' part can remain on-site while you use the pick-up truck normally

or 'slide-ins' in the USA. Extendable legs allow the body to be raised, allowing the truck to be driven out from below the body and used as normal.

The second is the fifth-wheel travel trailer, and also involves a pick-up truck. In this instance, the fifth wheel is actually a strong point that sits in the truck's pick-up bed and accepts the motorhome body's towing point. This arrangement spans the gap between a dismountable and a towed caravan. The truck can again be used normally, leaving the 'caravan' part on site. The towed body can be large and luxurious, with the expected American heavy but high-quality construction. Fifth-wheelers can be seen in the UK and Europe and there is one UK company, based in Wales, that builds them.

Stepping further back in time, there are a few rarities. A motorhome version of the Reliant Fox was available, with a tiny, coachbuilt body. The Fox superseded the Reliant Kitten, itself a version of the Reliant Robin but with a fourth wheel. You will also see older Land Rovers with motorhome bodies; many were Dormobiles, converted by Martin Walters between 1958 and 1960. And there are a number of DIY conversions that started life as ambulances. As in any classic, self-built, modified or kit-built conversion, the success of the exercise is entirely down to the skill of the builder.

Before examining the various kinds of motorhome in more detail, it is worth looking at the way light commercial vehicles are made into motorhomes. If you know how a vehicle is built, you will know more about what is to be found aboard a motorhome and, just as importantly, how it gets there. As motorhome construction is broadly similar across most of the main types, we will look at just two.

Panel Games

A panel van conversion starts out as the sort of middleweight commercial van we see every day. A typical vehicle of this kind has a boxy steel body fronted by a two-door cab. The vans used as motorhome base vehicles generally have a sliding side door and a pair of rear doors. Front-wheel drive is the norm nowadays, which leaves the maximum amount of space. But there are elements that might surprise you.

Modern base vehicles invariably have intercooled turbodiesel engines. These are transversely mounted, four-cylinder engines whose fuel is delivered by an electronically controlled fuel injection system. A four-, five- or six-speed gearbox shares the engine bay and, where an automatic gearbox option is available, this will be servo controlled with a clutch and gear selector mechanism. This kind of transmission will do the gear changing for you, also offering some measure of manual control. It is generally tougher, more efficient and more frugal on fuel than the kind of fluid-based automatic gearbox you may have encountered in the past.

In and around the cab will be items you may not expect to find. In a typical motorhome cab, the steering wheel is ultimately attached to a power steering rack; most are proportional, i.e. the greater the turn, the more the power assistance. Underfoot you will find a pedal controlling a servo-assisted braking system. In front, whether the vehicle is manual or automatic, you will encounter a floor-mounted or more probably a stubby, dash-mounted gearchange lever. Before you will be an instrument binnacle, with at least some information conveyed by an LCD panel. There will be a driver's airbag; there may be a passenger's one or it may be available as an optional extra. You will be sitting on a comfortable, supportive seat, perhaps with armrests and an adjustable lumbar support. In most panel van conversions, the cab seats can be unlocked and swivelled to face into the vehicle. Close at hand, there are likely to be controls for heated, electrically adjustable door mirrors.

Cab air conditioning is commonly included, while a heating system of impeccable efficiency is *de rigueur*. And when you switch on the ignition, warning lights indicating the presence of unseen but desirable additions are liable to illuminate. So, as well as lights telling you that the airbags, electronic control unit and handbrake are present and correct, and that the doors are closed, you could see lights telling you about the state of the anti-lock brakes and the traction control. Equally, it is reasonable to expect an on-board immobilizer, actuated by the proximity of the code transmitter-equipped ignition key. You may also find electric cab windows, electrically actuated central locking and a good radio/CD player with decent speakers. In some vans, you even get a lockable cubby in which to carry a laptop computer. In short, modern vans tend to have the equipment you would expect in a modern car, and more. Moreover, they have become increasingly car-like, to ride in and to drive. They are relatively quiet, comfortable, user-friendly and well fitted to their purpose – covering long distances efficiently while keeping their drivers and passengers relaxed, comfortable and safe.

Inside Story

To appreciate how a panel van is converted into a motorhome, you need to consider the starting point. Delivered to the convertor as a standard van, the vehicle has a huge load space. The convertor will then try to maximize the use of this space. But the load space will be subject to temperature changes, which

State of readiness: this high-top conversion has its window apertures and some insulation. The floor goes in next

A typical linear kitchen, which has everything you need to prepare tasty meals – and wash up afterwards! The microwave oven is usually an option

result in condensation and transmit the chill of the outside air while letting internal warmth dissipate. Insulation is therefore applied to the side walls and roof. What happens at floor level depends on the conversion but it is usual for the base vehicle's floor, which is normally ribbed, to be converted with a flat wooden floor panel, cut to fit the space precisely. In the vehicle pictured on page 28, the floor is made of plywood 10 mm thick. The inside is lined with Acoustitherm, a sound-deadening, insulating material of the same thickness.

A motorhome generally has a heating system, a water system, a washroom with a WC, a refrigerator, a kitchen area with a sink, at least one additional battery, electrical systems using mains voltage and 12 volts, an electrical control panel, a liquefied petroleum gas (LPG) system, a fresh-water tank, a water pump and a waste-water tank. Most of these have fittings that provide a service aperture through the van's side wall. In addition, windows and rooflights are fitted, which also require apertures. Consequently, a number of holes of varying sizes are drilled through or cut out of the original steel panels. All the windows, rooflights and external fittings are sealed into place with modern sealants, which let the convertor give at least a three-year guarantee against water ingress. And modern windows are acrylic, double-glazed bubble windows, in cassette form, with an integral frame and an opening/latching mechanism.

The van is also fitted with furniture, which is usually pre-built. This is likely to include bunk/sofa units, a kitchen unit with a hob, grill and possibly an oven, and a location for a refrigerator. There will probably be a washroom, head-level and/or low-level lockers, a wardrobe and perhaps one or more travel seats – seats with three-point, lap and diagonal seatbelts. The convertor also adds specially made cushions, often together with upholstered wall pads and document pockets. One or more tables will be included, perhaps with folding legs, or a pedestal table with a floor socket for its mounting column.

The furniture includes swivelling plinths for the cab seats, blind and flyscreen units for the windows and for those rooflights that do not already have them. To screen the cab glass at night, there are curtains or a set of blinds in cassettes. The side windows' blinds will be augmented by curtains, which may be fully lined functional ones or decorative *faux* items to soften the appearance of the van's interior. Interior lighting will also be added, in the form of recessed or aimable halogen lamps, fluorescent lights and, in some conversions, LED lights. A hob extractor or a roof vent with a reversible 12-volt extractor fan may

Part-way there ... the inner lining work is complete and the furniture and fittings are being installed. Note that the electrical work is in progress

be fitted, and sometimes a fixed ventilator is included in the roof of the wash-room.

Behind the scenes, as it were, more hardware is fitted. The fresh-water tank is usually located beneath the van's floor, as is the waste-water tank. Both might be insulated and may even have electric heaters to guard against damage from freezing in winter. Each must obviously have the means of being filled and emptied. Fresh water is replenished via a lockable external filler cap and a tap beneath the vehicle can be used to drain the water if need be. Just as in a house, the waste water is drained, from the shower, washroom basin and sink via small plugholes. In motorhome terminology, this waste water is called 'grey' water. And the water system's most important component, the water pump, must be mounted somewhere accessible and linked to the fresh water and 12-volt electrical supplies.

The WC is essentially a self-contained item, with a bowl, seat and flushing pump in the washroom and a removable cassette underneath for the waste material. In a motorhome, the chemically treated effluent is called 'black' water. The waste cassette is usually accessed via a hatch on the side of the conversion although, in some instances, there may be a hatch fitted into a panel just inside the rear doors. The heating system is also self-contained but must have an inlet, an exhaust, a gas supply, possibly a mains electricity supply and several outlets within the vehicle for the warm air the system provides. The convertor must incorporate a mains/12-volt transformer/battery charger unit.

The LPG may be in a fixed, underfloor gas tank but, more commonly, a gas locker, housing a pressure regulator and fittings for one or more gas cylinders, is installed. Such a locker has to be sealed but must also have floor vents to let out any leaking gas. Finally, gas lines, fitted with marked shut-off valves, are led to feed the items that use LPG. Similarly, 230-volt and 12-volt electricity cabling runs to and from the items that need or distribute electrical power.

As you can see, fitting all this equipment into even a fairly large base van requires a certain amount of skill. And extras such as an electric step, a TV aerial, a flat screen television or a reversing camera will require further expertise.

With panel van conversions, it is usual to retain the base vehicle manufacturer's paintwork. Equally, it is common to 'colour-key' exterior fitments, so the outer housings of, say, an awning, the cab mirrors and, in some cases, the various external fittings of the interior hardware, are painted in the same colour as the base van's bodywork. Further decoration is added, in the form of exterior graphics. Contrastingly coloured self-adhesive panels designed to enhance the looks of the conversion join bespoke badges that leave the onlooker in no doubt about the name of the convertor and the model of conversion concerned.

The result. The L-lounge's seating forms part of a double bed and the washroom is in the tail

So making a light commercial vehicle into a motorhome requires a considerable amount of work and a substantial number of pre-bought and convertor-built components. As well as fitting these, the convertor has to ensure that they work. Trained personnel are able to verify the safety and correctness of the electrical and gas installations. Sometimes qualified people are employed in-house, though inspection by an independent specialist may be needed before the necessary certificates can be issued. It is accepted practice for motorhome manufacturers to provide across-the-board warranties, covering the base vehicle and all elements of the conversion.

Coach Approach

This description also applies to coachbuilt motorhomes to some extent. Elements such as paintwork, interior equipment and trim, exterior service points, windows and vents are fitted in much the same way as to a panel van. But the construction of a coachbuilt motorhome differs markedly from that of a panel van conversion, and to understand the differences, we must once again go back to basics.

Let us start with a chassis cab. As its name implies, this is a cab unit, complete with an engine and gearbox, dash, steering wheel, pedals, seats, a windscreen, doors and so on. But from the B-pillars – the parts that the doors close onto – backwards, the chassis is naked. Behind the cab is the unclad ladder chassis, so the rear axle is visible, as is the propeller shaft if the chassis cab has rear-wheel drive. The exhaust system, whether it has a side or rear exit, can also be seen, as can the rear axle, handbrake cable, brake pipes, suspension components, etc.

Recently, great strides have been made in new chassis cabs built by Fiat and Peugeot, making them better for motorhome manufacturers. These vehicles' cabs have a truncated roof panel and no rear wall, saving the motorhome manufacturer from having to cut them away as used to be necessary. Motorhome-friendly electrical wiring components, a lower chassis profile and a wider back axle have also been introduced, together with a range of superior engines and six-speed gearboxes.

The making of a coachbuilt motorhome often begins with the mounting of a floor panel on the chassis cab. Some manufacturers then build the majority of the furniture onto the floor panel, before adding the body. One manufacturer works in a slightly different way, building the furniture into the body before lowering it into place on the chassis cab. But what is important is the construction of the body.

Standard Fiat Ducato chassis cabs, waiting to be made into motorhomes. Note that the cabs have temporary rear panel/roof sections

The material used is a special type of board that usually consists of three skins bonded together. The inner skin is a thin layer of plywood. Next comes a thick layer of polystyrene foam, clad in a thin aluminium skin. A number of manufacturers offer an outer skin that has a glossy glass reinforced plastic (GRP) surface, which is tougher and more scratch-resistant than painted aluminium. The composition of the material means that this is known as 'sandwich construction'. Of course, the exclusive use of a flat material would make for a very 'boxy' bodyshell. Relatively recently, manufacturers have therefore wholeheartedly embraced (GRP) moulding techniques. As a result, motorhomes now have curvaceous panels on their corners, roofs and tails, and for the transition panels – those that join together the cab and the bodywork. The side skirts and tail panels that form the lower edges of the new body might be in GRP, ABS (Acrylonitrile Butadiene Styrene) plastics or aluminium. But as in panel van conversions, the use of colour-keying, contrasting colours and special graphic treatments makes the whole both coherent and attractive. Some manufacturers favour a one-piece, moulded GRP bodyshell. Such a body is unarguably tough and, having no panel-to-panel joints, is less likely to develop damaging water leaks.

Of course, the luton – the section over the cab – is an important part of a coach-built motorhome. Whether it accommodates a set of storage lockers or an overcab bed, it has to fit the existing cab precisely. Like the rest of the bodyshell, the luton's joins to its neighbouring panels can be bonded and sealed with reliable compounds; again, lengthy guarantees against water ingress are given in most cases.

A largish 'luton', the location for an overcab bed in a coachbuilt motorhome

It is not unusual to see similarities in the bodies of a manufacturer's range of motorhomes. While coachbuilt bodies are not exactly built by the metre, tail panels, overcab mouldings and other elements can be shared across the range. The same goes for interior furnishings and fitments, cushions, beds and trim schemes.

The interiors of coachbuilt motorhomes differ from those of panel van conversions. The latter must accommodate factors such as the profile of the base van's bodywork and the height of the roof, which are obviously fixed. In coachbuilt bodies the height of the roof, the width of the body and, within reason, the positions of the windows, door and those fitments that penetrate the walls can be decided by the manufacturer. The internal layout can therefore be tailored more or less at will. However, as in a panel-van conversion, a coach-built motorhome's interior is custom-built. Lightweight materials are favoured and most manufacturers can produce attractive, curved panels in materials that can seem unbelievably light. Motorhomes can have all mod cons, a comfortable interior with beech-sprung beds and plenty of storage space, and still have enough load-bearing capacity for the vehicle to carry its owners, the essential onboard equipment, water, gas *and* the owners' clothing, food and assorted goods and chattels. This is testimony to the manufacturers' ability to address the challenge of specification versus weight.

Generally speaking, a coachbuilt motorhome has more interior space and fewer limiting factors than a converted panel van. This gives manufacturers the freedom to offer a greater variety of layouts and incorporate a number of features that would be hard, though not impossible, to accommodate in a panel van conversion. So, layouts can incorporate a fixed bed, a caravan-like 'U-lounge', bunk beds or twin beds. An L-shaped seat, a half-dinette with a travel seat, a full, Pullman-style dinette with two facing bench seats, or a pair of facing side sofas can become a forward bed. There can be underbed lockers, with or without external access doors, and in 'garage' models, a huge locker can be included beneath a transverse tail bed. In one instance at least, this bed can be raised, so the 'garage' can accommodate bicycles or a scooter. The possibilities are not endless but they are not too drastically limited either.

The size and configuration of coachbuilt motorhomes leads to certain common factors in their interior fittings. Often, the washroom incorporates a separate shower cubicle that can be closed off from the WC and basin by a domestic-style shower screen. Mounting the fresh-water tank beneath the trailing seat of the dinette is common; apart from being much bigger than an underslung water tank, an inboard one can be expected not to freeze in cold weather. The heating system tends to be bigger, and more powerful, and have a greater number of warm-air outlets. And it has to be said that, for the most part, the equipment is more easily accessed for servicing.

Bed making for beginners:
assembling a forward bed usually
entails a lot of cushion-hunting

Other elements within these larger vehicles can include a bigger and more comprehensively equipped kitchen, a larger refrigerator or a fridge/freezer and a bigger wardrobe. Some vehicles have a small, domestic-style cooker, often with one electric hotplate to go with its three gas burners, and some have a microwave oven. Some also have a separate, completely private 'master bedroom'. All have a vast amount of storage space, especially as their more angular bodyshell allows more and larger head-level lockers to be installed. But where the cabs are concerned, coachbuilt motorhomes differ little from their smaller counterparts. Chassis cabs generally use the same cab units as panel vans, so the equipment is the same.

As I have said, low-profile, full-height coachbuilt and A-Class motorhomes are very similar as regards their construction and interior appointments. The building methods and materials used can vary to a degree, as can the overall quality of construction, and factors such as these are generally reflected in the price. But overall, motorhomes are built in a generally similar way, to accepted standards.

In the construction of a coachbuilt motorhome, the floor is fitted directly to the chassis cab. Note the chassis extensions under the tail

2 A Matter of Choice

Choosing a motorhome can be fun but ensuring that you get the right one for your needs takes some care. You need to know the types of motorhome available and what each offers. A motorhome represents a substantial investment, but avoiding problems is easy enough, provided you have the knowledge to make an informed choice.

Before examining the available options, it is worth looking at the mistakes buyers – especially first-timers – tend to make. First-time buyers often crave an American motorhome. After all, what could be better than a huge, luxurious wheeled mansion, in which you can live on a full-time basis? Of course this is no good if you cannot master driving it. Attempting to pilot a large, left-hand drive US A-Class motorhome on narrow country roads can end in tears, not to mention damage. This is why many American motorhome dealers offer driving tuition to their customers.

Choosing a less ambitious vehicle makes sense but care is still needed. In the coachbuilt sector, the range of available models is huge. Which do you want? A full-height coachbuilt? A tag-axled model? A low profile? The one you choose is ultimately up to you but basic factors need to be taken into account. Petrol or diesel power is perhaps an easy choice; the popularity of the latter may help you make your decision. The number of berths you need is also relatively easy to decide upon. Similarly, the choice between, say, a garage model and a rear lounge conversion is easy. The trap into which first-timers fall concerns the layout. Coachbuilts come in a variety of lengths and offer a huge variety of internal layouts. Look at any dealer's forecourt and you will see a number of nearly new motorhomes with minimal mileage. They are often trade-ins because someone chose a layout they could not live with.

The first-time buyer needs to take the time to make an informed decision. Whether you have an idea of the type of conversion you want or you are starting from scratch, the following information will help you make an informed decision. Armed with this information, the search for your ideal vehicle is simpler and quicker.

An English van abroad – the Marquis Mirage 6000U New Life in Northern Spain

Panel-van Conversions

The panel-van conversion makes a good starting point in more than one sense. Its simplicity makes it easy to understand, and for many people this makes it the ideal first motorhome.

The obvious example is the Combi, the VW camper. Beloved of many, hippies and surfers among them, it has a well-deserved place in popular history. With a simple, practically unburstable engine driving a proven chassis surmounted by a workmanlike, 'boxy' bodyshell, it was compact enough to go practically anywhere. Parts could be sourced more or less worldwide, repairs were comparatively easy and it gained a reputation for soldiering on regardless. Simplicity was the conversions' theme, with interior appointments generally consisting of a bed, some lockers and a sink.

Although you can buy a new Combi camper, many are cherished classics with prices to match. And there are pretenders to this particular crown. Panel-van conversions of this kind are based on standard, light commercial vehicles with a normal roof, as opposed to the taller vans which are often used for carrying large but light loads. The type of van concerned here is called a fixed-roof camper.

Fixed-roof conversions have many of the elements described in Chapter 1. You can expect to find a side sofa that can be pulled out and laid flat for sleeping. This, a 'rock and roll bed', has a cantilever mechanism that lets the sofa's base and backrest form the basis of a double bed. Alternatively, a side sofa will have a set of boards, or a pull-out bed base, on which the sofa's back can be laid to form a bed. The kitchen area, basically a linear unit with a flat top and lockers below, will probably house a small sink and a simple, two-burner gas hob, perhaps with an integral grill. An onboard water reservoir and a pump will supply the sink.

The heating system may be gas-fired or could use the same fuel as the engine and while it will provide warm air circulated by a 12-volt, fan-driven system of vents, water heating may not be offered. Like any modern conversion, one like this will have a second battery, interior lighting, roof vents, blinds and curtains. While a small refrigerator might be included, a coolbox-style refrigeration device is more likely. Where a WC is included, space dictates that a small chemical toilet is housed in a special locker, to be pulled out for use and for emptying. A mains electricity system, capable of transforming mains voltage to run 12-volt lighting and charge the batteries, will also offer one or more 230-volt sockets. A small, pedestal table is likely, as is locker space with racking for plates and cups and a cutlery drawer. Add a suitably ventilated LPG gas locker, or possibly a fixed gas tank, and the conversion is just about summed up.

Danbury Motorcaravan's duo on Fiat Doblo. Campers don't come much
more compact than this

The main advantage of the fixed-roof camper is a function of its size. Though base vehicles vary in size, one converted to a camper is no larger than its commercial equivalent. Smaller conversions, such as the Danbury Dynamic, based on the Fiat Doblo, are essentially large cars you can sleep in. Bigger fixed-roof campers are still car-like in that they can cope with less restrictive car-park height barriers, while tight situations and modern traffic leave their drivers unruffled. The keyword is usability. You can, with a little care, use a fixed-roof camper as a second, or even first, car. The disadvantage is the roofline that helps make them so usable; standing headroom is not available.

Rising Stars

Motorhome makers addressed this problem with their usual proficiency. The simple solution was to make it possible to create standing headroom with the vehicle at rest, by adding a roof section that could be raised. Early attempts included all manner of ingenious solutions to the problem of making a folding roof waterproof. Some had an intricate array of folding side panels, others had flexible fabric side sections and many had extending 'concertina' sections. These worked with varying degrees of success, but as with most mechanisms, modern materials and techniques have wrought significant improvements.

Rising-roof campers combine headroom with on-road usability

These vehicles are called 'rising-roof' or 'elevatory roof' campers although the less formal name 'pop-top' is often used. As with fixed-roof campers, a panel van is the basis of a rising-roof model. The current practice is for the convertor to cut away the van's steel roof, usually removing a rectangular section just inside the line of the vehicle's roof gutters and trim the roof's stiffening ribs. A pre-made frame, usually of welded tube section steel, is attached to the inner skin of the remaining edges of the roof panel. Then the rising roof is fitted. This is a specially made, moulded GRP item, tailored to the base vehicle. Modern rising roofs tend to be high-quality, double-skinned mouldings whose exterior, usually finished in body colour, can be made as glossy as the base vehicle's bodywork. Whether hinged at one end or rising on cantilever struts at both ends, it has side curtains made of a waterproof fabric. This may have ventilating panels with fly-mesh inserts and can even have opening, flexible clear panels to let in light. Regardless of their method of mounting, rising roofs and their side curtains are sealed to the base vehicle using modern compounds and are unarguably waterproof. And when the roof is in its closed position, it will be held firmly in place by latches, straps or a combination of the two.

The result of this kind of conversion is a vehicle that can offer the advantages of a fixed-roof camper, without the limited headroom. Since the roof is well secured for travelling, the vehicle feels much like its fixed roof counterpart when driven. The stiffening effect of the original roof panel is replicated in the new roof's frame and, with the possible exception of a small amount of wind noise at speed, the vehicle is just as quiet as it was originally. Like their fixed-roof counterparts, rising-roof campers tend to be car-like to drive. As with fixed-roof campers, many height barriers present no obstruction and most out-of-town car parks can be used.

Unsurprisingly, the interiors of rising-roof campers are much like those of fixed-roof models, including the linear kitchen, chemical WC, coolbox-style refrigerator, heating system, dedicated gas locker, fresh water, a 12-volt power supply and the ability to use a 230-volt input to charge the batteries and power the on-board electrical systems. The addition of a rising roof provides no additional interior space when the roof is closed, so the conversion's character is the same as that of a fixed-roof camper. But erecting the rising roof gives not only headroom but also a significant amount of additional interior space. On site, the vehicle can feel remarkably spacious and airy.

As rising-roof campers have been so well developed since the days of the old conversions with solid-sided roofs or flexible 'squeezebox' side curtains, they offer a quite practical solution to those who want to use their motorhome as a family car.

A high-top camper has the on-board essentials – and more – in a compact package

The Height of Luxury

Look around, in any city or on any busy motorway, and you will see examples of the archetypal 'white van'. Often, working vehicles of this kind have a tall roof. Used within their specified carrying capacity, these vans – 'high tops' – can carry more goods than their low roofline counterparts, simply because they offer more interior space by courtesy of their tall roof. Some commercial vans of this kind are fitted out with internal shelves and racking, for the carrying of tools and/or parts essential to the trade with which they are involved. Provided it is not overloaded, a high-top van can carry a surprisingly large amount of cargo.

Motorhome manufacturers have taken high-top base vans very much under their wing. In the past, many conversions included a tall, moulded GRP roof to replace the original steel roof of a standard, low-roofed panel van. Nowadays, panel van makers tend to offer high-roofed models, and motorhome manufacturers have embraced them and developed conversion materials and techniques to suit.

So what advantages does the high top offer? The obvious answer is space, but the ways in which manufacturers use this additional space are many and varied, and there is a range of high-top models that can rival coachbuilt motorhomes in terms of comfort and usability.

To best understand how, we need to look at the starting point – the unconverted base vehicle. Look inside an empty, unconverted high-top panel van and it will immediately become obvious that it is cavernous. This is the convertors' raw material. As in the conversion of a low-roofed van, the convertor will begin by making holes in the side panels and roof for double-glazed, acrylic 'bubble' windows and roof vents, and to allow for the addition of a mains electric input, the fitting of a chemical WC service door and the inclusion of a fresh-water filling point, an air inlet and heat outlet panels and exhausts for a refrigerator and a heating system. The convertor will add a fresh-water tank, either under the van or, in some cases, inside it, and often a waste-water tank is fitted beneath the floor.

The convertor will then add internal panelling to insulate the painted steel walls and floor of the van. This stage often includes linings for the inner walls of the insulating material. These, the visible internal panels, vary from wood-effect wall sections to fabric-faced roof and wall lining panels.

The next stage involves the fitment of furniture and further hardware. This is where the high-top base vehicle's main advantage becomes obvious. As the roof is a fixed part of the bodyshell, the internal furniture can run from floor to roof. Since there is full standing headroom, a full-height washroom can be

A motorhome's windows are called 'double glazed' but they actually have two skins of a moulded acrylic material. They're also called 'bubble windows' for obvious reasons

included, as can a wardrobe that extends all the way to the van's roof. High-top camper vans generally have a fixed chemical WC, complete with an external service door through which the waste cassette can be removed for emptying. The additional advantage of a tall, fixed roof becomes obvious from the configuration of a high top's upper storage lockers. These can be fitted at head level, occupying space that cannot be used in a fixed or rising-roof conversion. So a full-width overcab locker can be added, giving more than enough storage space for bedding, for example. Lockers can be fitted above the kitchen, over a dinette or above a side sofa or pair of sofas that become part of a large double bed.

The high top's substantial interior space is also used to the full in the siting of low-level lockers. Though the base vehicle's floor space may be the equivalent of that in a low-roofed alternative, the additional height allows greater flexibility in the placing of the internal elements. This means that high-top conversions can accommodate a variety of interior layouts. The basis is generally a van with a sliding side door and two opening rear doors but add a different wheelbase measurement and the ability to accept comparatively large pieces of interior cabinetwork and the result is flexibility. So, a high top may have two

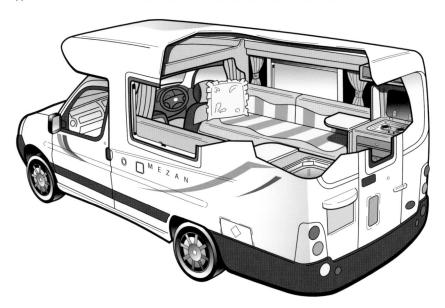

Micro motorhomes bridge the gap between panel vans and coachbuilt models

facing side sofas that can be converted into a bed, one L-shaped side sofa that can be similarly converted, a pair of forward-facing, seatbelt-equipped travel seats that can become part of a bed or a dinette that can become a small, single berth but that still incorporates travel seats. The possibilities are many – and every one has been investigated and, if practicable, incorporated. Flexibility is the watchword as regards high-top camper vans.

Small Beginnings

Although micro motorhomes are generally smaller than the average high top, they are built in much the same way as their coachbuilt counterparts. So we have a breed of vehicle in which the conversion bodyshell is not built by the base vehicle's maker but by the motorhome manufacturer. Consequently, this kind of motorhome represents a stepping-stone between the camper van and the coachbuilt type as regards construction techniques.

They are based on base vehicles of a slightly different kind from those used for the conversions already mentioned. Instead of the larger type of commercial delivery van, micro motorhomes use vehicles that are often recognizable as car-based. With the odd exception, they would not be able to accommodate two sleeping individuals – at least not without some arrangement that increases the available interior space. Although motorhomes based on such vehicles are available with a high top or rising roof, the majority of micro motorhomes have the kind of bodyshell associated with their coachbuilt counterpart. They have a recognizable, commercial vehicle cab, on a chassis bearing a bodyshell that is wider than the cab and that extends over its roof to form an overcab section.

The construction differs from that of panel-van conversions. Some micro motorhomes have a one-piece, moulded GRP bodyshell. Others, though perhaps using GRP mouldings for their overcab, roof and tail sections, have flat wall panels of sandwich construction. As we have seen, coachbuilt motorhomes use these techniques, the latter being the most common. The main difference lies in the overall size of the vehicle.

Micro motorhomes' construction starts with a base van that retains its cab, windscreen, doors, cab floor, engine bulkhead and so on. Unlike many coachbuilt vehicles, micros rarely have the typical, flattish light van nose. Instead, they have a car-like bonnet and front wings. Aft of the cab, the base vehicle's body panels may be kept, making a part-built micro motorhome essentially akin to a pick-up truck. In these panels, the necessary apertures for the mains electricity input, the fresh-water filler point and perhaps for external access to a gas locker may be found. But the apertures for the acrylic windows, roof vents, refrigerator vents and external entry door are cut into the motorhome bodyshell. This is wider than the cab and, with the addition of the overcab section, is taller. Part of the manufacturer's skill lies in making the motorhome bodyshell marry neatly to the base vehicle's remaining bodywork.

Though micro motorhomes are compact by definition, having a bespoke bodyshell offers a major advantage. Almost without exception, coachbuilt motorhomes have vertical walls. This means that interior space is maximized.

The compromise between a small overall size and the need to include as much in the way of accommodation and services as possible, gives the designers of micro motorhomes a tricky task. That they address and undertake this so effectively is testament to their ingenuity. Generally speaking, the layout of a micro motorhome comprises two facing sofas that convert into a double bed in the waist of the bodyshell. This leaves the tail of the vehicle to accommodate a kitchen that usually consists of two facing cabinets, one topped by a sink, the other carrying a hob/grill unit. The refrigerator sits in one of these cabinets, while storage locker space and a cutlery drawer occupy the other. Head-level lockers are also used while a small chemical WC fits in a special underbed locker.

If this seems modest, remember that all this equipment is fitted, kept and used in the space available from the doors backwards in a car-sized base van. Behind the scenes, fresh water, a heating system, a second battery, an electrical system, a gas locker and its associated fittings *and* a surprising amount of storage space are provided. In the final analysis, a very creditable attempt is made at putting a quart into a pint pot.

Practicality is the micro motorhome's strong suit. When arriving at a camp-site, its owner can replenish the fresh-water tank, turn the gas on, connect a 230-volt supply and be self-sufficient in minutes. This can equally be said of many motorhomes, but the important difference lies in the vehicle's compact dimensions. Similar to those of a large car, these allow a motorhome of this kind to be a first car. Although most multi-storey car parks cannot accommodate a micro motorhome, virtually any open car park can. Add the economy of a lighter kind of base van and the ease of driving and manoeuvring so small a vehicle and the micro motorhome has much to recommend it. The disadvan-tages, as with many smaller panel-van conversions, are that two berths, or rather, a double berth, is the norm, and that when the vehicle is set up for sleep-ing, some aspects, such as front to rear access, go by the board. For a couple, however, this is a small price to pay for the micro motorhome's versatility.

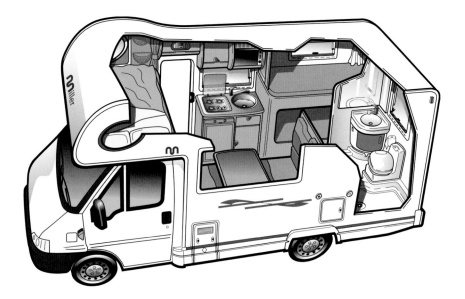

A coachbuilt motorhome is the archetypal family vehicle

Coachbuilt Choice

Mention the word 'motorhome' to anyone unused to such vehicles and the picture that will come to mind is predictable enough, a middleweight commercial vehicle with an added bodyshell that extends over the cab. This is an archetypal coachbuilt motorhome. But this mental image does coachbuilt motorhomes an injustice. These vehicles come in a variety of shapes and sizes and offer a wide range of layouts. Some are fairly compact, some approach the colossal, some larger ones have six wheels. Let us begin with an outline of this type.

The first aspect to consider is size. A motorhome is frequently referred to by its make and model but sooner or later its size, or more accurately its length, will be referred to. This will be expressed in metres. A 6-metre model (19 ft 6 in long) is thought of as being compact. By contrast, a vehicle over 7 metres long is verging on the large side. In a current listing of new vehicles, the shortest coachbuilt motorhome is 5.5 metres (18 ft long) while the longest measures exactly 8.8 metres (29 ft). Most models hover around 6.5 metres.

Width and height are the next measurements to be aware of. The width of a motorhome is the measurement across its bodyshell, and coachbuilt bodyshells are invariably wider than their cabs. Although there are some minor differences between models, the width is generally around 2.3 metres, which is a little more than 7 ft 6 in. It is worth pointing out that the width given by manufacturers is usually measured with the vehicle's cab mirrors folded, i.e. it is the minimum possible width. Height is complicated by the bodyshell configuration, but the lowest vehicle measures 2.67 metres (8 ft 9 in), and the highest is 3.35 metres (11 ft) while most are just under 3 metres (10 ft).

The weight is less visible but is tremendously important because, as we have seen, the category of licence needed to drive a motorhome depends on its weight.

Low-profile motorhomes have lockers in place of an overcab bed

Low Cunning

Traditionally, motorhome users fall into one of two groups: the family that wants a lot of berths; and younger and older users who often require a basis of two single berths, or a double bed. This has led to the increasing popularity of a new kind of motorhome. A conventional coachbuilt motorhome has a bed in the luton (the section over the cab) and to give an acceptable amount of space above the bed, this section is made higher. Couples may use the luton simply as a storage area but many do not need such a large storage space. Enter the low-profile coachbuilt motorhome.

Low-profile motorhomes vary. Some are called 'low profile' or 'low line' models but are not much lower than what we might call their full-profile equivalents. All the manufacturer has done is make the raised section of the overcab luton lower. Other models have a very low overcab section, which makes no pretence at being anything other than a storage area. Regardless of which of these configurations applies, the area over the cab is always equipped with one or more lockers, storage cubbies or a combination of the two.

The low-profile motorhome's advantages may not be immediately obvious. Losing the luton certainly gives a reduced frontal area, which means less wind resistance. Similarly, the reduced side area makes the vehicle less susceptible to crosswinds. Moreover, taking away the overcab bed, the lights that serve it, its windows and, often, its roof vent removes a considerable amount of weight from

Island beds are a fairly recent introduction to European motorhomes. The bed head is against the motorhome's rear wall here; some island beds are transverse

You have to go up in the world to access an overcab bed. The ladder is included

a place where weight is not too welcome. The clearest result is superior fuel consumption from the reduced frontal area and lessened weight. The other advantage is less evident but soon becomes apparent. Reducing the vehicle's weight in an area well above chassis level may allow more to be carried aboard the vehicle but it also lowers the centre of gravity. This reduces body roll as well as pitch and dive. Most motorhomes' suspension systems do a splendid job of controlling the bodyshell's dynamic excesses, but often the on-road behaviour of a low-profile motorhome is noticeably better than that of a similarly sized but full-height coachbuilt model.

Internal Affairs

As outlined in Chapter 1, coachbuilt motorhomes are built on a standard chassis cab, or one with the lower, lighter, Al-Ko chassis conversion. Regardless of the profile concerned, the motorhome manufacturer produces a bespoke bodyshell tailored to the chassis cab. Using sandwich construction materials and GRP mouldings, the body has vertical walls, a flat tail panel and a flat, or flattish, roof. Subject to certain constraints, the location of windows, vents, blinds and service fittings is up to the manufacturer, as are the length, width and height of the bodyshell. Manufacturers use this internal space in a variety of ways, so motorhomes can have different internal layouts, even if the bodyshells are of a similar size.

Layouts vary tremendously but there are some common factors. All motorhomes necessarily incorporate the base vehicle's cab. There may be a bed in a luton above the cab. This may be fixed, but in many models it can be raised and locked to provide headroom in the cab. In a low-profile motorhome, the overcab area will have storage facilities; often these are mounted well forward, giving a more airy feel and easier access to and from the cab seats.

What happens behind the cab varies, depending on the overall length of the motorhome. In a smaller model, the main bed may take the form of two facing sofas from which pull-out bases extend to receive the sofas' base and back cushions to become a double bed. Sometimes, the bases can be pulled out to a lesser extent, allowing the sofas to double as twin beds. In some models, a half-dinette – so-called because the cab seats swivel to face the table – stands behind the cab, opposite a single side sofa, or a linear kitchen, a wardrobe or just storage lockers. The half-dinette's rear seats are often travel seats, with seatbelts and head restraints. Larger motorhomes may have a full Pullman dinette, which has a pair of facing bench seats with a table in between. The area below the seats is a favoured location for a fresh-water tank. And where a non-dinette arrangement is used, manufacturers use one or more pedestal tables, each with a single, removable support that fits into a floor socket. Or there may be a specially designed folding table that is stored in a dedicated space when not in use. Often, in full-height coachbuilt motorhomes, a similar location is provided for the small ladder used to ascend to the overcab bed.

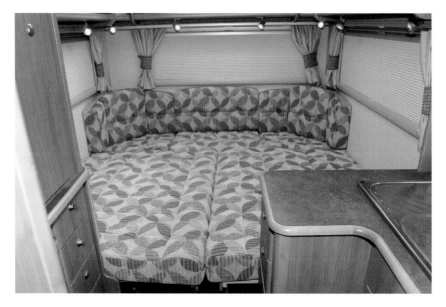

Fit for a king: A U-shaped tail lounge can be transformed into a huge double bed

This French bed's cut corner improves access to the adjacent washroom. The bed needs no assembly and provides storage space beneath. Then again, it takes up space …

Again depending on size, a motorhome can have a more ambitious lounge arrangement. Some have short, facing side sofas and some have an L-shaped type. Where the lounge is in the tail of the motorhome, a system used in caravans is often included. This is the U-lounge, which has a pair of facing sofas joined by a shorter, transverse seat with a backrest. Like the simpler facing sofas, the U-lounge's seat bases can be pulled out and the cushions arranged to make up a bed. This can be big enough to warrant the description 'King Size'.

Unsurprisingly, the conversion of seating into berths is extremely common in motorhomes. Most half-dinettes and full dinettes can be converted into beds, while L-shaped sofas, facing sofas and asymmetrical arrangements can be made up into berths, using existing cushions, attached bases or special infill boards and cushions. Some larger motorhomes have two lounges, the rear one of which can usually be screened off for privacy. And in some models, a fixed rear bed is included. This may be a transverse double bed or a full-length double bed that has a cut-off corner to allow access to an adjacent wardrobe or washroom. This is known as a 'French bed' and is commonly found in European models, although some British manufacturers offer them.

Another kind of fixed bed is a recent innovation, in European motorhomes at least: the island bed you can get in and out of on three of its four sides. Some ingenious ways of accommodating an island bed in a coachbuilt motorhome have appeared. Some models have a cutaway plinth, allowing foot room around the bed. Some have a bed that can adopt a chaise longue attitude, being raised to a reclining position at the head end by an electric motor. In most cases, an island bed offers a huge storage space beneath. Conversely, in some motorhomes, intrusions such as boxes to accommodate the base vehicle's rear wheel arches compromise accessibility by taking up floor space. Compromises such as these highlight the difficulties of fitting an island bed into a coachbuilt motorhome. The new generation base vehicles are wider than their predecessors, and so have allowed the use of island beds. The idea, however, originated in American motorhomes, where there is space to spare.

Order of Service

There is obviously more to motorhomes than seating and beds and it is relevant to discuss the service items here. Again, the dimensions and placement of these are dependent on the size of the motorhome and on its layout; there are all manner of solutions to this.

Motorhome kitchens are, by definition, not separate rooms, as their name implies. Sometimes, they are single units; often layouts dictate that some kitchen items have to be placed away from the kitchen unit itself, but it is rare for them not to be in the same general area.

The linear kitchen is the simplest kind, being a longitudinal unit, with storage lockers below and head-level lockers above. The kitchen usually has a gas hob, with two, three or four burners under a hinged glass lid. The kitchen sink tends to be mounted adjacent to the hob and is normally made of stainless steel, with a mixer tap and, again, a glass lid. In essence, it is just a miniature version of a domestic sink, and manufacturers often provide a clip-on draining board. The kitchen storage areas have such items as a wire crockery rack and a pull-out cutlery drawer with a moulded liner with compartments. Some kitchens have additional racks for mugs, paper towel holders and so on. In larger or more luxurious vehicles, there will be an over-hob extractor.

Like lounges, kitchens can be more ambitious. Larger motorhomes tend to have a domestic-style cooker, complete with a grill and oven, and a pan drawer at the foot. Sometimes, these cookers feature a low-wattage electric hotplate, as well as gas burners. Motorhome refrigerators can also use more than one source of power. Called 'three-way fridges', they can be powered on site by mains electricity or LPG gas. The 'three-way' name comes from the refrigerator's additional ability to maintain their internal temperature during travelling by using a 12-volt power feed from the vehicle's main electrical system. Refrigerators range from small, 60-litre items with an internal freezer compartment to tall units with three times this capacity, and a separate freezer compartment. A smaller refrigerator may be mounted in the kitchen unit but larger ones often occupy a separate stack. The same goes for separate gas-powered grill or oven/grill units. Having an ignition button and a light, these compare with domestic grills, albeit reduced in size. And if the various items are not mounted directly within the kitchen, they will be within easy reach.

There are variants of the linear kitchen. Where a forward or central seating/bed arrangement is used, a tail kitchen will be needed. This is basically a linear kitchen mounted across the rear of the vehicle. Like its longitudinal counterpart, it is likely to have a 'kitchen' window and it is rare not to have at least one light above the hob. Most smaller kitchens also have pull-out or lift-up extensions, to offer additional work space to that given by the worktop itself – such extensions are useful when the hob and sink lids need to be open.

Where space permits, there may be two facing kitchen units but in bigger motorhomes, the L-kitchen can provide a surprisingly large amount of working and storage space while remaining relatively compact. In an L-kitchen, the additional island part may be bow-fronted and can have dedicated storage for plates, cups and cutlery. Sometimes a bin is included but it has become increasingly common for the motorhome's side entry door to house an integral bin. This is naturally placed within reach of the kitchen.

Interior space also dictates the size and location of a motorhome's washroom but all coachbuilt motorhomes have a separate, private one. Accessed via a conventional door, or through a space-saving sliding door, this will have a hand basin, a tap that doubles as a showerhead, an integral shower tray and possibly a shower curtain. The WC will be a chemical unit, with an electric flush pump and a waste cassette that is accessed from outside the vehicle for emptying and for replenishing the chemical. Some washrooms include an electric extractor and all have one or more mirrors, as well as storage lockers, lighting and a heating vent.

As with kitchens, bigger motorhomes can have more luxurious, better-equipped washrooms. The room may be positioned in the waist of the vehicle, towards the front or in a corner in the tail, but additional space provides surprising levels of sophistication and usability in so small a room. In a larger washroom, you can find a completely separate shower cubicle, with its own showerhead on a riser rail, its own lighting and perhaps its own extractor. These washrooms frequently have one or more domestic-style shower screens, though modern ones often have a cylindrical shower cabinet with a curved sliding screen. Some appear at first glance to have no shower cubicle, but the wall that carries the hand basin may be hinged and able to swing out revealing a fully lined, waterproof showering area that can be curtained or screened off for use. Small, medium or large washrooms also have specially made interior furniture, incorporating lights, mirrors and storage areas. Essential items such as toilet roll

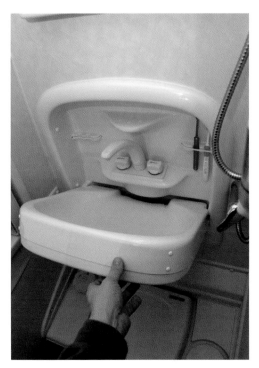

Tipping 'Pullman' basins drain when lifted. They're a space-saver because they fold flat against the wall

holders, towel hooks or rails and toothbrush and tooth-mug holders can be found, as can a frosted or blind-equipped window for privacy. Like their kitchens, motorhome washrooms are miniature versions of their domestic brethren. Although they cannot accommodate a full-length bath (nor could the on-board systems fill one), they offer all the other facilities of a domestic bathroom, in a surprisingly small space.

Storage Story

You have doubtless deduced by now that motorhome interiors attempt to emulate houses, in miniature. To do this successfully, they have to maximize the usage of the available interior space and years of development means they can do so surprisingly well.

The best way to understand a motorhome's storage facilities is to think in terms of two aspects, access and capacity. It is obvious that underbed lockers are hollow and can be used for storage. Not quite so obvious is the need to include certain service items within the lockers. The motorhome's heating system, for example, is unexpectedly compact but it must go somewhere and it is often placed under a bed. Using LPG gas, gas and mains electricity or the motorhome engine's fuel as a power source, it heats a small amount of water and distributes warmed air to the vehicle via a system of vents that emit the air using a central 12-volt blower fan. It has an air inlet and exhaust outlet as well as a water inlet facility. Some have a visible, convector heater with fan assist and all work quietly and efficiently. The convector kind of heater often has blown air heat distribution and usually stands at the foot of the wardrobe.

Though the underbed lockers' size may be slightly compromised by the presence of a heating system, they are still capacious. Many can be accessed from outside the vehicle, via a locker door let into the wall. This is convenient for storing equipment that can become wet or dirty, such as the electrical cable used to connect into a campsite's power supply, umbrellas, and other pitching gear. External doors also make for easy access to another service item, the motorhome's leisure battery – the second battery that powers the on-board 12-volt items.

There are two derivatives of external lockers that warrant special mention. Some motorhomes are equipped with a special locker, usually with GRP walls, that is designed to hold such items as skis, wet coats, wetsuits and wellington boots. This is called a 'wet locker'. So-called 'garage' models have a massive tail locker, called the garage. This can accommodate huge amounts of equipment and in some cases bicycles or a scooter. A garage is usually placed beneath a transverse tail bed. This is necessarily high mounted but in at least one case, the

The storage space in a motorhome may be enhanced with a roof box, or a tail box like this one

bed can be raised electrically, to provide enough room for a bicycle standing upright. What might be considered external lockers also accommodate LPG gas. The gas locker has to be sealed when closed and have vents to let escaping gas out safely. A further external door communicates with the underside of the WC, allowing the waste cassette to be removed for emptying. There might also be external underlockers – shallow lockers that can be used for pitching gear and the like.

The internal storage arrangements also follow common practices. Head-level lockers are placed all around lounge and dinette areas. Some have shelves as well as the locker base and many have their shelves lipped to prevent items from tumbling out when the locker door is opened. Wardrobes – and some vehicles have two – are smaller versions of their domestic namesake. They have a hanging rail, which might slide out in some models, as well as locations above and below for shoes, scarves, hats and so on. They are often illuminated.

Since motorhome interior furniture is specially designed and manufactured on a production-line basis, you will find some models with a vast array of special storage items. There are small chests of drawers whose tops unfold to become small, sturdy tables. There are ranks of drawers, internal shelves in wardrobes,

Some motorhome wardrobes have a pull-out hanging rail. This half-height wardrobe has an interior light, as do many

storage nets, storage pockets and little secret lockers. Where the use of the low-depth Al-Ko chassis permits it, motorhomes can have a double floor, with service items placed between the floors, giving additional space for more storage areas that are more secure than visible lockers. Every last cubic millimetre is used and the storage facilities are designed to keep items secure during travelling – locker doors with positive latches or strong, sprung hinges keep cargo literally behind closed doors, tie-down hooks, nets and straps within exterior lockers and garages keep your possessions under control and shelf lips and fiddle rails keep smaller items secure.

Like all motorhomes, coachbuilt models have three conjoined electrical systems. The 12-volt system is much like any other. It charges the vehicle's battery, powers the engine electrics, the lights, wipers, heater fan and so on. The only significant difference is that it also powers the motorhome's refrigerator and charges the second battery – the leisure battery. This powers the second system, the motorhome's 12-volt electrical system, which may be simple or very complex. Lighting is an obvious consumer of power but some motorhomes have heavy-duty electrical items, such as an electric step, a motor-driven awning or a reversible, roof-mounted extractor. The third system is that which distributes

Motorhome washrooms are usually a symphony in space-efficiency. There's a lot of equipment in here but the mirrors make it look far bigger than it is in reality

the 230-volt power that comes from a campsite's mains supply. This goes to a special device that is tucked away in a locker or wardrobe. The transformer charger distributes charging current to both the leisure battery and the engine battery and provides a 12-volt power feed for use by the motorhome's domestic power consumers.

While a number of these service items and furnishings appear in panel-van conversions, the average specification of a coachbuilt motorhome outstrips all but a few of the latter. One reason that coachbuilt motorhomes are so popular is the huge choice available. From a compact, sub-6-metre model up to a six-wheeler with a garage and a private rear lounge/bedroom, there is a coachbuilt motorhome to meet the needs of practically everyone. Manufacturers are increasingly wooing the younger market with sprightly, luxurious, low-profile models but still offer larger, full-height models with a berth count to satisfy even the extended family.

A Class Act

A-Class motorhomes, including some of British manufacture, look from the rear like coachbuilt models. But when the cab comes into view, one notices that they do not have a recognizable 'face'. Cognoscenti can look at an overcab-type coachbuilt motorhome and identify the cab as being the work of Fiat, Peugeot, Renault or Ford. But when the cab has a full-width windscreen and the motorhome maker's panels, only a badge gives away which base vehicle lies beneath.

From the rear of the cab backwards, an A-Class motorhome is identical to a coachbuilt model. The same methods of construction are used, the interior layouts are common to both and the onboard hardware is identical. But the cab is different, although more similar than might be thought. As mentioned in Chapter 1, A-Class motorhomes are built on a chassis cowl, rather than a chassis cab. The van manufacturer's cab floor, engine bulkhead, dash panel, chassis rails, engine, gearbox, steering, suspension, brakes and wheels remain. The same may be true of the chassis aft of the cab, although an Al-Ko chassis may be used. For this reason, you can look inside an A-Class's cab and see the dash of a Fiat Ducato, Peugeot Boxer or Ford Transit. However, special panels will surround the dash. The cab front, windscreen, cab roof, wings, bonnet and doors will be the motorhome manufacturer's work.

A-Class motorhomes tend to have an overcab bed arrangement in all but the smaller models. There is no luton and the bed does not usually hinge upwards to give headroom, which is of little consequence as A-Classes are generally fairly tall. Instead, the 'drop-down' bed does exactly what its name suggests.

A-Class motorhomes are just like coachbuilt models – from the cab backwards

Carried on sturdy, cantilever arms, often assisted by gas rams, it descends from the overcab area to rest at around chest height above the folded cab seats. Drop-down beds are double bed-sized and frequently have a set of fabric privacy screens that close off their front and side faces. These operate automatically as the bed descends, and some have further screens or blinds to close them off completely. Lights, vents and even a heated air outlet complete the comfort aspect. Virtually all have a bed access ladder.

This configuration, with the coachbuilt types of layout, makes for a very capacious interior. Once again, swivelling cab seats may be used, in conjunction with a half-dinette, or similar layouts to the other coachbuilt motorhomes can be found. Frequently, although an A-Class motorhome has the low, light Al-Ko chassis, it may still be tall. This is because double floors are often incorporated, which allows most of the service hardware to be hidden away between the two. Housed in this way, the service items do not compromise the available interior space but are protected from road dirt and debris. Equally, between-floor mounting protects the water and waste-water tanks, heating systems and pipework from damage through freezing.

'A-Class' is no misnomer. Such vehicles are often seen as being top-of-the-range among motorhomes, and many have high-quality levels of construction, materials and appointments. However, recently manufacturers have been striving to offer affordable A-Class models. The choice is consequently pretty broad.

Apart from the obvious advantages of the panoramic view from a full-width windscreen and the undeniable benefits of a drop-down bed, some customers buy an A-Class because they dislike any association with a commercial vehicle. Since there is no way an A-Class can be thought of as van-like, its configuration offers an ideal solution.

A reduction in size among A-Class ranges is another recent development. Motorhomes of this kind are available in a variety of sizes, from fairly compact two- to four-berth models to impressively large, six-wheeled, extended family versions. But still smaller two-berth models have appeared. Although these do not offer a drop-down bed, they have the accoutrements of a small coachbuilt motorhome, without the 'white van' image. Aimed at younger customers, some such models may have a quite powerful engine available as an optional extra. They offer all the advantages of a smaller vehicle: ease of driving, manoeuvrability, the ability to be parked more easily and, of course, superior dynamic qualities.

In many respects, A-Class motorhomes are just as versatile as their coachbuilt equivalents. In essence, they are coachbuilt, from nose to tail. More importantly, they are available in a range of sizes, with a range of layouts. These include the accepted front and rear lounge layouts, as well as longitudinal and transverse beds, U-lounges and island beds.

Transatlantic Travellers

Our final category of motorhomes provides the utmost in comfort, to the extent that many can outclass even a well-equipped family home. They tend to have every last accessory and can be lived in for extended periods. Some people use them full-time. They are all left-hand drive, have automatic transmission and are built with scant regard for weight saving. In the USA, any kind of motorhome is called an RV, a recreational vehicle. To everyone in the UK and Europe, they are American motorhomes.

Not all are the massive, coach-style type, however. There are 'day vans' (although these actually have beds), there are coachbuilt motorhomes and there are A-Class models, but American terminology and construction practices are as different from European ones as the vehicles themselves are. And before even considering a motorhome from the USA, it is important to understand which kind is which.

Let us start with what we call camper vans, those vehicles that are based on panel vans and have a fixed or rising roof, or a high top. In America, such vehicles bear the generic title 'B-Class'. An American coachbuilt motorhome, regardless of profile, is called a C-Class and the various sizes of luxury coach-like vehicles are A-Class. This may not sound so far removed from European terms, but there are important differences.

In conjunction with swivelling cab seats, a half-dinette maximizes the use of space.
The table extension swings out after having been unlocked

Wide open ... space. The interior of an American A-Class –
better than some houses

American B-Class vehicles equate to European camper vans in the sense that, stripped of their motorhome conversions, they would be middleweight delivery vehicles. However, they are bigger than the medium-sized commercial vehicles we encounter. There is also most likely to be a big, petrol burning V8 engine under the bonnet, with an automatic transmission.

American coachbuilt motorhomes, that is, C-Class models, resemble their European equivalents in looks but differ markedly in terms of size and weight. Some of the bigger models tip the scales at 6 tonnes and the largest currently available C-Class is 11.28 metres (37 ft) long (the Gulf Stream Super Nova).

American A-Class motorhomes start smaller than this, at 8.26 metres (27 ft 1 in) (the Winnebago Sightseer 26P 2-slide). And the largest is a whopping 12.41 metres (40 ft 8 in) long, 2.54 metres (8 ft 4 in) wide and 3.74 metres (12 ft 3 in) high (the Winnebago Vectra 40FD 4-slide). This sleeps only four and has a maximum weight of 15,600 kg.

High, Wide and Handsome…

The oft-confirmed characteristic that everything in America is bigger applies here. The base vehicles used for B-Class motorhomes are usually from Ford, Dodge or Chevrolet. In current listings, the engine sizes range from 6 to 6.8 litres, some of the former being V10 engines. Every one is a petrol engine. With one exception, a comparatively modest, 7.26-metre motorhome based on a 2.7-litre, diesel-powered Mercedes-Benz Sprinter chassis cab, all the C-Class models listed have a 6- or 6.8-litre engine; only two run on diesel fuel. All are Ford or Chevrolet based.

Rather than using a chassis cowl as a basis, American A-Class motorhomes use tailor-made lorry- or coach-type twin-wheel chassis. Again using a big engine – the smallest is a 5.9-litre turbo diesel, the biggest an 8.8-litre with the same fuel and forced induction – they always have automatic transmission. And 'pusher' models, like some European passenger coaches, have rear-mounted engines, which makes for quieter progress, as the engine is a long way behind the cab.

US A-Class motorhomes have a high-mounted single-skin plywood floor panel with underslung lockers. Younger examples have 'pass-through' lockers, which run transversely across the vehicle, between the chassis and the floor. This space is also used to house service hardware and the pipe runs associated with it. Then there is a framework made of welded, square section alloy tubing, which carries the bodywork. Further frames, made of 1½ in-square alloy tubing, are used to support the vehicle's exterior walls and its internal furniture. On many American motorhomes, the walls themselves are made of a vacuum-bonded sandwich construction material with a plywood inner skin, a polystyrene foam

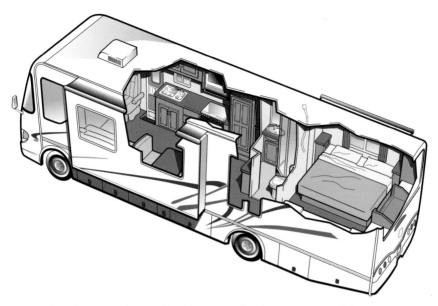

American motorhomes, like this one, tend to be seen as top of the range

interior and a GRP outer skin. Front and rear 'caps' – moulded GRP nose and tail panels – and a moulded roof panel that is domed to encourage rainwater to run off complete the bodywork. The thickness and quality of the bodywork materials add weight but most models also have sealed-unit double glazing. The use of toughened glass, rather than moulded acrylic material, for the windows underlines the fact that lightweight construction is low on a US motorhome maker's agenda.

American motorhome interiors tend to be built on a simple principle: not what can be left out but what can be included. Even the more modestly sized models have carrying capacity to burn and the interior furniture and fittings are consequently impressive. Aiming for domestic quality as well as domestic size, manufacturers fit big sofas, massive beds, huge lockers and solidly built furniture. The service hardware is on a matching scale. You can therefore expect to see a gigantic fridge freezer, a domestic-sized gas cooker, a microwave oven and more. Two roof-mounted electric air-conditioning units are normal, as is powerful, blown air heating and a water boiler with a 6-gallon capacity – three times that of the average European motorhome's boiler capacity.

The archetypal US motorhome washroom would put many a British domestic bathroom to shame. There is no bath, of course, but there will be a ceramic, rather than moulded plastic, WC and a full-sized shower with a toughened glass screen. Elsewhere, you could find a dishwasher, a washing machine and a tumble dryer. The fresh- and waste-water tanks are of an appropriate size.

The 'office' of an American A-Class, complete with reversing camera monitor and audio entertainment

The space for such equipment and for the large, comfortable furnishings and fittings is often enhanced by a clever piece of equipment known as a 'slide-out'. This is a section of wall with top and side shrouds; most accommodate a sofa or bed. At the touch of a button, the entire slide-out extends sideways, taking the sofa or bed with it, and adding greatly to the interior space. While one slide-out is common, many US motorhomes, C-Classes included, have two. And some A-Class models have up to four. Each slide-out has an automatic roll-out awning and electro-hydraulic floor jacks, used to level and support the vehicle when on-site, to prevent it tipping on its suspension and to give a solid base on which to walk.

These are impressive specifications so it is small wonder that many new motorhomers would like to go American. US vehicles certainly suit those seeking a luxury lifestyle on wheels. But there are three important disadvantages. First, American motorhomes are fit for American roads. They are fine on British and European motorways and dual carriageways but on minor roads they can be a handful at best; at worst, there are places where they simply cannot be taken.

The second factor is thirst. Diesel-powered models remain comparatively rare and, for example, a 6.5-litre, turbocharged diesel V8 will give only 14–16 mpg. A fuel-injected petrol-powered V8 can be expected to give about 10–12 mpg.

A slide-out, slid out. The unit, from the vertical strip in the foreground to the mirrored wardrobe at the rear, moves outwards electrically, to enhance the interior space

The common practice of converting petrol engines to run on LPG offers a less costly option, as this fuel is far less heavily taxed than petrol and diesel. But it is also less efficient – about 8–10 mpg.

The third factor is UK licensing laws. Many American A-Class motorhomes weigh more than 7.5 tonnes. This means that to drive one, you need a Category C licence, which means undergoing costly training and meeting a rigorous medical standard. Passing the relevant DSA test and repeatedly proving you meet the medical requirements can be expensive.

On the other hand, an American motorhome offers a level of luxury unparalleled among its UK and European rivals. Large enough and sufficiently luxurious to put a whole new slant on camping, it can accommodate users from a couple up to a large family. They have their limitations but when it comes to a sybaritic lifestyle on site, they are hard to beat.

American Excess

Since American motorhomes of any size are so often seen as ideal starter vehicles, it'd be wise to look at them in a little more detail. Why would it be wise? Because as in any field of human endeavour, knowing more about what you are dealing with will help.

American vehicles' electrical systems are designed for their own electrical supply, which runs at 110 volts. Dealers modify the system to suit use in the UK and Europe. Mains-powered items, including air conditioners, the refrigerator and microwave oven, require 110 volts but the remainder of the system can be converted to a 240-volt input. So light bulbs are changed and the two-pin electric sockets are changed to the standard UK three-pin type. To cater for the remaining 110-volt equipment, a transformer unit that steps 230 volts down to 110 volts is fitted. It is also common for American motorhomes to have a fixed onboard generator.

Another possible problem is that in the USA it is illegal to change a motorhome's wheel by the roadside. For this reason, an imported American motorhome will only have a spare wheel if a former owner or the dealer has added one. You could use the levelling jacks to lift all four wheels off the ground but you would be unlikely to get far with changing a wheel yourself, because it will be big and very heavy. So you would need a commercial breakdown outfit, such as that operated by the National Farmers' Union, to come out and help you. In fact, it is a good idea to carry not a spare wheel but a spare tyre – your breakdown company would be able to fit it for you at the side of the road.

American motorhomes can be so big that the term 'garage' is not a misnomer. In European motorhomes, this term describes a large locker, big enough to accept, say, a couple of bicycles or a scooter. But the American Gulf Stream Gladiator, for example, has an 11-ft garage – that is big enough to easily accommodate a Smart car. You can have an electric lifting ramp or drive-up ramps to ease loading and unloading.

In principle, using an American motorhome on a campsite is no different from using any other vehicle. However, many campsites have a range of different-sized pitches and all will ask you for the length of your motorhome in metres. Always assuming the access roads to the site can cope with a big US vehicle, you will be given one of the larger pitches. Driving on to the site and pitching are much the same as with a smaller motorhome, apart from the bigger American motorhome's automatic self-levelling jacks. These electrically powered, hydraulic items are used to level the motorhome but they can often lift it so its wheels are completely off the ground. On many sites, and especially on grass pitches, it is a good idea to place load-spreading blocks beneath the jacks before lowering them. Moreover, the 230- to 110-volt transformers used in American motorhomes are polarity sensitive, so the on-site electrical system's polarity must be checked and a reverse-wired adaptor may prove essential. Running generators, even the 'whisper quiet' kind, may not be allowed on site, or the times they can be run may be limited.

American vehicles' use of a site's outdoor amenities differs from European motorhomes' use only in terms of scale. In a large American A-Class

Chausson make a range of family motorhomes. The 5.76-metre Flash 02
has a Ford Transit base vehicle

motorhome, a fresh-water capacity of 60 gallons, with 40 gallons of grey-water capacity, is not unusual. This means that filling and draining the water systems, which is done in exactly the same way as in a European motorhome, simply takes longer. The good news, however, is that these tasks need not be done as frequently. When it comes to LPG, big American models have a fixed gas tank, refillable at an Autogas station. This is probably fortuitous as, in place of the European norm of 18 litres or so of LPG, US vehicles can carry 80 litres – exchanging the equivalent amount of LPG in cylinders would be hard work!

Unlike their European cousins, which have a fixed waste-water tank and a portable chemical toilet waste cassette, American motorhomes have a full on-board waste system. Two fixed tanks, one for grey water and one for black water, share a common outlet. This system is designed to be emptied into a special ground drain, but such drains are few and far between in the UK. A compromise is therefore necessary. American black-waste systems can be used with European WC chemicals added. Such systems do not have to be emptied as frequently as with European motorhomes. In fact, with an American C-Class model – the equivalent of a European coachbuilt motorhome – with a 30-gallon waste capacity, or an A-Class's 50-gallon capacity, draining down on-site may not even be necessary. If the need arises, most campsites can arrange for a manhole cover over a ground foul drain to be opened to permit drainage of both black and grey waste. And if all else fails, you could use a caravan-style, wheeled water container to ferry waste to a conventional drain point – although this would be a lengthy task!

Finally, a word of warning. According to one importer, some people have been tempted to go to the USA, buy a new or used motorhome there and ship it back to Britain. Quite a few have found themselves with their purchase stranded on a dockside in America because they had not reckoned with the cost of shipping it back to Britain. These costs include the shipping itself, which depends on the size of the vehicle, insurance and the various duties, VAT included. The various charges can add up to almost the same as the cost of the motorhome. Even if you could bring the vehicle home, the cost of modifying it for use in the UK and Europe could double the original purchase price. Given that you still would not have any form of warranty or support in the UK, the idea of self-importation may not seem so attractive after all.

3 Choosing and Buying

The Basics

Now that you are aware of the different kinds of motorhome that are available, you can choose the one that will best suit your needs. Just as you must build a house on a good foundation, so you must build your motorhome-buying decisions on thorough planning. Unless you are very rich, a motorhome is likely to be the second biggest purchase you will make. Being a homeowner will give you some inkling of what is involved in buying something costly, but a simple rule applies to all: buy in haste and you will have ample time to repent at leisure. Take your time at all stages.

Before you consider what to buy, you should first consider the use to which you want to put your motorhome. Is it to be a second car or a holiday-only vehicle? If it is to fulfil the former role, will it be compact enough to fit where you have to take it? Equally, if it is to be the latter, will it fit where you intend to keep it, or will you have to factor in secure storage when it is not in use? The value of such questions becomes immediately apparent when you start looking seriously at potential choices. But let us start by considering some questions that are still more basic.

The term 'motorhome' has two elements and the 'motor' part is just as important as the 'home' part. The first thing to consider is simply this: will you be able to drive the vehicle you desire? Modern vans are easy to drive but they are still big. Drivers can find that the experience of driving even a compact motorhome can be daunting. Practice makes perfect, of course, but often, first-timers buy a motorhome that, because of its size, proves tricky to handle. Be realistic. Moreover, you need to consider what you are *qualified* to drive.

You also need to do some research. You can use the various specialist magazines to get a feel for motorhoming, while reading their comprehensive vehicle tests to discover what elements warrant attention and to read expert opinions on particular vehicles. Then there are the advertisements;

A Mobilvetta P81 Top Driver in a top location in Cumbria

motorhome manufacturers advertise in the specialist press. Studying readers' letters and road tests will enable you to see past the gloss and discover what a given vehicle is really like. You can also use magazines to give you up-to-date contact information, so that you can order a few brochures and look into the detailed specifications of motorhomes.

The Internet is another immensely valuable tool for researching your choices. You can usually download motorhome brochures from websites, ask questions by e-mail and find out just about every last detail about the vehicles that tempt you.

Your Ideal Motorhome

Now for the detailed questions to which you need answers. The list below can be modified to suit your particular circumstances. Use the information in the previous chapter and that in magazines, on the Internet and in brochures and so on to help decide which type of vehicle you really want.

1. **What is your budget?** Establish this early on, so that you do not waste time and effort on researching vehicles with significantly higher or lower prices. Do not set too rigid a figure, however – deals can be made.

2. **Do you want a particular make or model?** Tests in magazines, information in brochures and on websites, and owners' recommendations will guide you towards making a shortlist.

3. **Which layout do you want?** Too many buyers choose the wrong layout and have to change, losing heavily as a result. Hire a vehicle first, to experience a layout in action. Study vehicles at shows, on dealers' forecourts, in magazines and on the web, being ruthless in ruling out unsuitable choices.

4. **How big should it be?** Will it go where you want to take it? Will you be happy taking it there? Have you the space to park it at home? Need you budget for storage? These are important questions that need answers.

5. **What accommodation do you need?** How many berths do you need? Do you want a fixed bed? Are you and other users agile enough to climb in and out of an overcab bed? Do you need additional travel seats, and if so how many?

6. **What facilities do you want?** Do you need an on-board shower? Do you need a big washroom? Is an oven/grill essential? Do you want a microwave oven? How many mouths will you need to feed? Will the fridge/freezer be big enough? Do you want gas, gas/electric or diesel-fired heating? Is wardrobe space essential? Altering an existing design, even if it is possible, is very costly.

7. **What options should it have?** Do you want a TV? If so, from where can a TV be viewed? Is a powered aerial booster included? Do you want satellite navigation, a reversing camera, reverse beepers, docking lights, a radio/CD player, extra speakers, a roof extractor? There are numerous special deals, show deals, included extras and cost options. Show displays, brochures, magazine adverts and the web will tell you about them.

8. **What base vehicle do you want?** Do you prefer a particular make? Do you want automatic transmission? Will the standard engine be powerful enough? How much fuel will the vehicle use? Do you want airbags? Will the vehicle be reliable? What warranty is offered? Are parts available for an older vehicle? What about servicing? And is the dealer network adequate? Does it cover Europe? All of this information and more is available.

9. **What special requirements do you have?** Do you need a vehicle that is easy to enter? Do you want to fit a cycle/scooter/motorcycle rack? Will you want to tow a trailer or small car? Will the vehicle accept a roof box or tail box? Will it carry what you want to take? Do you want a 'wet locker'?

10. **What is the real cost?** Obtaining precise information here is essential. Get exact figures – and exactly what they buy. This not only includes the vehicle and its various options. Apart from the obvious costs, what about insurance and breakdown cover, bedding, pots and pans? Go into the buying process with both eyes open!

Cycle racks adorn many a
motorhome's tail. This twin rack
and two bikes weigh very little

The Eyes Have It

There is no substitute for examining motorhomes in the flesh, as it were.
Happily, there are plenty of opportunities to see all manner of vehicles. The key
is to remember that just because the vehicle you are looking at is on sale, there
is no obligation to buy it. Applying this dictum can demand a considerable
amount of willpower, but remember what I have said about buying in haste.

So where do you look?

Showtime!

A motorhome show makes for an absorbing day out and offers much that is of
value, especially to first-time buyers. Every show's content can be split into
distinct sections, each useful in its own right.

Motorhome dealers, aware of the value of the shows, put a lot of effort into
their displays. Potential customers are generally free to climb aboard the vehicles
and study them in detail. Motorhome manufacturers, who are in competition

What's up, dock? A Fiat Ducato-based Timberland Freedom II
goes sunseeking in Whitby

and want to show off their wares to the best advantage, offer the same facilities. Both dealers and manufacturers will have a stock of brochures for you to bring away and there will be staff on hand to answer questions; do not be afraid to ask. Smaller dealerships may not be able to put quite so much into their roadshows but they still tend to display a large number of motorhomes; often these are used models. It is common for the dealerships to offer stocklists with prices, as well as printed matter detailing the various deals on offer.

Manufacturers of the hardware used with motorhomes also turn out in force at the shows. Some products, such as heating systems and refrigerators, may be of more interest to those who already own a motorhome than to those wanting to buy one, but seeing the range of extras can be useful. You will encounter just about every product associated with motorhoming, from flatscreen TVs to equipment for use at a campsite. Once again, a little brochure-collecting never goes amiss, even if you have some experience of motorhomes. The same goes for those support industries that offer a service rather than a product, such as finance, insurance, breakdown cover and motorhome hire. And the smaller concerns' stalls will give a valuable insight into products such as crockery, cutlery, guide books and maps.

Of all the people to be found at a show, arguably the most valuable to a newcomer are the club members. There are two main clubs for motorhome users, caravanners and campers, and some members attend all a season's shows to meet their fellow enthusiasts and exchange information. Information from club members and any other motorhome owners is immensely useful both to buyers and to motorhome enthusiasts in general. Such people are invariably friendly and communicative. They have already done what you are planning, so they can advise you. There are of course those to whom a particular model is the only choice, but others will have owned a variety of makes, models, shapes and sizes. There is just one word of warning. Occasionally, a deal or service that follows it can go awry. If you encounter someone who is bitter about such an experience, be aware that not everyone's experience is necessarily the same. A damning report warrants investigation and finding someone else who has experience of that situation should not be too difficult. Of course, if you find two or more stories coinciding, take notice.

Talking Shop

In addition to the shows, there are showrooms up and down the country. Many dealerships also have an accessory shop, a café and a children's play area. All have experienced staff and most have an after-sales facility.

A visit to a dealership, particularly a big one, can be a day out in itself. It is easy to be dazzled by the vehicles, the chrome and glass, the plush carpets and the pictures of motorhomes taken in stunning locations. The secret of handling

Massed motorhomes on a dealer's forecourt. A good few were pristine, low-mileage examples

your visit is simple enough: look at the motorhomes, accept the information and advice offered by the staff, but never forget that the choice of what to buy – or indeed whether to buy at all – is yours alone.

Keeping this in mind, you can gain a lot from visiting dealerships. Few motorhome manufacturers sell directly to the public so, like shows, dealerships are a showplace for new motorhomes. Some dealers specialize in particular makes or types of vehicle while others sell models across the range. Most staff are well enough informed about motorhoming matters to advise both first-timers and seasoned motorhomers alike. And dealerships invariably deal in used vehicles as well as new ones.

Smaller dealerships may not have the same sort of displays as those holding several agencies. Such dealerships may hold one or two franchises to sell new models, others may deal only in used stock. But smaller dealerships are not any less attractive because they do not have prepossessing premises and do not run multi-page advertisements in magazines. A smaller stake does not mean a lack of experience, less tempting sales packages or poor after-sales service. Sometimes, there are advantages in dealing with a smaller, more family-orientated concern.

Classified Information

Another place that deserves attention is the classified advertisement columns of magazines, specialized vehicle sales publications and newspapers. These carry a mixture of different types of advertisement, from full-colour multi-page offerings through box ads placed by motor traders to private insertions.

The classified ads can include bargains, some advertised by non-specialist used-car dealers. This can happen when someone decides to give up the hobby and trades their motorhome in against a car. Similarly, older vehicles bought in by motorhome dealers often appear in the classifieds, as they cannot meet dealers' benchmarks of price or age.

Often, advertisements on the Internet offer a faster presentation and even a quicker turnover than an on-paper ad can muster. The major motorhome magazines' websites carry classified advertisements and there are also Internet forums and dedicated sales sites that carry such advertisements. Internet search engines have links to such sites, as do most of the motorhome forums themselves.

Hire Feelings

Motorhome shows and visits to dealerships can help you make up your mind, but spending an hour or so in and around a motorhome cannot possibly give you the sort of hands-on experience you need if you are a first-time buyer. Similarly, although a dealership might offer a test drive, fifteen minutes at the wheel will not give you more than a limited knowledge of a vehicle and its capabilities.

It therefore makes a lot of sense to hire before you buy. When hiring a motorhome, you will be taught the basics of driving it and using it. You will experience exactly how the layout suits you. You will have a taste of life at a campsite and what it is like to travel, eat, wash and sleep in a motorhome. And all this is available at a cost that is insignificant compared to that of buying a motorhome.

Many motorhome hire companies offer short breaks. Even a weekend's use of a hired motorhome will either confirm or undermine your decision to take up the hobby. You will find out about pitching, heating, lighting and all the other aspects involved.

Most motorhome hire firms are sufficiently experienced to know exactly what their customers want. Rather than offering an empty motorhome and leaving you to your own devices, the concern will incorporate extras in its holiday package. Most companies include a kettle, plates, dishes, cutlery and even some washing-up liquid! Bedding will be offered, as will washroom consumables like soap and shampoo and the chemicals for the WC. Less palpable aspects also tend to be taken care of, such as secure parking or transport to and from the nearest main railway station. And packages include vehicle breakdown insurance and usually a telephone helpline in case of unforeseen circumstances.

Many hire companies also offer a try-before-you-buy arrangement, often in conjunction with a sister motorhome dealership. So if you decide to buy the kind of motorhome you hired, or even one with a different specification, the company will reimburse the hire charge.

A brief search of magazine advertisements, the Internet and/or Yellow Pages will track down a hire company. As is the case when looking at vehicles for sale, comparing hire costs is worthwhile. And do not forget to compare the cost of your time away with the real cost of buying your own motorhome. Doing this will put matters into perspective.

Best Buys

Motorhomes are made both throughout Europe and in the USA. The question that frequently arises is, quite simply, which one is the best? This spawns a counter question: what is your definition of 'best'? The central point of this is more about which motorhome is best for a given task, rather than which is the best per se.

With motorhomes, as with anything else, you get what you pay for. However, the bigger the manufacturer, the more efficient the production methods, which

This Dethleffs Globetrotter Esprit RT6874 has a memorable colour scheme.
Motorhomes do not have to be white!

is reflected in the price. And across a particular model range, you will see shared parts, be they tail panels or internal furniture components. The same occurs across makes, with particular accessory manufacturers holding a sometimes total share of the heating, WC unit, window and ventilator markets.

As we have seen, motorhomes vary greatly in form and, to some extent, function, but it is worth noting that an entry-level model will never be anything but that, just as a top-quality motorhome will always command an appropriate price. Moreover, developments in base vehicles, materials and manufacturing methods invariably mean that newer is better. Motorhomes are big business, and big dealerships offer extensive selections of vehicles. Moreover, healthy new vehicle sales sustain an equally healthy used market. Buyers are also protected by sound trade organizations, who maintain standards so that there is little danger in buying a motorhome, nor in financing and insuring it.

New or Used?

Whether you buy a new or, to use sales speak, a 'pre-loved' motorhome simply involves balancing the pros and cons.

For a start, a new vehicle cannot have a hidden past. You will have the reassurance of warranties, on the base vehicle and on the motorhome conversion or bodyshell. Such warranties can be surprisingly comprehensive, many including an anti-water-ingress guarantee lasting some years.

Depending on circumstances, you will be able to specify options and additions and some may be included in a specially priced package. You will be able to take advantage of the dealer's experience and expertise, and you will receive help and support with various matters, including finance, insurance, breakdown cover and essential accessories. Dealers offer a thorough pre-delivery inspection and, when the vehicle is ready to be collected, will give the buyer a 'walk-through', a hands-on lesson on how the motorhome functions.

On the other hand, you must consider the cost. A new motorhome, whatever its size and basis, is not cheap. Secondly, the minute you drive a new motorhome, its value will immediately depreciate considerably. Thirdly, ensure that the price shown is the OTR, or on-the-road price – some find out too late that the costs of road tax, number plates, delivery and so on add significantly to the list price.

Used motorhomes have their supporters, often with good reason. First, the depreciation from new becomes the original owner's problem. Moreover, owners tend to look after their motorhomes, and many use their vehicle infrequently. So it is common to see models in pristine condition with a minimal mileage. Some newer ones might even have unexpired warranty coverage, sometimes on both their bodyshell and base vehicle. Any teething troubles will have occurred when the vehicle was in the hands of a previous owner.

The disadvantages of used motorhomes are many, however. While many used models have a minimal mileage, some, especially micro motorhomes and camper vans, which can be used as second cars, may have a very high mileage. Some used motorhomes, though comparatively young in years, may have belonged to people who used them full-time. Consequently, you can encounter vehicles with three-figure mileages and badly worn interiors and interior fitments. And of course not everyone treats their motorhome well.

As regards pricing, depreciation rates vary markedly between motorhomes and secondhand cars. Used motorhomes hold their price and dealers are aware of it. They can often afford to offer comprehensive warranties of their own, even when the manufacturer's warranty coverage has run out, because, by and large, they are covering a safe bet. But used motorhomes, just like used cars, can have been stolen, written off, had their mileage wound back or have finance payments owing. So a valid HPI check (HPI Ltd has been checking the histories of used motor vehicles since 1938) should be offered.

Having said all that, if you buy from a respected dealership, you can often find a used motorhome in remarkably good condition and pay a fair price for it. Used-vehicle dealers rarely pre-prepare their stock but if you spot items that need attention, the chances are that problems will be rectified before you take

Tight spot: panel-van conversions, like this Adria Twin, will go where most cars can go

over the vehicle. You can expect a fairly comprehensive package, with a new MOT certificate if necessary, new consumables such as tyres, and good advice on matters such as finance, insurance and breakdown coverage. But be aware that the older the vehicle, the more wary you should be.

Buying from a private source rather than from a dealer can present its own problems. People sell motorhomes privately for a variety of reasons. Often, buyers and sellers want to take the dealer's profit on the sale out of the loop. This is fine inasmuch as it should make for a less expensive asking price. However, sellers sometimes pitch their prices at or only a little below a dealer's price. Buying at an inflated price without receiving a warranty of any kind and probably also having to pay for an HPI check, and possibly a professional base vehicle examination, makes no economic sense at all. So even if the price looks good, it still makes sense to factor in all the costs – those checks, the vehicle's MOT status, its condition and the fact that you have no comeback of any kind against the seller. Always compare private prices with equivalent dealer prices.

Older motorhomes tend to find their way into the private market. Many dealers set an age limit of around twelve years, selling vehicles older than this that have been traded in into 'the trade'. However, the private sector is not necessarily full of problems. Sales instigated by bereavement and other personal circumstances can be advantageous to the buyer. A non-specialist dealer or a private seller who knows little about motorhomes could advertise at a low price and accept less from a buyer.

Bargain Hunt

Having read this far, you are prepared to look seriously at motorhomes you might have a realistic intention of buying. Having visited shows, dealerships or both, you will know enough to understand what you are looking for…and what you are looking at. Bear in mind the risk of letting your heart rule your head. Excitement at the thought of soon owning your dream motorhome is a totally human trait. Unfortunately, so is leaping before you have looked sufficiently well. The best advice is to remember that you can be thrilled, exultant, overjoyed and smug later on. Wait until a deal is struck before giving your emotions free rein.

One way to do this is to consider time. The saying 'time is money' is a rather inaccurate truism but time is certainly a commodity and it is yours, to manage sensibly. Pressure salesmanship is less prevalent than it used to be and most dealers are aware of its negative effects. But at any stage during choosing and buying, you have an option. If you feel pressured, if the motorhome seems in any way questionable or if there is something about the deal that does not ring true, you can always walk away. As well as your time it is, after all, your money. How you spend both is up to you.

The Auto-Trail Excel range consists of four affordable and manageable motorhomes

Examinations in Progress

Once you have made the relevant decisions, you can think of examining your vehicles of choice as looking not at 'a' motorhome but at 'the' motorhome. There is likely to be more than one 'the motorhome', but just consider each you examine as 'the one' and give it the necessary degree of attention.

It is most likely that you will start your detailed examination inside the vehicle. This is appropriate, considering that you will spend more time living in it than driving it. You will be lounging, cooking, eating, washing and sleeping inside it for what could be many weeks.

Evaluating the suitability of a motorhome's interior layout is very much a personal matter. You may have one particular favoured layout or several in mind. In either case, sitting inside the motorhome for a few minutes is not enough. Try all the seats, including the cab seats, swivelling them if they have this facility. Here, a little imagination is appropriate. Imagine, when seated at the table, that you have a meal in front of you. Imagine, when seated on a sofa, that you are going to stay there for some hours. Can you see the TV location, even if there is no TV? Would you be able to position the TV so that it can be seen from the bed? Is there a light that is well placed for reading? Somewhere to put your coffee cup?

If the vehicle has a rising roof, have the salesman show you how it works then fold and re-erect it yourself. In a high-top, try the sliding side door and make the journey from the domestic area to the cab and back. If either is awkward or difficult, it will not necessarily improve with practice.

Examine the motorhome's interior when it is set up for all possible roles. Have the salesman demonstrate the bed or beds. Are they easy to assemble? Are they big enough, comfortable enough? Too firm? Too soft? Try passing from the beds to the washroom. Is it an easy trip? Similarly, imagine yourself using the cooker and sink, imagine preparing vegetables or washing up. Is the refrigerator big enough and easy to use? Will you have enough work surface area? Can you reach the oven easily? All potential users should obviously do this. Can the children use the overcab bed? Will they trip on the way to the washroom? It might take a bit more imagination but pretend to have a shower in the washroom. Check that the washroom cabinets will hold your personal necessities. Also, try the WC's seating position. You will use it for real soon and if it is set too high or is short of elbow room, you need to know.

Open all the lockers. Check that you can access them all and, equally important, that you can get to the service equipment. Manufacturers make layouts work as painlessly as possible but their idea of easy access may differ from yours. Open and close the windows and vents one by one. Try closing the blinds and then try out the lighting.

The basis of your inspection should be that, if anything jars, that aspect will become an issue sooner or later. Some elements can be modified. For example, if the vehicle's entry door has a mechanical step and you hate it, an electric step can be fitted – at a cost. But the costs of modifications mount up and there are some aspects that cannot be modified at all. The cost of adding accessories also mounts up. You can always have an awning, a bicycle rack or a tow bar fitted, but will they be within your budget? All these facets need checking and you need to be ready to reject a vehicle that does not at least come very close to meeting your needs. If this process is time-consuming, do not worry – the sales staff are paid to be there.

Outer Limits

As with the interior, looking around the outside of the vehicle can tell you a lot about how you will get on with it during daily use. For example, motorhomes with GRP-clad sandwich construction bodywork will resist scratching far better than those with a painted aluminium exterior. Similarly, moulded GRP or alloy skirt and bumper panels are tougher than those made of ABS plastic. Even the untrained eye can spot where corners have been cut during production. And if particular fittings or exterior items seem particularly weak, they probably are.

You may be puzzled by the presence of a badge bearing the designation 'EN 1646'. This system came in around ten years ago and the designation replaced the British Standard for motorhomes. Among other elements, it covers gas, electric and drinking water installations. EN 1646 inspections are validated and policed by the National Caravan Council (NCC) and supported by the Society of Motor Manufacturers and Traders. NCC personnel inspect vehicles, ensuring that they deserve their official EN 1646 badge, which makes it a feature worth seeking on a motorhome.

Open all the external lockers' doors, for two reasons: first, to verify that they actually work and secondly, to see what is inside. You may find some surprises behind those doors. For example, you may find that the vehicle has a wet locker for outdoor clothing and equipment. You may find that the WC's waste cassette is mounted well inboard; will you be able to cope with it when it is full and therefore heavy? Other items you could find include tie-down points and cargo nets in garage models, a location for an awning handle in a low-level locker or a leisure battery

An EN 1646 badge means a motorhome meets rigorous standards of quality and safety

mounted beneath the floor of a locker. It helps to know every detail of your potential purchase.

Look out for additional accessory items included in the purchase price. A small, perhaps shrouded, box mounted high on the tail could be a reversing camera – a lens is a dead giveaway. If one is fitted, there will be a monitor screen in the cab. A less obvious row of button-like fittings at the rear could signify the presence of reversing beepers. There will be a speaker and possibly an LED display in the cab of a motorhome with beepers. While the electrical system is switched on, try any electrical accessories such as an electric step or an awning motor. And even a new motorhome could have some pre-delivery damage. If you are paying the price, the motorhome should be perfect. If it is not, any scratches, marks, dents or damaged fittings should be repaired, or at least reflected in the price.

The Wheel Truth

Sometimes, experienced motorhomers do not bother to test drive a new vehicle they intend to purchase. Those new to motorhomes do not have the benefit of experience, so a test drive is an essential part of the buying process. After all, even if its interior is gorgeous and its outside is imposing, you will not be happy with a motorhome that is unpleasant to drive.

The sales staff at motorhome dealerships are used to giving test drives so there is no need to worry, even if you have no experience of driving a motorhome. Your test drive should be long enough and cover a route sufficiently varied to let you explore the vehicle's dynamic behaviour. There really is no other way to get the feel of a motorhome – to sample the weight of steering, the sharpness of the brakes and the performance of the vehicle in the gears. Check that the all-round vision meets your expectations, make sure that the cab mirrors give an adequate rear view and, above all, try the vehicle in the sort of conditions you expect to meet. It is wise to include a short stretch of motorway in your test, as well as a few bends and some roads with traffic lights – the salesman will know the local geography. Undertaking a few simple manoeuvres, such as reversing and parking, is also important. As with the interior, these can be imaginary manoeuvres – you need not really park it or reverse it into a tight spot. And ensure that the vehicle has the fitments you want. For example, you can have cab air conditioning fitted after you buy a motorhome but doing so, whether you want the vehicle maker's system or an aftermarket one, is extremely expensive. It is better to buy a vehicle that has all your desired items in its specification.

The buying process is all about ensuring that the motorhome concerned has what you want. Establishing this may involve taking a list along but it also means having an eye for detail. You should also be prepared to cross-examine

Long story: the Lunar Roadstar 900 is a tag-axled motorhome suitable for an extended family

the salesman throughout your inspection of the motorhome. The sales staff often have the answers you need at their fingertips. If they do not, they will be happy to find them. And do not be inhibited by being inexperienced. First-time buyers are common enough to motorhome sales personnel who, just like you, had to start somewhere.

Second-hand Rows

Looking at used motorhomes involves the same considerations but there are additional aspects to consider, so hone your eye for detail. While many used motorhomes are presented in pristine condition inside and out and are effectively as new, not all will be so nearly perfect. It will be largely up to you to spot what is wrong.

As with a new motorhome, inspecting a used model starts with the interior. While you will probably still be experimenting with layouts, remember to use your eyes. Of all the problems that affect used motorhomes, water ingress is unarguably the most serious. The result is damp and, if this is present, you will smell it. If you find yourself with breathing difficulties caused by the overpowering scent of air fresheners be very suspicious. Someone could be trying to cover the unmistakable, musty odour of damp.

Not so commercial: this 'white van' is in motorhome guise, complete with awning, alloy wheels and all mod cons

As a general rule of thumb, at any point where the motorhome's bodywork has a join, water could get in if the sealing method has failed. Apart from its characteristic smell, damp shows as staining or, in extreme cases, mould. The sections inside the joins are an obvious place to look but remember that water finds the lowest level – dampness can travel. Open every locker door and look inside, preferably using a torch. The evidence of long-standing water ingress will be obvious; you will be able to see the damp stains as well as smell damp, and feel it in carpeting. Be wary of a creaky floor, which suggests that the panels underfoot are delaminating.

Many motorhome dealerships run a dampness check as a matter of course and often issue a certificate to prove it, which is helpful. But if you do encounter a motorhome with a dampness problem, walk away. Anything can be repaired if enough money is spent on it but damp kills motorhomes. It is too big a problem to ignore.

Just what you can expect in a used motorhome depends on how 'used' it is, and what you will accept depends on your requirements and your budget. But here are a few tips on what to look out for, apart from damp, and what to avoid.

In a well-used vehicle, you can obviously expect to see evidence of its use. Cushions can lose their supportiveness, curtains can fade, woodwork can become scuffed, fittings can work loose and surface finishes can become worn. You could have the curtains and cushions replaced, repair the woodwork, tighten the fittings and refinish or replace the worn items. Whether you choose to do this is up to you but ask yourself these two questions. First, is this the only motorhome of your chosen type on the market? Second, will the necessary work be done free of charge?

The aspects to consider when examining the inside of a used motorhome, particularly an older one, are fairly simple. For example, newer models usually have removable carpets, held in place with pop studs, but in older vehicles – and in some newer ones – the carpets run beneath the internal structures. Replacing thin or holed carpets means cutting out the old ones and having a removable carpet set made. This is an expensive exercise and only works if the floor under the carpets is in good shape.

When it comes to internal fixtures and fittings, loose fittings can be tightened, provided the woodwork that carries them is in good order. But if there are broken hinges and latches, would you be able to get replacements and, if so, at what cost? You need to know. The same goes for older service items. If the firm that made an older refrigerator is still in business, it is likely that spare parts will be available, but if the unit is obsolete or if its manufacturer is long gone, any significant problems spell replacement – again, a costly proposition.

Another point to look out for is do-it-yourself improvements. Some motorhomers are extremely good with their hands and are capable of making intelligent and good improvements. Conversely, there are those who can wreak havoc with their so-called handiwork. Aspects of a motorhome that's suffered repeated attacks by the 'Provisional DIY' probably will not work very well – if at all.

When assessing the exterior of a used motorhome, bear in mind that you could come across the odd battle scar. European motorhomes are built with weight saving in mind so they do not take kindly to even minor impacts, and their effects are hard to eradicate. If there is a cracked rear light lens or a split tail panel, you could make buying the vehicle dependent on a satisfactory repair. The same goes for damage to wall panels. Happily, such damage is usually no more than cosmetic but beware of any damage close to where panels meet. If the sealant is visibly cracked, there is a possible spot for water ingress so check the corresponding area inside the motorhome. Also, do not forget that damage is not restricted to eye level or below. Roadside trees and overhanging parts of buildings can assault motorhomes' upper bodywork. Take time to check the roof panel, borrowing a stepladder if necessary, to look for hidden damage. Another, less potentially serious kind of damage happens to motorhomes' acrylic windows and roadside trees are often to blame. Acrylic is a very soft material and even wiping a dirty window with a dry cloth will create a network of fine scratches. Being raked by passing tree branches can gore an acrylic window quite severely, though it takes serious abuse to actually break one. As a rule, any scratches that do not catch a fingernail can be polished away, but deeper marks are there for life. Also, prolonged exposure to the ultra-violet component of sunlight can cause windows to deteriorate. If a vehicle has one or more really bad windows, ask the salesman about replacements, or a substantial discount on the price.

Many of the riskier facets of buying a used motorhome have little to do with the conversion part or the manufacturer's bodyshell. The base vehicle may be a light commercial and therefore be capable of covering an intergalactic mileage. But a lack of mechanical sympathy, poor servicing, extended periods parked or in storage and much short journey work can take their toll.

Often, spotting a questionable base vehicle is easy. If the speedometer is nice and shiny but is not quite as shiny as the pedals, you can bet that the mileage registered is not the real total. Similarly, if the screws around the instrument binnacle are butchered, someone has removed the speedometer – perhaps to rewind the mileometer. Other clues to the kind of use the motorhome has undergone can be spotted. Detectable wear on the steering wheel's rim and on the gear lever knob suggest that they have had a great deal of use, such as happens during many short journeys in traffic. Wear in the driver's door mechanism and window are the consequences of much use, and if the driver's seat is also bursting and the seatbelt is furry, it is evidence that the vehicle has been used as a second or first car. If the motorhome has a towbar, what has it towed?

A small box trailer or motorbike trailer is fine but a big, heavy trailer can make inroads into the transmission in the form of heavy wear.

Reassurance lies in the fact that no matter how assiduously a seller has polished and valeted a motorhome, certain problems cannot be disguised. A baulky gear change, sloppy brakes, a smoky exhaust, a clattering engine and lots of slack in the transmission spell a hard life. Panel vans and the cabs of coach-built motorhomes are made of steel and can rust as much as any car body. Plastic filler and paint can be used to gloss over corrosion but a magnet will not find plastic attractive; use one during your inspections. And looking under the bonnet can tell you a lot, even if you are not mechanically minded. There may be a little corrosion on underbonnet fittings and perhaps the odd patch of missing paint. But if the engine bay is filthy, smelly and has tatty wiring and scruffy or broken plastic panels, it means previous owners have not been looking after the mechanical bits.

The good news is that there are ways of protecting yourself against all the nasty practices that go on in the world of used vehicles. An HPI certificate is one way of getting your hands on an accurate report of a vehicle's history. An HPI search unearths evidence of whether the vehicle has at some point been 'clocked', stolen, written off and rebuilt or have outstanding finance owing on it. You may have a knowledgeable friend who can help you assess used motorhomes but if you do not, professional inspections are available. The AA offers them, AIM Vehicle Inspections offers a dedicated motorhome base vehicle inspection service for motorhomes up to 3.5 tonnes gross weight, and the RAC also inspects base vehicles up to this weight and its 'Essentials Plus' service includes an HPI certificate. Whilst both HPI certification and vehicle inspection cost money, they could save you a great deal. This is especially important if they uncover something serious in the vehicle's past or its present condition.

You need only pay for your own HPI certificate when buying privately. A good dealership has to meet certain standards and must provide HPI certification by law. Most dealers carry out a damp check and also a habitation check. The latter verifies the fitness of safety-related items including both the gas and mains electricity installations. Dealer warranties can cover some unexpected elements so studying the small print is worthwhile. You will also have the chance to examine the motorhome's paperwork. This will include the registration document, on which you can verify the vehicle's date of first registration and the number of former keepers. Old MOT certificates will show whether there is a suspicious change in the mileage figure and the service record will illustrate if, when, where and by whom the vehicle has been serviced.

Some motorhome owners take great pride in their vehicles and this tends to show in the paperwork associated with it. If the document pack includes every bill, for servicing, repairs, the fitment of accessories and of consumables such as

The neat little Ace Capri, at home in Dinan

tyres and batteries, the motorhome in question is a good prospect. If, as is sometimes the case, there are also handwritten or typed notes detailing every trip the motorhome has made, down to the destinations, dates and fuel consumption measured, you are probably on to a winner. Rather than just being pre-owned, the vehicle has indeed been 'pre-loved'.

The Colour of Money

Motorhomes cost tens of thousands of pounds, so finance is often central to buying one. Finance is often seen as the best way to get a motorhome. Dealerships offer packages involving well-known finance houses such as Black Horse Ltd and the Bank of Scotland's Capital Bank plc, under the beady eye of the Financial Services Authority (FSA), the body that maintains a register of dealers and regulates the financial services they offer. Protection exists in the Financial Compensation Scheme (FCS), which is the UK's statutory fund of last resort for the customers of authorized financial service firms. Finance packages generally include payment protection policies and vehicle insurance at competitive rates. There is data protection, the right to cancel, full terms and conditions statements and a complaints procedure. In short, there is security in the small print.

Normal Service

There is no typical finance deal, but I can give an example that comes close to being typical. All such arrangements naturally differ to some extent but there are common points and the following will outline the sort of factors you can expect to encounter. But first, let us consider one point that applies to new motorhomes bought by disabled customers. If you are wheelchair-bound and the vehicle is adapted for you, say with a tail lift, or a hoist for an electric scooter, you need not pay VAT on the motorhome. To receive VAT exemption, you need to sign a form to state that you are a regular user of a wheelchair; the dealer will give you the relevant form to complete. This has to be backed up with a letter of verification from your doctor but once this paperwork has been completed, you save the VAT part of the motorhome's purchase price.

Motorhome loans tend to reflect the low rate of depreciation enjoyed by these vehicles. A ten-year agreement, with a deposit of 5 per cent of the purchase price and a fixed rate of interest, is normal. The payments are likely to reduce every eighteen months or so but loan figures can vary so it is always worth shopping around to see what is available.

Is it a good idea to pay cash if you can? Not necessarily. Depending on the figures, it may be that funding your purchase with a loan and retaining your cash makes more sense. In some instances, the compound interest on your capital could outstrip the simple interest you pay on a loan. Such investment can leave you in pocket; if necessary, you can take advice from a reliable expert.

Loan Arrangers

While the imprecation to shop around is good advice, you obviously need to know what you are shopping around for. At this point, outlining the various ways in which a motorhome purchase can be financed will add yet more power to your purchasing elbow. Let us look at the available options in more detail…

Hire Purchase

The point here is that the dealerships' financial package may not be the most advantageous and you do not have to accept it. Banks and building societies also offer loan packages. But do not think that a loan is a loan is a loan. Some deals are better than others. However, certain safeguards mean that borrowing money is not the minefield it used to be. You still have to be wary but nowadays you have a safety net.

The commonest sort of finance is an unsecured loan. You pay a deposit and the lender pays for your motorhome. Then, the lender charges you a monthly sum, so you pay back the money in instalments for the time specified in the agreement. But of course you do not just pay the cost of the motorhome. The lender charges interest, which will be shown in the agreement, and you may be surprised at the total figure involved. An unsecured loan is the type of finance usually taken out by people who do not own their home. With an unsecured loan, you are not offering the lender any collateral, so you will pay more interest than you might on other types of finance. Moreover, the upper limit on unsecured loans is relatively low. Currently, the ceiling stands at around £25,000, which is not enough to buy a new motorhome.

Of course you need to know what will happen if things go wrong. In the worst case, should you default on payment, the lender will take you to court for non-payment of your debt. This can lead to a visit from the bailiffs, who cannot take your home if you do not own it but can still seize enough property to repay the debt. If you do happen to own your home, it can be taken from you. In any event, since the lender bought the motorhome, it remains their property even though it may be registered to you and in your possession. This is a double-edged sword: if you have problems with the vehicle, the lender may help you; if you default on payment, the lender can demand that the vehicle is returned.

Another point to bear in mind is that you do not pay off the value of the motorhome in equal segments. The monthly payments may be identical but it takes time before you pay anything but interest – the capital outlay reduces later in the term of the agreement.

Another kind of finance is a secured loan. The lender can offer you a more attractive rate of interest if you offer some security. Homeowners can get a loan of this kind by offering their house as collateral. This does not mean that you must actually own your home outright. Your mortgage is what is called the first charge on your home. If you secure a loan for a motorhome against your house, the motorhome will become the 'second charge'.

Because this arrangement puts the lender in a more secure position, they can afford to lend you more. At the time if writing, loans of £50,000 – twice the ceiling of unsecured loans – are possible and some lenders will go further still. The lender can also afford to tempt you with a lower rate of interest. After all, they can seize your house if you default on payment; for this reason, it is common for the lender to arrange an assessment, to verify that your house is worth what you claim. Those who are self-employed and people who do not have a very good credit rating are likely to be able to take out a loan of this kind.

In some respects, hire purchase represents both good and bad news. The dealership from which you buy your motorhome will almost certainly be geared to provide the necessary service by acting as an intermediary for one of the finance houses. But it can be costly and some loans are costlier than others. Where a dealer is offering a highly tempting sale price for a motorhome, or is including

The Mercedes-Benz based Frankia T8400GD offers four berths and four travel seats in its coachbuilt bodyshell

a vast selection of 'included' items, you may well find the cost of both is reflected in the total cost of the loan. In this instance, you should shop around; you will find the web addresses of some loan comparison websites in the contacts list at the end of this book.

The consumer has some rights in this context. The Consumer Credit Act of 1974 demands that lenders must offer you insurance cover and access to payment protection schemes. So if you lose your job, fall ill, have an accident or die, your debt will be repaid. As with any form of insurance, the price varies so comb the fine print. Indeed, combing the fine print is a must when it comes to the credit agreement the Consumer Credit Act requires you to sign. You will have time to do this as the Act also gives you a seven-day 'cooling off period', within which you can change your mind. The snag is that the Act applies only to secured loans up to £25,000 value. When you borrow more or when your loan is unsecured, it has no relevance.

Elastic Plastic

On the face of it, using your credit card to pay for a motorhome may seem like a good idea. But do not be misled: with an existing card, the annual percentage rate (APR) of interest is likely to be ferocious. At the moment, credit card companies are seeking new clients by offering low or even zero interest rates for a fixed period to new cardholders. So if you could pay off your debt within the agreed period, credit could cost you nothing. The snag is that new cardholders tend not to be given credit limits that even approach the price of a new motorhome. However, that zero interest might come in useful in the short term, perhaps to top up another loan or to add some accessories. Just be careful that you calculate realistically – some people have come spectacularly unstuck with credit cards.

An agreed overdraft with your bank or building society is another finance option. Banks and building societies can offer overdrafts at interest rates below those of loans and you only pay interest for the days you are actually overdrawn. This sounds tempting but sailing this close to the wind financially can have its dangers. You need an intimate knowledge of the bank or building society's terms and conditions. You may discover that there is a hefty overdraft fee. And if you slip over your agreed overdraft by a few pence, you could find yourself faced with a substantial charge.

Remortgage

Remortgaging your home sounds like a good way of raising the funds for a new motorhome, since mortgages mean a small outlay over a period of time. But

The Four Winds Chateau Citation is a 'Mini' C-Class motorhome in US terminology. Mini or not, it has two slide-outs and all the expected American motorhome features

while it is all very well having low monthly repayments they are liable to go on … and on … and on … for far longer than the average motorhome loan. So how much do you pay overall? In the end analysis, it can become a case of how fast you can pay off the debt versus how much you pay in total.

A current account mortgage is an alternative to a remortgage. It is effectively an overdraft riding on the back of your existing mortgage, and it can seem a good deal because the repayments are made attractive by a low interest rate. However, do not try to con the lender into thinking that you are going to spend a lot on your house when you are actually going to use the money to buy a motorhome. The idea is to improve that which is mortgaged, i.e. your house. Some lenders might play ball if you reveal the real purpose of the current account mortgage – but if you do not, trouble looms.

Credit Check

Any lender will check your credit rating. And if you have difficulty getting a loan, the chances are there are black marks affecting your credit rating. You can also check *their* deals. There are websites at which you can compare the deals lenders are offering in the comfort of your own home, with no sales pressure whatsoever.

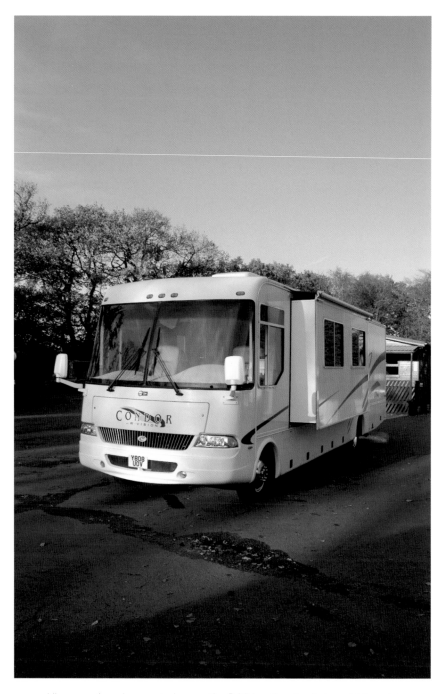

Like many American motorhomes, the R-Vision Condor features 'slide-outs'
that maximize interior space

Calling the Shots

There are any number of deals on motorhomes. There are show deals, special offers, deals including special equipment packs, end-of-season deals – you name it, there is a deal for it. These deals are there to attract buyers, and being a buyer you are in a position of power.

You want to buy a motorhome and the dealer wants you to buy it from him. To induce you to do so, the dealer will entice you with special offers, facilities, inclusions and so on. These can range from allowing you to trade your car in against a motorhome to providing a full quota of accessories, from a TV to a set of teaspoons. Such 'sweeteners' can mount up to a valuable set of acquisitions. Some motorhome manufacturers include special packs with new vehicles. These tend to consist of a set of accessories you would otherwise have to buy and fit yourself, or pay to have fitted. It may be that you do not want all of them but these packs can include useful additions such as a special CD/radio, a Freeview TV receiver, an awning, a reversing camera or a more upmarket interior trim scheme. Equally, there are some items that are essential to using a motorhome, and sometimes you can sweeten the deal further simply by asking for them. The costs of hardware such as a campsite mains cable, a water filler hose, an LPG cylinder, a spark ignition gas lighter, awning pegs, levelling blocks and the like mount up. A dealer's including items, bought in at trade price, can make the difference between a successful sale and a 'no deal'.

The dealer will be aware of what he is doing, so you also need to be aware. You can persuade the dealer to include more with the motorhome or to accept less for it – he will know when to stop. Provided you also know when to stop as you are offered optional items, services or memberships at a 'special' price, you will not go far wrong. You can always ask if you are unsure of some detail, and of course at any point you can always call a halt to the proceedings and go home to think things over.

There are some highly important matters you have to find out about, and it is a good idea to make a list of them so you can tick each off as you go. They are:

1. What is the exact price of the vehicle and what precisely does this figure buy?
2. What precisely is covered by the warranty and for how long is it covered?
3. Are there separate warranties for the base vehicle and the motorhome builder's additions?
4. Are these warranties extendable and, if so, at what cost?
5. When can the motorhome be collected?
6. Will it have been given a pre-delivery inspection (PDI) and will there be proof of this?

7. Will there be certificates covering the gas and mains electricity installations?
8. Will it have a road fund licence?
9. Will it have a new MOT certificate if required?
10. If used, will the motorhome have been valeted?
11. Will the essential documentation be provided, including a certificate of motor insurance?
12. Will a walk-through be provided on collection?

In a private sale, you cannot expect to have all this. As well as items like an HPI certificate, you will need to arrange your own insurance and possibly get road tax and perhaps organize an MOT test soon after collection. The available protection for a private purchase is, of course, minimal but there are two steps you can take to cover unfortunate eventualities. One is to ensure that the details are written down. If you leave a deposit with the seller, as is generally accepted, make sure you are given a signed receipt for your money. For collection day, draw up a simple sales agreement, with your details, the vehicle's details, including the registration number, mileage, date of first registration, MOT test status, any accessories fitted and the price you and the vendor have agreed upon. Make two copies of this agreement and make sure that both you and the vendor sign both copies, keeping one each. If you point out that the document exists to protect both the vendor and yourself, he or she should be happy to sign it. It will protect you to some extent should a dispute arise. However, a motorhome sold privately is 'sold as seen', so there is very little comeback against the seller.

Insurance

When arranging insurance cover for a motorhome, there are elements you need to understand, and this applies even if the cover is part of the dealer's sales package. Both the dealership and the specialist insurance brokers you might contact on your own account offer the same kinds of insurance policies. These are similar to private car policies but there are some important differences relating specifically to motorhomes.

Road risks insurance is an essential requirement. This sort of cover is fairly obvious – it insures against accidental damage to the vehicle, to other people and to their vehicles. And it includes cover against claims for personal, legal and property damage. Matters like fire damage or destruction and theft are catered for and it is likely the insurance cover will be fully comprehensive, with an agreed policy excess. A no-claims discount, the vehicle's value, the age of the drivers and their status and mileage-related adjustments all affect the cost of the

Motorhomes may be big but they aren't as tough as they look. This one lost an argument with a motorway barrier

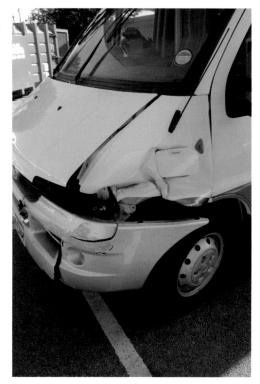

premium. The premium can usually be spread over a period of time for an additional fee and the instalments are generally paid via a direct debit arranged with your bank.

This is all standard stuff so there is little matter for concern. All you need to know is that the insurance company concerned is reputable. Should the premium seem excessive, it may be worth shopping around and there is merit in making certain that the insurer involved offers the services that are to be expected, including an accessible claims procedure and the choice of any additional specific cover you may need.

GAP Insurance

One possible addition is guaranteed asset protection (GAP) insurance. This should not be necessary but some insurance policies make it essential, at least during the early years of owning a motorhome. If your motorhome is written off, the insurance company will pay out what it believes the vehicle was worth. If that value is less than you think it should be, or even less than what you still owe on the motorhome, a GAP insurance policy will replace your motorhome on a new-for-old-basis. This should apply for at least two years from the date of purchase. So you can buy cheaper insurance, and special GAP insurance as well, but you should check which is the lesser of the two evils – a higher premium or a lower one plus GAP insurance.

Fortunately, many companies summarize the special elements in the insurance policy for you. But make sure you read the summary carefully. For example, you will probably find a key clause, which might, for example, state: 'Your policy does not cover loss of your motorcaravan, accessories or spare parts if your ignition key or card is in an unoccupied motorcaravan, unless kept in a fixed, locked safe.' So, putting your keys in a drawer or hiding them in the wardrobe will not do.

There are other aspects you might need to explore. A motorhome policy should cover the carrying and use of LPG gas, and such policies generally do. A typical policy will insure items such as a TV, a CD/radio and a satellite navigation unit, provided that the selling dealer fitted them and their value is reflected in the insured value of the motorhome. If such items were fitted elsewhere, they can be insured subject to an agreed value. In these circumstances and in a typical policy, the items are covered only up to a limit of £750 for a single object. Similarly, £2,000 worth of personal belongings insurance with £500 cover for valuables is included, the limit for a single article being £250.

Lastly, it is worth verifying that continental use insurance, or cover for use further afield, is an option.

Rescue

The final consideration at buying time is breakdown rescue. It may be provided as part of the dealer's sales package or you may have to arrange it yourself. But it is essential to stress-free travelling. If your motorhome breaks down on the road, you are not going to be able to push it, even off the carriageway. Arranging breakdown assistance with the major providers will not be a problem, but if you do this yourself, ensure that the company concerned knows what it is protecting. A provider geared to offering only private car breakdown assistance services will certainly struggle when presented with a 6-metre vehicle. Make certain the company has records of the exact size and weight of your motorhome, as well as of the vehicle it is based upon.

A typical breakdown cover arrangement includes, or will offer, help with starting the vehicle at your home. Roadside repairs are a given, as is recovering your motorhome if it cannot be fixed at the roadside. Recovery may entail transporting it to an appropriate garage or simply taking you, your passengers and your motorhome back to your home. This all sounds perfectly simple and it is but for one point. If you break down on the Continent or even further afield, you will need repatriation as part of your breakdown and/or insurance cover.

Other options worth considering at home or abroad might include an arrangement for overnight accommodation, or for a temporary replacement vehicle. Depending on circumstances, this might be another motorhome. And remember that most breakdown service providers operate using a switchboard manned 24 hours a day.

Insurance and breakdown cover can be purchased using a simple common rule. It is better to buy what you need rather than find out the hard way that you need what you have not bought.

4 Understanding Your Motorhome

When you come to use your motorhome for real, you need to know exactly what you are dealing with. This chapter takes you through all the motorhome's onboard hardware, explaining what each system or item does, how it works and how best to use it.

In an ideal world, the walk-through you are given on collection, plus the various instruction books provided with the vehicle, should make you *au fait* with the various systems and their controls. In the real world, there are reasons why this does not happen. A walk-through on collection is merely that; it is a short time in which to absorb a lot of information. Some handovers are excellent but elements can be forgotten, especially in the excitement of the moment. And even if the instruction books are all present and up to date, which is not always the case, they can vary between the highly informative and the practically impenetrable. Although some motorhome manufacturers make a creditable attempt at producing a more accessible instruction book, not all do.

I will not be able to provide information on every function of every control on every kind of item, but this chapter will explain the general principles involved, as well as how to make using your motorhome easy, comfortable and, above all, safe. It will also explain how, and why, some of the items and systems interrelate.

Liquid Asset

Before outlining the best ways to handle driving a motorhome, we can consider the on-board elements that you need to know about. In a very broad sense, the service systems in a motorhome are equivalent to those in your house. That they do not work in exactly the same way is irrelevant; what matters is that they provide what you expect, wherever you live. So, you have hot and cold water, heat, light, drainage systems and so on. The way in which motorhome systems

The American Damon Avanti is more svelte than its stablemates, making it
well suited to European use

work mimics domestic practices and we can start with the simplest element, the water system.

The first point about a motorhome's waterworks is fairly obvious. At home, you have an uninterrupted water supply, fed from a water main. Being mobile, a motorhome cannot tap into the water mains so the water supply is finite, although it can be refilled as necessary. A motorhome has one or more fresh-water tanks mounted low down in the vehicle. When mounted beneath the vehicle, they are called 'underslung' and an underslung water tank is liable to be insulated and may be provided with a low-voltage immersion or contact heater to prevent freezing and the damage it causes; heating units run from the motorhome's electrical system and are thermostatically controlled so that they only operate when the temperature of the water falls below a particular level.

Alternatively the water tank may be mounted either between the floors in a double-floored model or inside a seat or locker. Some such tanks might still be heated and all are made of a food-safe plastic. Capacities vary depending on the kind of motorhome concerned but, broadly speaking, panel-van conversions have around 60 litres minimum, while a large coachbuilt motorhome is likely to have twice this capacity. Fixed tanks of this kind are equipped with a filler point, which resembles a car's petrol cap and is lockable. A method of draining the system is also provided. Some tanks have a simple drain tap mounted low down at the side or tail of the vehicle or beneath it. Most tanks have an inspection/service hatch and some are drained by pulling out an internal plug reached via this hatch.

The water is used for a variety of purposes. The hot-water system uses this fresh water, so the tank initially fills and then replenishes the water heater. The hot and cold water taps in the shower, hand basin and sink are rarely separate nowadays. Instead, motorhomes generally have miniature versions of domestic mixer taps. These 'monobloc' taps have a hot and cold water feed and rotating the tap controls the temperature. The hot-water capacity tends to be restricted to around 10–14 litres, so the working temperature is deliberately set high so that a reasonably lengthy shower can be enjoyed. In many instances, motorhome chemical WCs have an electric flush and it is also common for the flush water reservoir to be fed from the fresh-water system. And a number of motorhomes have an exterior shower connection, which may provide hot as well as cold water.

The need to replenish the fresh water will soon get owners into two habits that help conserve it. The first is monitoring the amount left, using the control panel's display. The second is making the most of the available supply, which takes longer to learn but pays off. Not leaving a tap running is obvious, as is using a reasonable amount of water for flushing a WC that is fed from the fresh-water system. But also, when showering, one can have a 'Navy shower'. This

The Romahome R20 is a popular micro, based on the economical
1.6-litre diesel Citroën Berlingo

means running the shower for long enough to get wet, then turning it off while
soaping yourself, and turning it back on to rinse yourself. Motorhome taps
generally have a lever control, so the temperature setting can be maintained
even though the water flow is stopped.

In general, motorhome washroom fittings are simply miniature, moulded
versions of those you find in any house's bathroom. However, one item which
may cause confusion among new motorhomers is the folding basin. This clever,
compact item normally sits vertically against the washroom wall. Folding it down
reveals a usefully sized hand basin, with a tap inside – the tap may double as a
shower head that can be pulled out for use. The basin itself has a moulded-in
soap dish but there is no plughole. When folded up, it drains into a hopper at the
back, and the water passes down into the grey-water tank via a hidden pipe.

The water pump is the central item in the water system. Like many of the
service and accessory items, it runs on 12-volt electricity. The power source is
the motorhome's leisure battery but, if a mains supply is connected, it has a
transformer charger unit that runs the 12-volt electrical items. Motorhome
water pumps are either of a reciprocating or roller type and are switched on or
off at the main electrical control panel. And they are clever. When a tap is
turned on or some other part of the system demands water, the pump will either
sense that the water pressure in the system has dropped, or it will be activated
by a microswitch in a tap. The muted pulsating beat you hear when this happens

is the pump in action and when the water pressure is re-established, or when the tap is closed again, the pump stops. If the pump continues working, it usually means the fresh-water tank is empty and the pump is trying to pump air, which cannot establish the pressure essential to shutting it off. Or, if there is a drain open – the one serving the heating system is the usual culprit – the pump cannot pressurize the water system and will run on *ad infinitum*. It is perfectly simple to tell what is wrong. If the pump runs for more than a matter of seconds, check the water level indication at the control panel. If this shows there is some water in the tank, go outside and listen for the tell-tale trickle of draining water underneath the vehicle. Closing the offending valve will solve the problem but you may need to refill the water tank, as the pump may have ejected all the available supply via the open valve.

The fresh-water system is usually filled using a special hose, which is coloured blue to indicate that it is a food-grade item. Sometimes, motorhomes are equipped with a hose connector that has neighbouring electrical contacts for use with an additional, external reservoir such as a water roller. This, favoured by caravanners, is exactly what it sounds like. It looks rather like a garden roller and, when filled with water, it can be trundled back to your campsite pitch with relative ease. A water roller, or even the type of container you have to carry, can be linked into your motorhome's fresh-water system via a separate, external electric water pump. The motorhome's control panel can be programmed to draw water from the external reservoir to top up the onboard tank for the desired period of time. This effectively increases the overall fresh-water capacity, but at the cost of carrying a separate water reservoir.

Campsites have clearly labelled drinking-water taps, which makes filling a motorhome water system easy. A hose about 6 metres long, with a standard, ¾ in in BSP 'garden hose' fitting will serve for most refills. Occasionally, campsites have plain taps, rather than ¾ in BSP threaded taps, so it is worth also investing in a universal tap adaptor, the kind with a rubber socket and a hose clip with a metal 'butterfly' that lets you tighten the clip without using a screwdriver.

Some panel-van conversions and micro motorhomes have different fresh-water tanks and filling procedures. As these models are scaled down in relation to coachbuilt types, so are their water systems. In these kinds, the fresh-water tank may be a jerrycan-style plastic container. This is still a food-grade moulding with a water pick-up pipe. However, as it is relatively small, taking it rather than the whole vehicle to the fresh-water tap makes for easy replenishment.

But where does the used water go? The grey water – the water you have used for preparing food, washing and showering – goes through a miniature version of a domestic drainage system. So from the shower tray and the sink and hand basin plugholes, the water drains down. On some smaller motorhomes, it simply goes overboard via one or more drainage hoses. At a campsite this naturally

This Auto-Trail Cheyenne 632 is by Lochranza Castle, on the Isle of Arran

makes you unpopular so it is wise to take along a caravan-style reservoir, or even just a bucket, in which to collect your used water for disposal in the drain point provided. On most models, however, there is a waste-water tank that collects the grey water. On campsites, it is usual to go to a motorhome service point, where you will find the fresh-water taps and a special drain to get rid of your grey water. Often, this is a 'drive over' drain so you can position your motorhome to allow the grey water to fall straight down into the drain. Some models also have a corrugated drain hose that requires less accurate positioning of the vehicle, and most service points have a dedicated tap and water hose for you to use to rinse the area clean afterwards. Incidentally, black water – chemically treated sewage – should never be drained into a grey-water drain point.

Maintenance of fresh- and grey-water systems is minimal. If the motorhome is used regularly, the fresh water is unlikely to go brackish in the tank, but motorhome accessory shops sell water purifying tablets and special chemicals to use to freshen water tanks periodically if you are concerned. You can also fit an inline water filtration unit or use a filter jug. Otherwise, you need only remember to drain off the fresh water if the vehicle is to remain unused for a while and especially if freezing is a danger, during the vehicle's 'down time' or at any time the vehicle is unheated during cold weather.

Grey-water systems also require little in the way of maintenance, although you may notice an unpleasant smell rising from the internal plugholes. If this becomes offensive during travelling, putting the plugs into the shower tray, hand basin and sink is a quick way to deal with the problem temporarily. The more permanent solution is to use a cleaning solution available from caravan and motorhome accessory outlets. Added to a nearly empty grey-water system, this will get rid of the odour as the system is used. The smell is usually caused by food particles decomposing in the pipes and tank.

In the Black

Motorhome WCs come in three guises and one brand has the lion's share of the market: Thetford. This is a British firm that manufactures chemical WCs for motorhomes, boats and caravans. Here is how these WCs work.

Like any domestic WC, a chemical one has a bowl, a seat and a lid. Within the bowl, there is a shutter that seals off a waste tank, which is held in, or forms the lower part of, the WC. Depending on the WC, you can introduce flush water into the bowl with either a hand-operated bellows pump or a button that activates the electric flush pump. It is usual to prepare the WC for use by first putting in a little flush water, and in some WCs a special chemical is mixed with the flush water to prevent waste matter from adhering to the bowl's inner surface and the closing blade. After using the WC, you open the shutter, allowing the waste material to fall into the waste tank under gravity, then flush it again and close the shutter. The chemicals added to the holding tank work on the waste material, combating smells and aiding decomposition. When the waste tank is full – which is indicated by either a level gauge or a warning light – you have to empty it.

Smaller conversions and micro motorhomes often have the type of WC in which the waste tank is also the lower half of the unit. Larger motorhomes have the type where you can extract the waste tank – properly called the waste cassette – via a special locker door on the side or tail of the vehicle or in a special panel reached through the rear doors of some panel-van conversions. Regardless of the type of waste tank, it will be completely sealed when separated from the WC bowl assembly. Campsites have special WC chemical disposal points into which you can empty the waste before rinsing out the cassette and adding chemicals and a little water. WC chemicals are available in liquid form or in water-soluble bags and the business of emptying and repreparing a WC waste tank is not at all unpleasant. All waste tanks have a pressure-equalizing valve; when you press the button air enters the tank as you pour out the contents and prevents splashing. All separate WC cassettes have a chemical measuring cup built into the cap of their emptying spout and the latest models, those for Thetford's C250 range, even have wheels to make taking the 18-litre cassette to the disposal point easier.

Not all the small conversion-type 'half-and-half' WCs are made by Thetford but the principles remain virtually identical. Such units are often housed in a special locker and are pulled out into the vehicle to be used. Cassette-type Thetford WCs appear in two varieties. One is the bench type, and as its name implies, it is fixed against and sealed to the existing washroom walls on three sides. Down below, one end communicates with an external cassette locker's door. The seat and lid are placed centrally in the moulding, which also has a location for a toilet roll, which has a splash-proof lid, to keep the toilet roll dry when the motorhome's shower is used. A rotary control operates the electric flush pump.

The second type of unit is a swivel-bowl cassette WC. This is much more like a domestic WC, although the moulded plastic bowl assembly can be rotated through a wide arc. This allows you to position the bowl at any angle within the arc, so you can find for

Grey water goes down the drain. Those motorhomes that lack an extension hose have to be parked closer to the drain

yourself the orientation that offers the greatest amount of room and the most comfort. Compared to domestic WCs, Thetford swivel cassette WCs have a small, low bowl and seat. This does not affect their functioning, though some motorhome manufacturers tend to mount the entire unit a little too high for some. And the newest models have a bigger, swivel-bowl assembly, the seat and lid being accordingly larger.

The third type of motorhome WC is rather more sophisticated and is not too often encountered, although similar units are to be found in American motorhomes. The Dometic vacuum WC has the advantage that the waste material can be carried quite some distance, via a pipe, to a remote waste cassette. It has a large, ceramic bowl that is

Swivel service: Thetford swivel-bowl cassette WCs can be positioned for maximum comfort and space

very similar to that of a domestic WC, but the flush mechanism is operated by a small pedal mounted low down near the bowl. The other advantage of the vacuum WC is that it needs no chemicals; the remote mounting of the waste cassette, allied to a special filtration system, removes odours. Conversely, American motorhomes have a fixed holding tank that is usually used for both grey and black water. Conventional WC chemicals can be used in this tank and its capacity means that it does not often require emptying.

Electrical Energy

In our homes, we take electricity for granted. You cannot do this in a motorhome because it obviously cannot have a fixed mains electrical connection. But you can have 12-volt electrical power on demand, as well as mains electricity when you are staying at a campsite with the required 230-volt power points. Motorhomes have two interrelated electrical systems.

Low Power

Let us begin with the base vehicle's existing electrical system. This powers the electrical hardware of the vehicle, be it a panel van, chassis cab or chassis cowl. It has a battery capable of starting a cold diesel engine. The battery is charged by an engine-driven power source, the alternator. Electrical items that make heavy demands on the battery, such as lights and windscreen wipers, are kept up to speed by the alternator's charging input.

When the base vehicle is turned into a motorhome, certain additions are made to the electrical system. The 'motorhome' part has its own 12-volt wiring system, feeding its lights and other electrical items such as its warm air fan, its extractor fan, its electric step and its awning motor. The power for these comes from a second battery, the leisure battery. This differs from a vehicle battery. A vehicle battery will be called on to deliver a massive power output for a short time, when starting the engine. A leisure battery does not have to do this but it does have to provide a consistent but smaller amount of power for a long time. Because the leisure battery is frequently discharged and recharged, it also has to be efficient at maintaining its relatively low output until it is at a low level of charge. For this reason, leisure batteries are deep-cycle batteries, capable of meeting these needs. The gel battery is a relatively recent development. It uses a gel rather than a liquid electrolyte and is resistant to extremes of temperature, shock and vibration. It also tends not to suffer electrolyte evaporation, and calcium plates rather than lead ones reduce gassing. Many manufacturers are including gel batteries rather than conventional lead-acid batteries.

The base vehicle's electrical system is altered to do two things when the engine is running. First, the engine alternator's charge current, which charges the engine battery, is also used to maintain the leisure battery's level of charge. Second, the vehicle battery is used to power the 12-volt element of the three-way refrigerator. This only happens when the engine is running as, without any input from the alternator, the refrigerator would flatten the battery in a very short time. Also, the 12-volt input can only maintain the chill in the refrigerator. Mains electricity or gas power is needed to cool it down in the first place.

So can using the motorhome's electrical items flatten the vehicle battery? The answer is yes and no. Motorhome manufacturers use one of two ways to get the alternator to charge the leisure battery. The simpler way uses a device called a split-charge relay. This, as its name implies, diverts some current from the alternator to the leisure battery. In consequence, the vehicle battery does not lose charging current. The more complicated method involves a special unit, the transformer charger. We will look at this in more detail later but, among other things, it can divert some of the alternator's current to the leisure battery. Normally, power for all but the 12-volt element of the refrigerator comes only from the leisure battery and it is usual for all the motorhome's 'leisure' electrical facilities to switch off automatically when the base vehicle's engine is started. So normally, the engine battery is in no way involved in powering the motorhome's electrical items when the engine is not running. However, many motorhomes have, on their electrical control panel, a switch that lets the motorhome take power from the engine battery. This is for use when the

This tag-axle Hobby was seven years old when photographed. Motorhomers generally cherish their investments

leisure battery has become flat, so if the switch is left on for too long the vehicle battery will be flattened too.

High Power

When staying at a campsite with this provision, you can connect your motorhome up to the mains. This is done using a special cable which runs from the pitch's mains connection to a dedicated plug fitted to your motorhome. The power runs safely to the motorhome's 230-volt electrical items and to its transformer charger unit through domestic-style circuit breakers. In the event of an electrical problem, the breakers will cut the supply, either totally or in a particular circuit. As the campsite's mains supply is similarly protected, your chances of getting an electric shock are practically nil.

Mains power is used in a variety of ways. All motorhomes have at least one domestic-style mains socket. All three-way refrigerators can use 230-volt power and some motorhomes can use electric power to heat the water in their hot-water system and, in some cases, to help with their interior heating. Some have a single electric hotplate in their hob or cooker and many have one or more mains-powered lights, while the transformer charger turns 230-volts into 12-volts to charge both the motorhome's batteries at rest. Because of this, you can be certain that you will only suffer starting problems if the engine battery is faulty, or if there is some problem with the engine itself.

Current Affairs

You need to be aware of your system's capabilities, and know how not to exceed them by being too demanding.

Starting with the 12-volt system, the leisure battery has a capacity. Knowing this and performing a simple calculation will give you an idea of the leisure battery's abilities. If the leisure battery is marked 65 Ah, it means it has a 65 ampere hour capacity. So when fully charged, it will supply an electrical item that consumes one amp for 65 hours. The bald figures probably mean very little but a further simple calculation will make matters clear. An amp or ampere is a unit of current, and the calculation for finding out how much current an item needs involves dividing its power in watts into the voltage to get the current. The equation therefore:

$$\text{Current (in amps)} = \text{Power (Watts)} \div \text{Voltage (Volts)}$$

So if a motorhome's halogen lamp has a 15-watt bulb in it: 15 – the wattage of the bulb – divided by 12 – the battery's voltage – equals 1.25 – the current in amps that the bulb consumes.

Motorhome leisure batteries are usually fitted somewhere unobtrusive and are often low or no-maintenance items. This pair lives in a locker, keeping their weight low down

Now we need to divide the battery's capacity figure by the current. So for our 65 Ah battery, we divide 0.8 into 65. Sixty-five amp/hours divided by 0.8 amps equals 81.25.

So, our 65 Ah battery will run our 0.8-watt bulb for 81.25 hours. Of course, you will be making much greater demands on your leisure battery than that one bulb, but calculating these individual current consumptions, adding them together and dividing the result into your leisure battery's ampere-hour figure will give you an idea of how long you can run the 12-volt items for from a fully charged battery. However, you also have to remember that wiring has a resistance, as do switch contacts, and batteries can lose a significant amount of their capacity in cold conditions. Nevertheless, these calculations give a usable guide to the battery's staying power.

This equation also applies to the mains current's capacity. At home, we consider the mains supply to be effectively infinite. At a campsite, the incoming electrical supply is usually a 450-volt three-phase provision because it not only has to run the campsite's own electrical services but also provide electrical power to many of its pitches. Transforming the 450-volt input down to 230 volts gives campers the required level of voltage. The top-of-the-range amperage is 16 amps, but some smaller or older campsites offer 10. It can be lower: 8, 6 or even less, especially on the Continent. Power consumption is cumulative so if all the campers were to run all their electrical items at any one time, the system would become overloaded and cut itself off.

So when you use a campsite's mains hook-up, there is a limit to the amount of current you can consume at any one time. If you use too much, the circuit breaker on your pitch's mains connection will trip out and you will have no electricity. At some sites, you can simply switch the power back on but not at every one.

To figure out what you can run, use the above equation, with mains voltage this time. Take a 2,000-watt kettle for example. The current this uses is 2,000 – the wattage – divided by 230 – the number of volts, which makes 8.7 amps. But what happens if you are boiling the kettle and want to switch on your 3-kilowatt fan heater? That makes another 13 amps. This gives a total of 21.7 amps – and the power supply will trip out. So you need to tailor your use of mains electrical items to the current available. There are special low-wattage items for use on campsites and you can run most fan heaters at their low setting, which is usually 1 kilowatt.

You also have to bear in mind that onboard units such as a transformer charger and the mains element of a water heater also consume current from the campsite's supply. One answer, apart from not using heavy current users together, is to switch one off while using another. You can, for example, turn off your mains water heating unit while you boil a kettle.

The Ace Capri, pictured here at Honfleur, is a manageable motorhome

Heart of the Matter

We can now turn our attention to the units that deal with the introduction and distribution of power within the motorhome, as it is important to understand this hardware. The mechanism may be a single unit or there may be separate pieces of equipment for the low and high voltages involved. The former is the more common so let us look at it first. The transformer charger takes the incoming 230-volt power and transforms it to around 12 volts, to charge the motorhome's engine and leisure batteries. Giving a higher current than that used for charging, it also provides 12-volt power for the low-voltage equipment in the motorhome.

But if you were to leave a battery on charge for a week, its internal electrolyte would probably evaporate away; the battery would 'boil dry'. However, transformer chargers can sense the level of charge in the batteries and distribute charging current accordingly. Rather than providing power to the motorhome's electrical components directly, it is usually tapped into the system upstream of the leisure battery. This lets it keep the battery charged as well as powering the 12-volt accessories, while using the same circuits as the battery does. The result is that the fuses in the 12-volt system, which protect the various electrical items, work regardless of whether the power is coming from the leisure battery alone or is being boosted by the transformer charger. Meanwhile, the unit monitors the charge state of the vehicle battery so that the motorhome will always start.

You only need to know two things about the low-voltage side of the transformer charger unit. First, it makes sense to examine it and its handbook, so that you know where the fuses are and which fuses protect which circuits. If a fuse blows, do not just blindly replace it unless you know why it blew in the first place.

Secondly, turning 230 volts into 12 volts creates some heat. Many transformer charger units are fan cooled to cope with this so the sound of a fan does not indicate a problem – it is meant to run constantly when there is a mains input and the unit is in operation. Remember that, as the transformer charger itself uses mains electricity, the current it consumes must be factored into your campsite mains amperage calculations.

This brings us to the mains side of the transformer charger. The first item you need to know about is the earth leakage circuit breaker (ELCB). If this detects even the minutest connection between the incoming mains live circuits and earth, it will trip, cutting off the power. The residual current device (RCD) does much the same, albeit in a slightly different way. It detects any minute imbalance between the mains system's live and neutral wires and cuts the power. In fact, the RCD has all but replaced the ELCB in motorhome mains systems. Regardless of which is used, these devices are sensitive enough and can trip fast enough to prevent you getting an electric shock. If you find your transformer charger has a residual current circuit breaker (RCCB) do not worry, it is an RCD by another name.

These mains circuit breakers are your first line of defence against electrical problems. But a motorhome's electrical system is divided into sub-systems, each of which is protected by a micro circuit breaker (MCB). MCBs are simply circuit breakers that do what the fuses do for the 12-volt system. Rather than blowing if there is a problem, however, an MCB switches off the power to the circuit it is protecting. You can, of course, switch it back on again but if you do not know what caused it to trip, that would be very unwise.

Many transformer chargers have a further facility. Some Continental campsites – and one or two in Britain – have an electrical characteristic called reverse polarity. Motorhome accessory shops sell plug-in polarity detectors but many transformer chargers have a polarity warning light. Most of the electrical items in motorhomes are not polarity sensitive, but some you might take along may be and there is a small risk of a shock such as when, say, changing a mains-powered bulb. Accessory shops also sell special site connectors that put the situation right by again reversing the polarity. Once you know the polarity is incorrect, you can connect using your reverse-wired connector and all will be well.

In those cases where there are separate units instead of one transformer charger – i.e. by a mains-powered battery charger, perhaps a separate power transformer and domestic-style mains circuit breaker boxes – there will still be fuse boxes, wiring and both main and subsidiary circuit breakers. The principles

The Esterel 43's GRP construction makes it curvaceous

are similar and so are the practices but you may have to spend some time hunting down the locations of the separate units.

One point concerns American vehicles. In America, the domestic mains supply runs at 110 volts – less than half UK and European voltage. Importers therefore either replace all the electrical equipment that cannot be switched to accept 230 volts with European equipment, or they add a transformer that cuts 230 volts down to 110. Since replacing the equipment is a big, expensive job, you are likely to find that a mains transformer has been added. This will be connected upstream of a 230-volt to 12-volt transformer and work in the same way.

It is also common for American vehicles to have an onboard generator, powered by the engine fuel. This is often mounted in a locker with excellent sound insulation and is consequently fairly quiet. However, it is usually inappropriate to use one of these, or a separate generator with a European motorhome, on a campsite. We will look into this in more detail in Chapter 5.

Power in Practice

Now we can look at the ways in which you use the power. In a motorhome, most if not all of the lighting is 12-volt-powered, as is the heating distribution, the provision of water pressure, any on-board entertainment and the flushing of the WC. In modern motorhomes it is normal for the 12-volt power system to be under the overall control of the switches on a dedicated panel. Usually, this is itself overridden by the base vehicle's electrical system, specifically its ignition circuit, so that the 'domestic' functions stop working as soon as the engine is started. The control panel has a master switch that activates the 12-volt system and additional switches for individual items, such as the water pump and perhaps some specific light units. Most panels also have indications of the level of charge in each of the batteries and the water levels in the fresh- and grey-water tanks – often rocker switches are used to activate the relevant display. Some control panels are a great deal more complicated than this, including displays of internal and external temperature, programmable central-heating control, external water pump runtime and so on.

The fixed electrical items include the light units. Fluorescent lights, either with a straight tube or one coiled round on itself, work in the same way as their mains counterparts, having internal circuitry and a starter. They use only a small amount of power and run cool. Halogen lights are common and they come in a variety of guises. The simplest are fixed downlights, with clear or frosted glass lenses, and are often used in washrooms, over the head end of beds and over dinette tables. An adjacent switch is a refinement, as is the ability to swivel the light. These halogen units are like miniature spotlights. They can usually be swivelled horizontally through about 100 degrees, as well as being tilted to suit where you need illumination. Halogen lights consume more power than fluorescent ones and it is important to be aware that they run hot. This applies especially to units you can aim – there is a risk of burning your fingers.

Manufacturers of motorhome lighting have made great strides in designing units for specific roles. Some lights have a special handle so that you can aim them painlessly, some can be slid along tracks so that they can be ideally positioned.

There are a number of special uses for tungsten lights, these include the illumination of the inside of ovens and grills, refrigerators, lockers and wardrobes. In the latter cases, it is common for the bulb to illu-

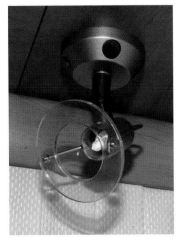

A typical halogen spotlamp. This one can be aimed and there's a switch on its bezel. Take care when adjusting one of these – they run hot

minate automatically when the door is opened; some wardrobes even have an illuminated hanging rail. Recently, LED lights have started appearing, they use little power and run very cool.

Fixed mains lights are not very common in motorhomes, although more and more manufacturers are including them, often adding a dimmer switch into the bargain. Such lights are usually fitted with low-wattage bulbs. The fact that motorhome interiors are small and usually light-coloured means that any mains light you add, such as a table lamp, is best equipped with a modest size of bulb.

Motorhome power sockets come in two basic kinds, one for each level of power. Twelve-volt sockets are usually identical to car cigar lighter sockets and accept the same kind of plug; the sockets are usually labelled to indicate a 10-amp restriction on current demand. Sometimes European 12-volt sockets are fitted. These have a much smaller diameter than UK or American sockets. Some 12-volt plugs have a dismountable collar that reveals a European plug but normally you need to use an adaptor, or change the plug to the alternative kind. In some motorhomes you may find a wall socket that accepts a plug with two flat parallel pins. These Clipsal sockets have been used in caravans and boats for many years but they are not common these days. You can get an adaptor with a Clipsal plug on one end and a standard cigar lighter socket on the other.

Mains sockets are simply a motorhome version of the standard, three-pin domestic mains socket. Most of them are switched and they are usually positioned in places convenient for the table and kitchen. Sockets of both kinds are placed in TV cabinets or near TV locations, usually next to a TV aerial socket.

This special edition Autocruise Stardream has been fitted with a number of accessories; note the special headlights and colour-keyed awning

Unless converted, American motorhomes naturally have US flat-pin sockets and it is not unknown for some imported motorhomes to have European ones. In either case, adaptors can be used but it is safer and more elegant to replace them with the UK type. And in some European motorhomes, you may find a mains socket in the washroom, in a panel or perhaps in a locker; it is obviously necessary to use caution where electricity and water are close together.

There are various kinds of 12-volt motors. Those used for the distribution of warm air, even where there is a convector heater, can be simple fan motors, which are often under the control of a temperature-sensitive resistor or a manual speed dial. Extractor fan motors can usually be run at two or more speeds, while in roof extractors the fan can often be run in reverse to draw air in, as well as being run at different speeds. Heavy-duty motors appear in electrically powered roof vents, which can be opened and closed using a rocker switch. Still heftier motors are used to power electric awnings and steps. Although these still run on 12-volt power, they are geared for maximum torque. So, although the awning or step may move slowly, a powerful motor is involved. An electric step usually has a rocking control switch mounted near the door the step serves. However, it is common for it to be retracted automatically when the motorhome's engine is started. Those steps without this facility might have a warning buzzer to remind you to retract the step but where there is neither, you have to remember to pull in the step before driving away. Checking the relevant cab mirror is a good habit.

Behind the scenes, mains power can in some cases be used for heating water as well as the motorhome's interior. It invariably provides one of the refrigerator's three power sources and it has a further role in refrigeration in some motorhomes. Electric air conditioning is popular in American motorhomes and it can also be found in quite a few European ones. Usually roof mounted, air-conditioning units of this kind use mains power to cool the interior of the motorhome when it is on site.

Gas

LPG is used as an adjunct to electricity in motorhomes. It comes in cylinders, which are housed in a special locker, or in a fixed tank, which is usually mounted beneath the floor of the vehicle. To use LPG properly, you have to know something about it, but once you do, you can carry and use this gas in perfect safety, exchanging the cylinder or refilling the tank as necessary.

Like their electrical equivalents, motorhome gas systems have developed over the years, and are safe, efficient and easy to use, but they have to be certified safe. It is recommended that certification is renewed on a yearly basis. A

CORGI (Council for Registered Gas Installers) registered engineer can do this provided he is qualified to work on LPG installations.

LPG is a colourless, odourless, non-poisonous, heavier-than-air gas. An odour is added by gas companies; normally, you will only detect it when changing a cylinder or refilling the gas tank, or if a burner fails to ignite, but smelling it at any other time suggests that there is a leak – which is why the odour is added.

LPG stored in cylinders or in a tank is not a gas but a liquid, which is the state it adopts when under pressure. And because it is stored under pressure quite a small cylinder or tank can run gas-powered equipment for some considerable time. When released, it can occupy approximately 200 times its stored volume. This also explains why one should shut off the gas supply before driving the motorhome.

Two types of LPG can be used in motorhomes. Butane, sold in blue cylinders, is a popular choice. Volume for volume, it is heavier than its opposite number and it burns more efficiently. However, in any LPG system, the fuel has to revert from a liquid to a gas to be used. If the ambient temperature is low, such as in winter, butane may not vaporize or it may freeze in the low-pressure part of the gas system.

The alternative is propane, which is sold in red cylinders. Although they are the same size, they have different weights; a 3.9-kg propane cylinder, for example, is equivalent in size to a 4.5-kg butane one.

Gas Class

Typical motorhome LPG installations using cylinders accept one or two standard-sized butane or propane cylinders, ranging from approximately 4 to 13 kg, and a pair need not be the same size and gas type. Note that when cylinders' sizes are quoted this refers not to the weight of the cylinder but to the weight of the gas inside it. So a 3.9-kg cylinder typically weighs 10.3 kg. If these overall weights seem a little daunting, there is an alternative. BP Gaslight cylinders contain propane and are made of translucent plastic; each weighs roughly half as much as a similarly sized steel cylinder. And apart from being lighter, you can see how much gas remains.

The basic arrangement for using LPG cylinders is simple. When a cylinder is empty, you exchange it for a full one. In the UK, Calor Gas enters into a cylinder rental agreement with the motorhome owner. You pay a rental fee at the beginning of this agreement and all the cylinders belong to Calor Gas. When you exchange your empty cylinder for a full one, at a campsite or other retail outlet, the charge involved is for the gas you are buying.

BP Gaslight cylinders are used in a similar way. You fill in a cylinder hire form, pay a deposit and subsequently pay only for the new gas when you exchange a used cylinder for a full one. Currently, two sizes of cylinder are available. The smaller, 5-kg cylinder can be bought or exchanged at some stockists of Truma heating hardware. The larger, 10-kg size is stocked at 293 Homebase stores in the UK and the company is looking at introducing 5-kg cylinder stocks.

One snag is, that though the two types of LPG are always the same, their containers vary across Europe. Although Calor Gas is easy to source in the UK, there are no outlets on the Continent. This can make life a little tricky. While you could ensure that you stock up with the maximum amount of gas you can carry before boarding the ferry, you will be unable to acquire refilled cylinders abroad. Any miscalculation of gas consumption or any gas leakage could leave you without gas and probably unable to heat your motorhome or cook aboard it.

There are ways around this. If you have a fixed LPG tank, you can fill your gas system at any Autogas filling station. Refillable gas cylinders are another option, and they can also be replenished with Autogas – we will look at these in Chapter 6. A third option is to buy one or more Camping Gaz cylinders. This company sells cylinders across Europe so you will always be able to get hold of LPG. In this instance, you purchase the cylinders, which remain your property. There is no rental agreement and, as with Calor cylinders, you pay for the gas inside the cylinder when exchanging. It makes sense to buy Camping Gaz cylinders in the UK. However, these are two minor snags if you travel abroad extensively. You must carry the appropriate fittings to allow you to use Camping Gaz, which is not too much of a problem, although some may not be totally comfortable with making the necessary modification. The main problem is that only one of the Camping Gaz cylinder sizes can be used in a motorhome, the Type 907, which contains 2.72 kg of butane. Although the LPG inside is the more efficient type, this capacity is comparatively small and frequent changes of cylinder can be costly.

Safe Houses

LPG is perfectly safe to carry and use in motorhomes because ways of storing, carrying and distributing it safely have been developed over many years. Being a petroleum product, it is, of course, highly inflammable. Being heavier than air, it is capable of collecting in sealed, low level areas; motorhome gas storage lockers are able to cope with both these characteristics. Gas lockers marked with the appropriate 'inflammable gas' symbol are sealed from the remainder of the vehicle's interior. But they are not completely sealed in themselves. As LPG is heavier than air, lockers have drop vents. These might be moulded plastic vents or simply holes in the locker floor, protected with plastic or metal mesh. If a gas leak occurs, the LPG falls safely out of the vents under the effect of gravity. The warning odour in LPG will let you know if there is any leakage but, in any event, you should never cover up or block off the locker's vents.

Refillable LPG cylinders fit into a standard gas locker while the alternative, a fixed tank, is usually attached horizontally beneath the floor of the motorhome. Fixed reservoirs of this kind can be refilled at any filling station that sells Autogas.

It is essential that gas lockers have no electrical components inside. Some systems have cylinder heaters for use in very cold climates, which are specially designed for use inside gas lockers. However, if someone has fitted a 12-volt lamp or a power socket inside a gas locker, it could cause a spark which would ignite leaking gas. Any such modifications should be disconnected and removed.

LPG cylinders are always used upright and gas lockers have fittings into which the cylinders can be strapped tight. It is essential to turn off the cylinders' main valve before travelling and when the gas system is not in use. The gas that comes from a cylinder cannot be used at full pressure, so there is another device within the gas locker that reduces the pressure to the specific requirements of the items that use it. This is the regulator.

Not long ago a range of gas fittings and delivery pressures was in use across the Continent. In the UK and elsewhere, sealed, factory-set regulator units attached directly to gas cylinders were the norm. Propane was delivered at a pressure of 37 millibars, butane at 28 millibars. Some gas-burning items could

Connecting a Camping Gaz adaptor. The flexible hose of the 'tail' leads to the
Euro regulator in the background

run on both types of gas, others could not, and some, particularly in German motorhomes, needed a still higher pressure. Depending on the type of gas concerned, male or female screw fittings were used, some with a left-hand thread. Clip-on regulators were also used, as was a screw-in type for use with Camping Gaz cylinders. Now, we have the Euro regulator, which was fully implemented in late 2003. By the time 2004-model motorhomes hit the show-rooms, the standardized system was universal. All motorhome LPG appliances were made to run, regardless of the type of LPG used, at the 30-millibar pressure given by the Euro regulator.

This makes life easier, but the LPG containers are still non-standardized. So some means of accommodating these differences is essential. Euro regulators have a short, flexible hose that runs to the LPG cylinder. This has an end fitting to suit the cylinder being used. Although there are adaptors that can be used with the existing arrangement, it is possible to change this 'tail' itself, from, say, one with a fitting for a propane cylinder to one with a butane fitting. Motorhomers who regularly travel on the Continent or further afield often have a collection of regulator 'tails' and swap them according to the availability of cylinders. Again, this is ideally work for a CORGI-registered operator but many motorhomers are capable of making a reliable, gas-tight joint and ensuring that it stays that way.

Downstream of the regulator, on the low-pressure side, LPG is led in tough, rigid pipework to the units that burn it. Modern gas systems incorporate gas-isolation valves, which may be situated near each appliance or may be ranked together in a special manifold. The point of such valves is that, should a leak or other problem develop in a particular appliance, its LPG supply can be shut off while other appliances remain unaffected.

Filling Stations

Replenishing your motorhome's onboard LPG supply is easy enough, provided you follow a few simple procedures. After a little practice, you will be able to predict when the cylinder's contents are going to run out although some systems are equipped with gauges to help you. You need only minimal mechanical knowledge to change an LPG cylinder. Clearly you should not change cylinders anywhere near an open flame or by the light of a hot bulb.

Step one is to ensure that the cylinder's gas valve is shut – close it as you would turn off a water tap. Then disconnect the regulator or the 'tail' connec-tion from the cylinder. This may involve undoing a clip fitting, unscrewing a thumbwheel or unfastening a fitting using a spanner. The rule is that all gas fittings except those on Camping Gaz cylinders unscrew the 'wrong' way – turn clockwise to loosen. BP LPG cylinders take a 27 mm clip-on fitting. A

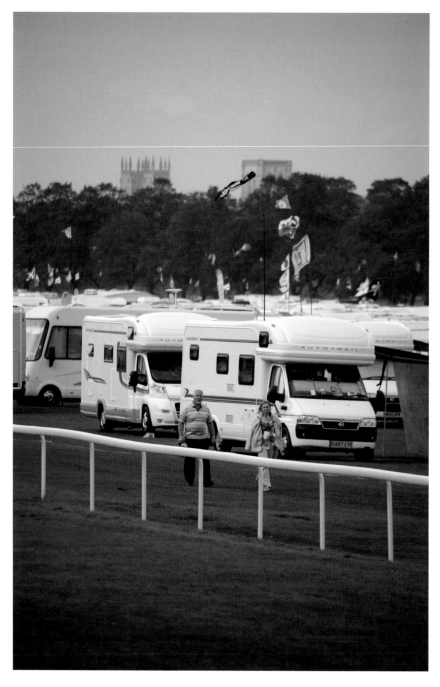

Outdoor shows, like this one at York Racecourse, attract trusted travelling companions as well as new models

cylinder-mounted regulator, or an adaptor to allow Gaslight cylinders to be connected to a standard LPG system, is available from Truma stockists. As you make this disconnection, you will be letting gas at cylinder pressure escape for a moment. A brief, sharp hissing sound, accompanied by the pungent smell of LPG, is perfectly normal.

You can now completely detach the fitting. Unstrap the cylinder, releasing it from its mountings, and take it out of the gas locker. Then, replace it with the new cylinder. You will have to remove a plastic or metal blanking plug so remember it will probably have a left-hand thread. Strap the cylinder securely into place and reconnect the fitting. LPG fittings do not need to be tightened too much; you need only tighten them firmly. Usually, the thread must be started and tightened anticlockwise. When the fitting is tightened, turn on the cylinder's gas valve. You will hear a short, muted hiss as the pressure is re-established but you should not hear anything more, nor should there be any smell of LPG. If there is a sound or a smell, there is a leak that you must find and fix. Shut off the gas valve, unfasten the connection and start again. Problems at connection time are usually down to either a bad sealing washer or a speck of grit on the gas fitting's brass 'acorn', or a damaged connection in the cylinder. All prevent the connection's seating correctly, making it impossible to achieve a gas-tight seal. If reassembling the connection with a new washer, cleaning any grit or using another cylinder does not stop the leak, you need professional help.

Gas in Use

If you encounter a smell of gas, do not switch anything on – not even a torch. To discover where the leak is, you can use the gas isolation valves. Turn them all off and ventilate the vehicle to get rid of the smell. Then, open each valve in turn until the smell becomes evident again – this will tell you which unit you must leave isolated until a professional can solve the problem. And if, on returning to your motorhome, you encounter an LPG smell that is particularly powerful, STOP! If there is a significant amount of gas about, open the gas locker and immediately shut off the gas supply. Do not switch on any electrical appliances, but leave the door, windows and roof vents open to ventilate the vehicle fully before seeking the help of a professional.

You should have any inspections, certification and modifications made by a CORGI-registered engineer who is trained to work on LPG installations. You should also have the system's flexible hoses replaced every five years, or sooner if you see damage or suspect it has occurred. Flexible hoses used for LPG are in fact date marked. And have a good fire extinguisher mounted in a place where it is accessible. You can also invest in a fire blanket if you wish and there are LPG detectors if you feel you would like to use one.

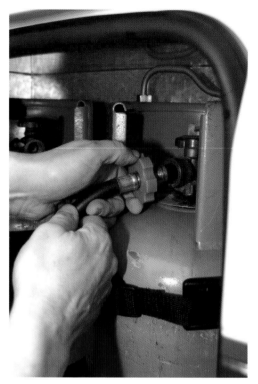

Connecting a propane cylinder in a gas locker. This connector doesn't need a spanner but it has a left-hand thread

Using LPG could not be simpler. To light a hob burner, turn on the relevant control knob and hold it in before igniting the gas. Many LPG-burning appliances have spark ignition – you just press the button to light the gas. Other appliances rely on a hand-held spark igniter, a cigarette lighter or a match. Regardless of which method of ignition you use, you have to hold in the lit burner's control knob for a few seconds before the gas will continue burning, because the burning gas heats a thermocouple, which will only let gas continue to be delivered at the burner if it is hot. This flame-failure mechanism protects you if a gas flame is blown out or stops burning for any other reason.

All modern hobs, grills and ovens have flame failure devices but some have much more. Where the hob is under a glass cover, closing the cover automatically shuts off the gas supply, dousing the flames. Some hobs are drainer hobs, effectively shallow sinks with a drain, useful when spillages occur. Sometimes, a simple hob has a grill beneath and concealed controls can make it tricky to find. Often, motorhomes have oven/grills, with internal burners top and bottom for the relevant function. Illumination and spark ignition are commonplace, while some ovens go as far as having an integral rotisserie.

One European characteristic particularly affects German-made motorhomes.

Sometimes, they have no oven or grill. In this event, a suitable unit can usually be fitted, while many such models are sold in this country with a 'UK pack', which includes an oven and grill or a combination unit. Paradoxically, many European motorhomes have facilities for doing other tasks outside. There are external LPG connections for use with a barbecue and there is sometimes an external shower point.

Those items that burn LPG unseen, such as refrigerators and gas heaters, also have a flame-failure mechanism so there are only two related aspects to consider. As will soon become clear, gas heaters and the gas-fuelled part of a refrigerator draw air in and let the products of combustion out independently. The only open flames in a motorhome LPG installation are the hob burners, the grill and the oven. Fixed ventilation in modern motorhomes means you can cook in perfect safety but the ventilation system is not designed to cope with open flames burning for very long periods. This means you should never use them as a source of heat. And if a gas heater or refrigerator's exhaust becomes blocked the products of combustion could enter the motorhome. So, if you use an open flame as a heat source, you will not be able to detect carbon monoxide and this is a killer gas. What will warn you more effectively, especially in the event of an unseen exhaust blockage, is a carbon monoxide detector. These can be used in motorhomes and are a wise investment. Another useful warning device is the smoke detector.

An American C-Class aimed at the European market. The Fleetwood Pulse 24D is relatively compact but it still has a slide-out and lots of space inside

In a recent development, accessory manufactures have been working on the 'gasless' motorhome. While electric-only refrigerators and non-LPG heating systems have been around for a while, non-LPG cookers and hobs are something new. They use similar arrangements to gas appliances for drawing in combustion air and safely exhausting the products of combustion. The difference is that they are diesel-fired.

Warming

In the dim and distant past, motorhomes used to have a single radiant gas heater of some description. These were undeniably efficient but required great care and attention, especially as regards fire safety and ventilation. Motorhome heating systems have changed radically, and they are now both efficient and safe.

The space in a motorhome is small compared to that of a house but is very large compared to a car. Base vehicles naturally have a heater and this is normally more than adequate during travelling, even in winter. However, it might be inadequate in a larger motorhome, especially in the travel seats behind the cab seats. This is why some motorhomes have a conversion heater. This works in exactly the same way as the base vehicle's heater. It has a matrix (a radiator) that is piped into the engine's cooling system. When the engine reaches its working temperature, the hot water that feeds the cab's heater also feeds the conversion heater. A 12-volt blower fan pushes the heat out into the area behind the cab.

The snag with cab and conversion heaters is that they work only when the motorhome's engine is running and is at working temperature, but you can hardly sit on site with the engine running. So, motorhomes have a 'static' heating system to heat the air inside, and water from the fresh-water tank.

There are two obvious energy sources that can be used for heating: LPG, and mains electricity. But you cannot safely have an open LPG flame inside a motorhome and the mains electricity supplies at campsites have limitations.

Hot Air

As we cannot burn LPG inside the motorhome, we have to heat its interior by burning the gas outside it. Sounds silly, does it not? However, doing just this is possible, courtesy of an elegantly simple device called a heat exchanger. Here is how it works.

Think of a hollow, sealed canister. If you put a gas jet and an igniter inside the canister, you can light the gas – but it will not burn for long; the flame will quickly eat up all the oxygen in the canister. So, you add an air inlet. Great, now the flame keeps burning – but not for long; the products of combustion fill the canister and put the flame out. So you add an exhaust outlet as well. Brilliant! The flame burns because it has a way in for the air it needs and a way out for the exhaust it makes.

If you added long pipes to the air inlet and exhaust outlet, you could take your canister inside your motorhome and warm your hands on it. Go one better and arrange a blower system with ducts and vents and you could blow air over the canister and distribute the heated air to the parts of the vehicle where it is needed. This, albeit put simply, is blown air heating, as used in motorhomes. Heating system manufacturers use refinements including flame failure devices, thermostatic control, underfloor air inlets and a side- or roof-mounted exhaust flue but the principle is the same. The heat exchanger is sealed, the flame burns inside it and the combustion air and exhaust gases respectively enter and leave the canister outside the vehicle.

The simplest form of motorhome heater is the Trumatic S, made by the German company Truma. This has an internal heat exchanger, in which gas jets are ignited, either manually with a piezo crystal igniter or automatically by a battery-powered spark igniter. Air enters the heater and exhaust leaves it externally and the output of the gas burners is under thermostatic control. Working solely by convection, the Trumatic S gives a 3.4–5-kilowatt output, depending on the model.

The Trumavent is a 12-volt-powered warm air distribution system that can be incorporated with the Trumatic S. It adds a fan to the rear of the heater and ducting can be led to points where warm air is required, such as in the motorhome's lounge and washroom. There is a version with automatic speed control. In this, a control knob fitted into the heater's top panel can be set to make the thermostatic control unit alter the speed of the fan, giving the required heat output. Electricity as a power source comes in a further option. This, the Ultraheat, is an electric, air heating element that is fitted into the Trumatic S's casing and adds up to an additional 2-kilowatt output.

Some motorhomes, especially smaller models and camper vans, have no visible heater, just warm air vents set into low-level panels. Such systems still have a heat exchanger but it is out of sight, inside a locker or beneath the floor of the vehicle. Propex Heatsource LPG space heaters are a good example of this kind of unit. The Propex Heatsource 2000 and its stablemate, the HS2800, have underfloor air inlet and exhaust systems. Full electronic control, thermostatic monitoring and self-diagnostic functions make them reliable and easy to use. So the only controls are warm air vents, which you can aim, open and close, and a wall-mounted control box. These units have outputs respectively of 1.6 and 1.8 kilowatts.

Liquid Fuel

LPG is not the only combustible fuel that can be used for heating motorhome interiors. Vehicles not converted to run on LPG necessarily carry liquid fuel and marine and truck applications formed the basis of systems that have been translated into motorhomes. The German company Webasto makes liquid fuel-fired heating units, ranging from the 0.9–2-kilowatt Airtop 2000S to a 5-kilowatt unit for severe conditions. Available in petrol or diesel versions, these units use very little fuel; the mid-range, 3.5-kilowatt Airtop 3500S uses just 0.42 litres per hour at full power. The units have a pressurized injection system to feed their fuel burners, which operate inside a heat exchanger, like LPG-fired heaters. And once again, there is fine control. The heat output can be varied and can be operated using a programmable timer. It is also possible, using Thermocall, to input commands to the system from your mobile phone – useful if you are heading back to your motorhome after, say, an afternoon's skiing.

Eberspächer is a German company that makes liquid fuel-fired space heater units that have a variety of remote control options, including a key-fob unit, a radio remote control and Calltronic, a system that allows the heating to be controlled via your mobile phone. Under the generic name Airtronic, these space heating systems include a 0.8–2.2-kilowatt unit, the D2, and a larger unit, the 1–4-kilowatt D4. Fuel consumption ranges from 0.1–0.51 litres per hour.

Heaters that use the vehicle's on-board fuel supply have a number of advantages. Often, the system can be configured to pre-heat the engine cooling

The blue cylinder is this Eberspächer Combitronic heating system's calorifier. It fulfils a role similar to that of a domestic copper hot water cylinder

system. Using the engine fuel is a more economical way of heating than using LPG and such installations do not require the stringent safety inspection and certification an LPG-fired system needs. Unless you plan to do a lot of cooking, you will probably find that, as the LPG system is not being used for heating purposes, the amount of gas you can accommodate will suffice for Continental trips. And there is a less obvious but highly significant advantage. A liquid-fuel-fired heating system can be used, legally and safely, while a motorhome is in motion. All you must remember is to shut the system down before approaching a filling station. With so many advantages to offset their initial cost – and a number of new motorhomes feature liquid-fuel-fired heating – it is little wonder that such heating systems are becoming ever more popular.

Water Signs

Heating the air inside a motorhome is only half the story. Some method of heating water efficiently is essential, for washing up, washing and showering. In the past, instant-heat through boilers were commonplace; rather like domestic electric showers, they heated cold water on demand as it passed through them. Nowadays, largely for reasons of safety, storage water heaters are the norm. Such units heat a fixed amount of water taken from the motorhome's fresh-water tank. The amount heated is relatively small – 10–14 litres is a typical capacity – but the water is heated to a high temperature, to be mixed with cold water for use.

Most units do not rely solely on LPG. The Propex Malaga 3 is a compact, LPG-fired storage water heater. Just like its space-heating equivalents, it has a heat exchanger, but this time the heat is transferred to the stored water rather than to air. This unit has a dry weight of only 9.3 kg but its heat output is 1.5 kilowatts. It uses LPG at the rate of 80 g per hour. The Propex Malaga 3E has an electric immersion heater that works just like its domestic equivalent. This 750-watt element can be used instead of, or in conjunction with, LPG and it is under the control of a thermostat.

Indeed, many motorhome heating systems can juggle power sources, making the best of what is available at a given time, while providing both space and water heating. A look at a popular LPG/electric combination heater will illustrate how such systems work.

The Trumatic C6002EH has both summer and winter modes. In summer mode, the unit can be set to use LPG or mains electrical power to heat its 12 litres of water to a pre-set 40° or 60°C. If you choose LPG operation, the heater automatically selects its lowest burner setting. If you choose electric operation, you can opt for a 0.9- or a 1.8-kilowatt output. The campsite's electricity supply has a bearing on which power level setting can be used and there is thermostatic control for both LPG and electric heating.

A Truma heating system is a common fitment to European motorhomes. Note the warm-air ducting used to send heat around the motorhome's interior.

Choosing winter mode brings this system's space heating facility into operation. If you select LPG operation at 2, 4 or 6 kilowatts, the unit uses temperature sensors to control its 12-volt, blown air heating fans. The speed and running time of these alters to provide the internal temperature you have chosen. If electric operation is chosen, one of the two mains-powered output levels mentioned can be switched on manually.

In adverse conditions, or for a fast warm-up, the C6002EH pulls out all the stops to output 7.8 kilowatts, bringing temperatures up as quickly as possible, then shuts down its gas burner when the required temperature is achieved and it always uses mains electricity as its primary power source. The C6002H can also drain itself to prevent damage from freezing if the temperature inside the motorhome it serves drops to 4°C. It can also select which power source – or combination of sources – it uses. Moreover, it is remarkably efficient.

Dual Fuel

This is a dual-fuel item in that it can use and combine mains electricity and LPG as sources of power. There are also systems that combine liquid fuel and electricity. Burning liquid fuel instead of LPG gives much the same result, whether it is air or water that is to be heated. However, the water heated directly is not what comes out of the tap. A closed-circuit water system, full of a water/antifreeze mixture, runs under pressure, the mixture being circulated by a pump. This mixture is heated by the system's heat exchanger and the heat it receives and stores can be distributed in two ways.

In one, where space heating is required, the mixture is pumped into one or more heater matrices. Air from inside the motorhome is blown through each matrix, which, just like the matrix in a car heater, warms it as it passes through its fins. Fan blades then force the warmed air through ducting, to be released at blown-air heating vents. The other system does exactly the same but it uses heated fresh water, rather than the water in a closed circuit.

The arrangement for water heating uses the same, circulating hot water/antifreeze mixture but this is passed through a water-to-water heat exchanger. The heat is transmitted from the mixture to cold fresh water inside the heat exchanger and it is this water that is used, for washing up, washing and showering. The inclusion of a mains-electricity-powered immersion heater means that this power source can be used with liquid fuel, or sometimes instead of it.

The Webasto Thermo Top C is the heart of such a heating system. Underfloor mounting means that this unit intrudes only minimally on the host vehicle's interior space. Inside the Thermo Top C, a plate-type heat exchanger allows the heat from the fuel being burnt to pass into a closed coolant circuit, in which the heated water is pumped through a second, water-to-water heat exchanger. In this, cool fresh water held in the 'demand' side of the system is heated and pumped directly to the motorhome's taps and two heater matrices with fans. These give warm air at ducts throughout the motorhome.

The German company Eberspächer built its reputation on manufacturing 'parking heaters' for trucks, vans, buses and cars. The term 'parking heater' is actually a misnomer, as such heaters can be used when the host vehicle is being driven; they can also pre-heat engine coolant. Eberspächer makes a variety of space/water heating units for a variety of applications but their Combitronic Compact, a relatively new system, works in a modular way. A single underfloor unit, which houses a liquid-fuel-burning heat exchanger, lies at its heart. This can output up to 5 kilowatts, depending on the model, and this output can be upgraded by up to a further 1.8 kilowatts by the addition of mains-electricity-powered air- and water-heating elements. Although it has a closed circuit full of coolant mixture, it uses a calorifier, which is essentially the equivalent of a domestic hot water cylinder. This has a mains-electricity-powered immersion heater as well as a water-to-water heat exchanging coil. The water in the closed circuit, when heated, can supply warm air via fan-

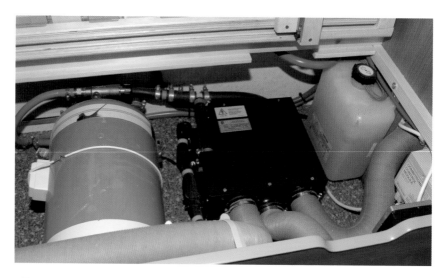

The Eberspächer Combitronic Compact is extremely versatile. The blue cylinder is the calorifier – the equivalent of a domestic hot water cylinder

assisted matrices and electrically powered PTC (Positive Temperature Coefficient) pads, which warm interior air that has passed over them by fan pressure. This allows electrical power to supplement liquid fuel power for the blown air space heating.

The Combitronic Compact is able to mix power sources to give a particularly fast warm-up from cold. Refinements, which include electronic speed control of the fans' output, computerized monitoring and diagnostic systems, a timer, an alarm, remote control functions and automatic frost protection make this system a particularly flexible one.

Power under Control

Using a motorhome heating system is much the same, whatever the type or fuel. The general principle is that one or more fuels are used to heat water and provide warm air. Generally, the more complex the system, the greater the number of facilities it offers and, consequently, the more control inputs and settings required.

While switching on a system and setting a thermostat are usually easy enough, making the various selections – LPG, mains electricity power or both, liquid fuel or electric power, air/water heating or both – differs, depending on the system concerned.

An important point here is that motorhome heating systems are designed to be fail-safe. It is usual for heating systems to be serviced at certain intervals

This neat unit is a dual-fuel water heater. It takes up very little room in a small motorhome or van conversion

and there is little in the way of between-service maintenance. That said, there are three important matters that warrant attention. First, many new motorhomers find that their heating system will not ignite because they have failed to remove the side exhaust vent's travelling cover, which proves that fail-safe works in this context! Simply unclip the cover and stow it away and the system will function. Second, whether the exhaust vent is side or roof mounted, it is essential to ensure that it remains clear. Roof vents in particular can become clogged by debris such as leaves in autumn, and they must be unobstructed to work properly and be safe. Finally, even where there is automatic frost protection, it makes sense to drain the water out of a heating system if it is to remain unused in winter conditions. The water's freezing and expanding can do a lot of damage, and such damage is rarely covered under a system's warranty.

A large, garage model A-Class, like this Hymer, makes an excellent long-distance tourer

Cold Front

Like most of the service items in a motorhome, the cold storage facility will vary in size, depending on the size of the vehicle. The smallest and simplest kind of refrigerator is a coolbox – a portable unit that is generally run from a 12-volt cigar lighter socket. The next is the compressor refrigerator, which is often found in smaller motorhomes, such as fixed- or rising-roof camper vans and smaller high-top conversions. Some compressor refrigerators are portable, and these bridge the gap between coolboxes and larger models. Others are fixed, generally in a kitchen area or under a bunk locker. Compressor refrigerators work in the same way as a domestic unit but on a smaller scale. While they are notably undemanding in terms of the space they occupy, they can put quite a load on the vehicle's 12-volt supply.

The kind of unit most often found in motorhomes is the three-way refrigerator. This gets its name from its ability to use three distinct power sources. Which is used depends on what is available at a given time, and this depends on how the motorhome is being used. The first source is 12-volt electrical power supplied by the motorhome's engine battery. When using this, the refrigerator runs constantly at its highest cooling capacity, without any form of thermostatic control. But of course this source is restricted to times when the motorhome's engine is running so that the vehicle's alternator charges the engine battery; without that charging current, the refrigerator would quickly run the battery flat. This power source cannot do more than maintain the refrigerator's internal temperature; it is necessary to use one of the remaining power sources to cool the refrigerator before it is loaded with supplies. The 12-volt system simply keeps your food cool as you travel.

The second power source is the preferred one – mains electrical power, whether from an on-site supply or from your home's mains electrical system. The third is LPG, which can be used when the vehicle is stationary and when a mains electricity supply is unavailable.

Motorhome refrigerators do not work in quite the same way as domestic ones. Being absorption units they use heat to create the circulation necessary to make their cooling system work. Apart from the limitation of 12-volt power, however, they work well with any of the three sources.

Like other items, motorhome refrigerators have undergone significant development. In the past, it was necessary to ensure that when parked, the motorhome was fairly level for the refrigerator to work at all effectively. Nowadays, refrigerators are tilt-tolerant and will work even if their host vehicle is parked on a modest slope. In most instances, the motorhome owner in the past had to opt for and switch on the available power system. While this is still sometimes necessary, many refrigerators have automatic energy selection

(AES), which does exactly what its name suggests; the refrigerator knows which power supplies are available and will use the most efficient – 230-volt electric power for preference.

Motorhome refrigerators of this kind usually bear the name Dometic or Thetford and they range from small, cabinet-type units with an internal freezer compartment to large fridge/freezers. Regardless of style and capacity, they work in the same way as domestic refrigerators, and have variable levels of cooling, controlled by a front-mounted dial. Like domestic units, they need to be defrosted on occasion and, what with ice trays, bottle locations, egg racks and the like, they differ little from home fridges. The only significant difference is a practical one. Motorhome refrigerators have a locking mechanism to prevent the door opening when the vehicle is being driven. It makes sense to adopt the habit of ensuring this is locked before driving.

Blind Ambition

In motorhomes, the windows are referred to as being 'double glazed'. In fact, apart from in some American motorhomes, they are made of a clear or tinted moulded acrylic material. This is double-skinned to provide insulation and sound-deadening but there is no actual glass involved. Windows of this kind work in one of three ways. Fixed windows simply stay put, sliding ones can be unlocked and slid open, and hinged ones can be raised on locking supports. Such windows are usually housed in an integral cassette, which is sealed to the panels into which it is fitted.

The maintenance required is minimal, but acrylic is a soft material so cleaning should be done with care; there are special products that can be used for this task. There are similar products to deal with scratches. But it is important to note that, compared to domestic windows, the materials and mechanisms used are fragile. For this reason, you should never force motorhome windows in any way. Equally, a window left open can be severely damaged by even the lightest of contacts, so remember to ensure all windows are latched before driving off.

The only other kind of motorhome window that is commonly seen is the opalescent kind used in washrooms. However, some of these allow the interior to be seen from outside at night. If this concerns you, have someone check – you may need to use a blind.

Motorhomes have two kinds of ventilation: fixed and opening. The fixed ventilation is fitted to comply with construction guidelines and, blockages apart, needs no further thought. Opening ventilators come in a variety of shapes and sizes and you need to know how to use them.

The simplest kinds of roof vent lift up, either on sprung side brackets or on

Cosy: with the blinds drawn and the doors locked, motorhomes are
comfortable, private and secure

a screw mechanism on the side opposite a hinge. You can vary the amount by which vents are opened and all you need to remember is that, like the windows, they are relatively fragile; it is best to close them all before setting off.

The more upmarket kinds of roof vents have the same kind of acrylic construction as windows. These may be opened and latched with a shaped, pivoted bar that fits into graduated stops in the frame. Others use a simple hand crank, which may fold into the frame for travelling, and some open electrically, and are operated by a rocker switch. Once again, you should close the vents before travelling, bearing in mind that force can cause damage.

To make the interior of the motorhome private it may have curtains that are fully functional, especially those used to screen the glass in the cab. Some are even fully lined. But in many instances, the windows are flanked by 'faux curtains', used to soften the lines of the windows. What makes for privacy are blinds. These can be used to completely close off the windows and roof vents and they are quite easy to operate. Like the windows, these blinds are cassette units fitted to the inside of the windows. There are plain blinds, effectively roller blinds mounted into the top or bottom of the cassette, which can be pulled up or down against spring pressure and sometimes latched partly open. They retract automatically. A little higher up the range are pleated blinds, which can be slid closed and fold themselves automatically as you open them.

If you want to leave a window or roof vent open at night but do not want uninvited guests, you have flyscreens. These are simple mesh screens that cover the windows and vents. They clip on to the edge of the blind, so it is possible to have a window or vent partially obscured and still insect-proof. A refinement of the same principle is a fly mesh that covers the entry door. Flyscreens work well except in one area: the female Scottish midge is big enough to nip you but is small enough to pass through a flyscreen's mesh!

Cab blinds are an effective and elegant solution to the problem of closing off the cab glass. Made by the German company Remis, these are available to suit the popular base vehicles and some motorhome manufacturers fit them as standard or offer them as an optional extra. Remifront blinds consist of two cassette units, shaped to fit the insides of the left and right cab doors. The pleated blinds in the cassettes can be pulled out from their fastening clips to close against magnetic holding strips. The windscreen part has two pillar-mounted cassettes, each containing a pleated blind half the width of the windscreen. When unlatched, these half-blinds pull out, sliding on transverse rods top and bottom, to meet and be held magnetically at the centre of the windscreen. The one place where such blinds cannot be used and where curtains on rails may not be used is in the cab of an A-Class motorhome. Closing off the coach-like cab glass here can be a challenge and manufacturers sometimes use special sliding blinds for this purpose, while at least one uses an electrically operated roller blind that descends from the windscreen header rail.

Bedding Down

In many cases, making a bed in a motorhome involves more than merely adding the bedclothes. Of course, fixed beds can usually be left made up and ready for use, but often you have to literally *make* the bed before you can use it. The complexity of this operation varies but there are some general practices that apply to most motorhomes.

Most beds, whether or not they need to be assembled, have beech-sprung bases. In these, a peripheral frame made of aluminium alloy or wood has lateral strips of beechwood. These usually have a convex upward curve and provide the bed's springing. In conjunction with a mattress made of good, fairly dense foam, beech sprung beds can be very comfortable.

A typical longitudinal bed, whether it is in the centre of the motorhome or in the tail, starts as a pair of facing sofas. The bases pull out to meet in the centre, and the bed is then assembled by placing the sofa backrest cushions flat to make a full double bed.

A bed that starts out as a dinette can be more complicated to assemble. The dinette table is usually an additional area of bed base. An extra, low-level wall

Motorhome beds have beech-sprung bases. Assembling the bed is a nightly task

mounting receives one end of the table and the table leg can be folded or shortened to suit the lower height. The complication appears with the addition of cushions. The dinette seat is usually also a travel seat and its base and backrest form most of the bed. However, you will need one or more additional cushions. The same goes for the additional cushions needed when a forward bed includes a dinette, a short side sofa, two opposing short sofas or an L-section to make up a full, transverse double bed. You will find the extra cushions somewhere in the motorhome, probably in the wardrobe or stored in the overcab bed.

Overcab beds sometimes need a little assembling. Unless it is fixed, an over-cab bed usually hinges down for use, its motion controlled by gas rams; often, a roof-mounted strap must be released first. With the bed base lowered, placing the cushions flat on the base completes the procedure. The bed access ladder may be stored in the overcab area or it may be kept in a wardrobe or a dedicated cupboard. Such ladders normally just hook into place on the edge of the bed. The final item is standard equipment in most coachbuilt motorhomes with an overcab bed – a net that stretches from the edge of the bed up towards the ceiling. Particularly useful when children are using the overcab bed, it can be clipped into place to prevent anybody falling out in the night. The overcab bed in an A-Class model works on the same basic principle, with an access ladder and possibly a net.

Alfresco Annexe

You may not want a motorhome that is so big as to be cumbersome to drive but you may still want extra accommodation. This is where an awning comes into its own. This is basically a massive roller blind that fits in a bespoke cassette attached to the side of the motorhome. It can give a pleasant, covered outdoor lounging and dining area that is protected against light to medium showers while offering shade in better weather. It is also possible to obtain side walls for most awnings to make a 'safari room', which can be used even in poor weather. As it is effectively a tent, of which the motorhome constitutes one wall, you can put camp beds, sleeping bags and even a heater in it. When closed for travelling, an awning simply sits in its cassette, securely latched into place.

When pitched, you can open and erect it quite easily. Although some awnings are electrically operated, most are unrolled using a long, hand crank. Open the awning so that its outer rail is about 1.5 metres from the side of the motorhome. Then unfasten each awning leg in turn, extending and locking them so that the awning's outer rail is raised and so that both legs are parallel,

Erecting an awning requires more patience than skill, provided it isn't windy

with their feet angled away from the vehicle. As you unroll the awning further, the legs will support the outer rail as they first achieve and subsequently go beyond a vertical position. Move the legs further away from the vehicle until the awning is unrolled fully, to the point where the fabric is taut. Then set the legs at a height that places the awning's outer rail a little below its attachment to the motorhome. At this stage, it helps to check that the motorhome's side entry door does not foul the awning; if it does, adjust the height of the legs accordingly. Ensure that the legs are vertical, and if it looks like rain, adjust one leg so that it is a little shorter than the other. This means that the fabric is given a 'fall'. Any rain will then run off with the aid of gravity.

There are refinements to this basic set-up. An awning is a big piece of fabric so, in windy conditions, it is necessary to pin its legs down, using rock pegs. These are special tent pegs that can be driven into the ground through holes in the awning's 'feet'. While this generally suffices to keep an awning under control, some motorhomers also use guy ropes. Obviously, a mallet is an essential addition to your on-board equipment. And if it becomes really windy, put the awning away before it does some damage.

Where side walls are to be added to make a 'safari room', the general principle is similar to that used for erecting a tent. A groundsheet may be included and tent pegs are used to pin down the walls. Then, you can add your internal furniture and put in heating and light.

Sometimes, you will see an addition that is neither a 'safari room' nor a tent. Users of camper vans especially use tent-like extensions that generally practically double the space in the vehicle. They are basically tents that use the camper van's tail as one wall.

Essential Maintenance

It is necessary to maintain your motorhome, but how many of the necessary tasks you carry out yourself depends on two things. You can undertake a number of the tasks yourself, with only average technical and mechanical skills. However, there are certain aspects that you would be unwise to tackle yourself. These include working on LPG and mains electrical installations.

The kind of jobs you can take on include basic vehicle maintenance and certain jobs on the water system. The former includes such items as checking underbonnet fluid levels and tyre pressures. Incidentally, some filling station or supermarket tyre inflators do not have the air power to cope with motorhome tyres. Some newer motorhomes come with a 12-volt electric air compressor. If yours is not so equipped, invest in one that is suitably highly rated or befriend the staff at a commercial vehicle service garage.

The Auto-Trail Excel 600B is a compact motorhome, based on the
Fiat Ducato X/250 chassis cab

Water systems generally need little maintenance. The repeated filling and
emptying of the fresh-water system normally keeps things fresh, although water
purification chemicals are available should the system show any hint of brack-
ishness. Should the motorhome remain unused for any length of time, it makes
sense to drain and flush the water system repeatedly, finally leaving the drain
points open. And grey-water systems respond well to purification chemicals as,
especially under certain conditions, odours can become a problem.

Protecting Your Asset

You also need to look after your motorhome carefully when you are not using it,
even in summer. If you do not, it will suffer damage at some level, and neglect
can be costly. Untended, it will suffer the effects of disuse. In time, the base
vehicle's battery will go flat. Its tyres can develop flat spots from constantly
carrying the motorhome's weight, the brake discs and drums will rust and the
clutch may stick to the flywheel. All these problems are curable but it is better
if they do not arise in the first place.

The same applies to the domestic hardware. The leisure battery will flatten
over time, even if the continuous demands on it are minimal. The fresh-water
tank's contents will go stale and movable items – taps, switches, hinges and

locks – may become obstinate. Unheated and with nothing other than its fixed ventilation in operation, the motorhome's interior will suffer. Even in summer, cool night air can cause condensation. You might see this on the windows and you will certainly feel it in soft trim items such as carpets and cushions.

These unwelcome developments are easily avoidable with minimal effort on your part. To keep the base vehicle happy, you simply need to drive it: once a month is pitiful, once a fortnight is desirable and once a week is best. The aim is to give your vehicle a little exercise so you have to be realistic – ten minutes with the engine ticking over is not enough. Take your motorhome out on the road and give the engine, transmission and brakes a workout. This means bringing everything up to its full working temperature, so the oil in the engine and transmission becomes hot enough to circulate fully. How far you drive depends on where you take your vehicle but on a mix of minor and major roads, 5 miles will suffice. This distance will help boost the batteries' levels of charge, circulate both oil and coolant and keep the brakes and flywheel rust-free. And because the vehicle has been moved, the likelihood of your parking it on the same arcs of the tyres' treads is minimal, even if you park in the exact same spot as before.

This exercise, apart from putting some heat into the motorhome, will not do much for the interior. Fortunately, there are other ways to keep the inside up to scratch without moving the vehicle. One way is preventative maintenance. Draining off the fresh water means it cannot go brackish. It goes without saying that the grey-water tank and WC cassette should be emptied too. If you open all the taps and leave all the plugs out, your grey-water system will be dry and ventilated, which will save you repeatedly flushing it with purifying chemicals. Leaving the WC's closing blade open and its cassette rinsed and empty will keep it fresh, and putting tape across the seat will remind everyone not to use the WC.

Ventilation is paramount to the welfare of the interior. Given fairly dry conditions, you can leave selected roof vents or windows open. If the weather is cool and wet for any length of time, some heat would not go amiss. Many motorhomers arrange a 230-volt feed from their home's electrical supply, which means that a small fan heater can be placed inside and left on a low setting for an hour or two. How often you do this depends on whether it has been raining; it is obvious that in the height of summer, additional heat is not going to be required. And do not forget that the ultra-violet element of sunlight can do harm to fabrics and tyres. Closing window blinds will save your furnishing fabrics from fading. As for your tyres, you can get silvered fabric wheel protectors but you can always cover the tyres with black plastic refuse sacks if your motorhome lives in a suntrap.

Cold Comfort

The same basic principles apply when a motorhome is unused in winter. You can reasonably assume that sunlight is not going to be a problem then but rain, frost, snow and ice are likely to be. This is why 'winterizing' motorhomes is a yearly chore.

Before taking it out of service, clean it thoroughly, inside, outside and underneath. A household vacuum cleaner will help with most of the interior cleaning chores but wash down the cooker, sink, basin and shower tray with the appropriate household cleansers. For the exterior and underside, use a hot jetwash. A thorough jetwashing will remove all the road grime and any salt deposits from seaside use or road gritting. When using a jetwash, remember that the high-pressure spray should not be aimed at items designed to cope only with rainwater, such as refrigerator vents. And the higher pressure of the rinsing spray's jet is capable of wrecking a tyre – keep your distance when aiming. Then, when you have driven the motorhome far enough to dry it, give it a treat; assiduous use of wax polish will preserve the paintwork over the winter months.

If the vehicle is to stay off the road for several months, you should make it fit to remain idle. It is better if you can drive it weekly or at least fortnightly. If you cannot or would rather not, you can preserve things with a little effort. Putting it up on axle stands eases the load on the suspension and tyres; some motorhomers remove their vehicle's wheels and store them somewhere cool and dark. For this you need a good trolley jack and axle stands – make sure they are tough enough to handle the weight of your motorhome. And as there is no point in taxing an unused vehicle, go to the Post Office and trade in your tax disc against a Statutory Off Road Notice (SORN).

You should 'lay up' the vehicle after it has been driven, so that the brakes are clean and dry. Preserving the brakes means ensuring that they stay rust-free and you can do this in one of two ways. If the motorhome is up on stands, there is no reason why you should not start the engine, warm it up fully and then engage a gear and let the driven wheels rotate for a few minutes. Gently applying the brakes will clean the brake discs or drums for you but you will have to rely on your end-of-season drive to clean up the brakes on the undriven wheels. If the rear brakes are drum brakes, simply leaving the handbrake off should keep them happy – put the vehicle in gear to prevent it from rolling away.

If you would rather not start the vehicle when it is aloft, you will have to protect the brakes' friction surfaces. Equally, you would be well advised to do the same for the undriven wheels' brakes. You cannot oil brakes but you can use a spray concoction, such as Metal Protect, to keep rust at bay. Ideally, you should remove the brake drums if you have them to coat their inside surfaces.

The coating can be removed when you 'recommission' your motorhome and any slight residual coating will be burnt off when the brakes are used.

Your motorhome's interior can be kept in good condition simply by the regular application of a little heat. This, allied to intelligent ventilation, will keep the soft furnishings happy. But never leave a fan heater running unattended.

In winter conditions, it is the cold that is the greatest threat to your interior hardware's wellbeing. Since motorhome water-system components are made largely of plastics, corrosion is not an issue but the risk of serious damage from a freeze-up is high. Most water-heater manufacturers specifically warn that damage from freezing is not covered by the warranty. Some water boilers have self-actuating drain valves that click open when the temperature falls. The simple solution is that if there is no water aboard there is no chance of its freezing. So draining down is a must.

One point on which the jury is still out is whether or not to store the majority of the soft furnishings away from the vehicle. Some people do this and are happy with the result. If you have a cool, dry loft or cellar, then keeping your cushions and mattresses indoors is fine, provided you do not have mice. And the one thing you should take care over is storing LPG cylinders. Storing these where any leaking gas could collect is extremely dangerous.

When the time comes to put your vehicle back into service, you might

A-Class motorhomes needn't be big. The Hymer Exsis-i is 6.15 metres long – that's just over 20 feet

consider a mechanical service. Some suggest that this is better done before you store it. Either way, it is obvious that you should ensure that the strength and freshness of the engine antifreeze is checked *before* the temperature drops. Prior to recommissioning, go around your motorhome's interior with a screwdriver and an aerosol tin of silicone lubricant. A little tightening and lubricating will save you having to sort out what you find needs fixing when you should be enjoying your motorhome.

If you cannot park your motorhome at home or do not have the time or the inclination to look after it all winter long, storage is an option, albeit at a cost. Proper storage puts your motorhome under cover, looked after by people who know what to do. The appropriate information concerning storage can be found in the contacts list at the end of this book.

5 Enjoying Your Motorhome

On the Road: Driving a Motorhome

No matter how experienced a driver you are, you will find that although the driving techniques will be familiar to you, there are some aspects of driving a motorhome you need to think about from the very start. Unless the vehicle is a micro motorhome, which is based on a van derivative of a car, you will encounter differences immediately you climb into the driving seat. For a start the driving position in a full-sized motorhome is higher than in a car.

You will find many elements of a motorhome's cab are like a car's. There will be a steering wheel and two or three pedals in front of you, a gear lever, an instrument binnacle and steering column stalks and a set of switches to control the various functions. Some of the controls will be obvious but use the manufacturer's handbook to ensure that you know them well. And you need to get used to its size – it will be bigger than a car!

Think of it as a box on wheels. Be aware of the length, width and height, and of all the protuberances that might cause problems. Use this mental representation constantly, when driving, when manoeuvring and when parking. One aspect warrants special attention. Driving a car you never have to consider its height. In a motorhome you have to bear that constantly in mind in relation to car-park height barriers, overhanging tree branches and jutting pieces of buildings. Some motorhomers make a point of putting in their cab a label showing their vehicle's height, just to remind them. Some owners of bigger motorhomes play safe by adding the width and length. Even if the label is just a reminder, it is a good idea, particularly if you have never driven a big vehicle before.

Another aspect is the length; in most cases, rear vision is not easy. There are accessories to help you with this but some of the most useful items will be there already. You may have a rear-view mirror in the centre of the windscreen, and it may even give you some rear vision, but you will find yourself using your door mirrors far more than in a car.

Practise makes Perfect

It might be a good idea to hone your driving skills in a safe place. Find a big, empty space in which to practise: most people know where to find such an area. There may be an out-of-town shopping centre, a factory or a station car park. In such an area you will be able to become accustomed to handling your motorhome without having to cope with other road users, narrow spaces or trees. But do not forget about height barriers!

Apart from your motorhome, you will need an assistant and four cardboard boxes. Start by simply driving around the space, just to get the feel of the transmission, steering and brakes. Get used to where the clutch bites, how easy it is to use the handbrake, how the vehicle feels to drive at walking pace and how the accelerator responds to your touch.

When this becomes easy or boring, stop the vehicle, and put two of your cardboard boxes very close to the sides at its widest point. Place the other two boxes to flank the tail. Drive forward and around in a circle, to approach the boxes from the other side. They show the narrowest possible gap you can drive through provided you are driving in a perfectly straight line. It will look very narrow from the driving seat! You would probably be better adding a metre per side to your narrowest gap, to account for any curvature in your course and the need to make steering corrections. Drive between the boxes a few times, looking

Practising driving your motorhome in a wide open space lets you get used to it without the risk of damage

Is there something behind you? You can only park by ear without an assistant – or a reversing camera

out for their position relative to your motorhome's bodywork. And remember to look in the cab mirrors as you go past.

Now put your four boxes in a line and pass them on your blind side, i.e. to the left in a right-hand drive vehicle and vice versa at a crawl, noting where they lie in your field of vision. Have your assistant call out the size of the gap between the boxes and the side of the vehicle. Simultaneously note the position of the boxes in your far cab mirror and you will see how close you can go when passing, for example, a line of parked cars.

Then place your boxes in a line a few yards away from the tail of your motorhome. Although you will be able to see the boxes at each end of the line in your mirrors, have your assistant count down the distance towards them as you reverse closer. When you are a few feet from the boxes, slow to a glacial pace and get your assistant to call out when you are a matter of inches away. Now drive forward, take the end two boxes out of the line and repeat this exercise. You will find that when you reach a certain point, the two remaining boxes directly behind your motorhome will be totally invisible, and you will be reliant on your assistant's spoken instructions.

Practising in this way means that, at worst, you will flatten a cardboard box, which will do your motorhome no harm. Not practising means that you could hit an obstacle, or even a car parked directly behind. This would do your motorhome no good at all and would be costly.

Open Road Adventure

With a better than working knowledge of your motorhome's cab and your new spatial awareness, you can take to the road with confidence. Developments in base vehicles mean that motorhomes can handle modern traffic conditions with ease. The features on current base vehicles can include proportional power steering, servo-assisted brakes, ABS, traction control and cruise control. Many have six-speed gearboxes, while most automatic models are a far cry from vehicles with conventional, fluid-driven automatic gearboxes. Instead, they have a servo-controlled manual gearbox with a clutch. The gearbox is fully automatic but it can be manually overridden to an extent. However, it is the servos that select the gears and operate the clutch, under the command of a computerized control unit, which takes instructions from a simple selector lever that is usually dash-mounted. And the driver has only two pedals, the accelerator and brake, to operate. In American motorhomes, there is usually a conventional automatic gearbox with a fluid-filled torque convertor; a 'stick shift' – a manual transmission – is a rarity in the USA.

Motorhome base vehicles have also benefited from developments in their engines' technology. Turbocharged, intercooled direct injection diesel engines are the norm. These engines, although they have the unmistakable diesel sound at low speeds, run quietly and smoothly at higher speeds. Nowadays, it is possible for 130 horsepower to be delivered by a 2.3-litre, four-cylinder diesel engine. Manufacturers now refer to horsepower rather than engine capacity for this reason and power outputs of this magnitude mean that there is more than enough power and, just as important, torque – the engine's twisting force – to allow realistic cruising speeds with reasonable fuel consumption.

However, motorhomes may now be car-like but are not quite like a car to drive. First, diesel engines give out power at relatively low engine speeds. When the power delivery starts to fall away in a particular gear, simply change up. The next point is that, compared to a car, a motorhome is heavy. Although they may be able to cruise at high speeds on a motorway, few motorhomes can accelerate like a car so allowances must be made when pulling out on to a main road and when overtaking. Similarly, braking has to be planned to allow for this weight. The base vehicles' brakes are totally adequate for the weight they must cope with but it is wise to be aware of this weight, especially when the vehicle is packed for an extended holiday. Moreover, being tall as well as weighty, motorhomes have more marked dynamic responses than cars. Although they are usually well controlled, there may be body roll, pitch, dive and squat. These mean that a motorhome cannot be driven with as much verve as a car can.

The size of motorhomes, even of panel van conversions, means that in addition to a commanding viewpoint, they have a commanding presence on the road. The bigger the motorhome, the more this applies. So in traffic, be careful to leave room for fellow road users, especially at roundabouts and complicated junctions. It is a good idea to glance regularly at each cab mirror, especially the one on the blind side.

When the road becomes still more open, such as when it is a dual carriageway or a motorway, progress can be very good. Although most lorries are governed to a speed of approximately 56 mph (their motorway speed limit is 60 mph), on good roads, motorhomers can drive faster and overtaking lorries is often simply part of maintaining a good average speed. But there are things to be aware of. One is crosswinds. Motorhomes present a considerable profile to crosswinds and a steady crosswind merely requires the motorhome driver to counter with a small amount of corrective steering. If the crosswind is gusty, or is blanketed by roadside obstructions such as hillocks, bridge pillars and trees, it can have a sudden effect, blowing the motorhome off course. Beginners tend to overreact as they are caught out by the sudden change in the pressure of the crosswind. Practise makes the steering correction finer and so the effect is less obvious. It is also possible to predict crosswinds. If you are about to emerge from behind a hillock, or bridge pillar, you can expect to have to make a steering correction. In gusty conditions, watching the countryside can help you predict when to steer more carefully. For example, when you travel through open countryside, the bowing of trees and the ruffling of crops indicate an approaching gust of wind. And if it is raining, the raindrops in your headlamp beams will illustrate the strength and direction of the wind.

Lorries are roughly cuboid in shape, and they displace a lot of air as they move along, creating a 'wash', much as a ship does on the water. Overtaking, or being overtaken by a lorry, disturbs your motorhome. This may be unnerving at first but compensating for it requires nothing more than a little well-judged steering. If you are overtaking, as you pull out you will feel as though your motorhome is being drawn towards the lorry. As you compensate by steering away from the lorry, the situation will reverse itself as you encounter the lorry's 'bow wave', which pushes you away. Because you are applying corrective steering to keep you away from the lorry, the bow wave will try to take you still further away until you have overhauled the lorry sufficiently for the effects of its 'wash' to subside. So you need to gently weight the steering, first away from the lorry, then towards it, and finally back to the customary centre position. The secret is to 'steer small', as they used to say in the navy. Overcompensating simply makes matters worse.

Another lorry-induced effect is less direct. In certain lights, you will see the tracks that lorries wear in the roads' carriageways. The spacing of these is

Ducks of Hazzard? No, a Marquis Starlet II by Windermere

slightly wider than the track – the distance between the wheels on one axle – of many European motorhomes. When you feel an uncertainty in your motorhome's steering, not unlike the effect of a crosswind, it means that the vehicle's wheels are trying to follow in the lorries' tracks. This feeling of there being a crosswind when it is totally calm is disconcerting but it is not danger-ous. Overzealous steering corrections will make matters worse as the motorhome tries to wander from the worn groove on one side to the one on the other. The trick is to relax, steering gently to iron out the minor degree of yawing. So hold the wheel lightly and let the grooves do the steering. This works, as the grooves are visibly straight, and if their effect becomes very marked, such as when the wear is advanced, steer a course to the left of them. You will see lorries doing this where the road is particularly badly worn.

Mannerly Behaviour

Driving a motorhome involves a mixture of power and responsibility. Being in charge of a larger vehicle, you are also in charge of a larger 'footprint' – the piece of road your vehicle is occupying at any given moment – than a car's. A lorry will have a larger 'footprint' than you or the car. Driving well involves commit-ment and manners. If you intend to pull out of a junction, turn off at a road junction or take a certain exit at a roundabout and so on, signal your intention, then do exactly what your indicators show you plan to do. This will gain you the respect of fellow road users; being timid, irresolute and making unpre-dictable manoeuvres will, quite rightly, make them angry.

On the motorway, you can learn from lorry drivers, who are professional drivers. When one has passed you, they will indicate to pull back in. If you flash your headlights, they will know the tail of their vehicle has passed you and will pull in, with a left-right-left flash of the indicators in thanks. Develop the same habit after drivers flash to indicate that your tail is past their vehicle's nose. It gains other drivers' esteem and puts you on a par with the professionals. However, remember that when a lorry pulls in front of you, you will have to drop back to maintain your braking distance. And do not ruin it all by baulking a lorry that is breasting a long incline. With its load and its governed engine, its speed needs to be constant.

On lesser roads, be courteous, do not prevaricate, but do not be a bully. The size of your motorhome gives weight to your actions but do not abuse it. Keep an eye on your mirrors, do not baulk anybody and do not tailgate slow drivers.

It is a fact of life that some other road users will treat you badly, simply because you are driving a motorhome. You will hear angry hooting of car horns, for no better reason than the fact that you are there. You will be undertaken – passed on the wrong side – even if you are travelling a little above the speed limit. You will be treated to gestures and choice phrases. Stay calm and consider who is making themselves look foolish. After all, it is their blood pressure.

Park or Ride

'Motorhome friendly' is a description applied to many towns, not all of which actually live up to it. Parking a motorhome, especially a larger one, can be difficult if not impossible in some places. And with a few exceptions among micro models and camper vans, a motorhome will not fit in a standard car parking bay, no matter how much you may want it to.

Parking a motorhome is an adjunct to driving it and the cardboard box exercises will have helped in your handling of the vehicle. But where to park? Generally speaking, 'doughnut' development, where businesses have moved out of town into retail parks and the like, is useful to motorhomers. Unless the area is desperately busy, you can usually take up a space and a half if you look carefully. Parking centrally reduces the likelihood of damage from neighbouring cars' doors and it is a good idea to remove any abandoned supermarket trolleys from the vicinity of your parking spot, because if a breeze blows up, they could roll and assault your prized panelwork.

Won't fit! Height barriers keep 'travellers' out of car parks. Sometimes, a warden will let a motorhome in

Park and Ride schemes are also useful, especially as many have dedicated motorhome parking areas. Using these, you can park out of town and take an easy, inexpensive bus ride to the shops. If you encounter a height barrier car park, you need not necessarily dismiss the location as unusable. Height barriers are put there to keep vans – specifically travellers vans – out of car parks. Unless you come across a particularly unhelpful car park warden, there is every chance that the height barrier can be swung open for you.

Given the space, on-street parking is entirely feasible. Here, however, 'the space' is important. If the street is broad and not too busy, your motorhome should be safe enough. Judging which parking spot suits takes a little practise but, as a general rule, if you *think* it is too busy or narrow, it is probably all right, but if you *know* it is, go elsewhere.

When parking at night on the road, most motorhomes will need to use their parking lights. Small motorhomes, those under 1,525 kg unladen weight, may park without lights only in an area subject to a speed limit of 30 mph or less, and the vehicle must then be parked with its nearside to the kerb in a two-way street, and not less than 10 metres from a junction.

Lastly, beware of this particular risk, whether you are parked, or using narrow roads either in or out of town. 'White Van Man' may be a pleasant bloke but he is generally driving to a schedule, sometimes a tight one at that. One passing you at speed from either direction can make a microsecond's miscalculation of scale. At best, you will clash cab mirrors, which is as close as two vehicles can get without serious damage. Whilst sympathy for your assailant would be utterly misplaced, some knowledge of his motivation does not come amiss. After all, he is working to time and it is not his van he is driving…be warned.

Site in Sight

For new motorhomers, the campsite experience can be daunting, but it need not be, and as with anything else knowing the ropes is an advantage. Broadly speaking, major UK campsites fall into one of two categories: club sites and commercial sites.

There are two clubs, which are run on similar lines. The Camping and Caravanning Club has nearly 100 sites up and down the country, while the Caravan Club has around 200. Online booking is possible for members of both, and the campsites are equipped to set standards, so you will know more or less what to expect. Both clubs also have a network of lesser sites. The Camping and Caravanning Club has 1,200 certificated sites that can accommodate five motorhomes or caravans and are exclusively for club members. The Caravan

Club has 2,500 similar sites, called 'certificated locations'. Sites of this kind vary as regards what they offer. Some are simply a flattish field, perhaps with a fresh-water tap and some waste bins. Others have hardstandings – pitches with a gravel, cement or tarmac surface – electricity supplies and other facilities. Some are in sensational locations; some are almost always used as overnight stops and others are close to a particularly enticing attraction or location.

Commercial campsites, sometimes referred to as independent sites, vary greatly. Some have a number of touring pitches, set among 'seasonal' – long-term – ones, and many have a large number of static caravans. These are 'static' in that they generally only move on their tiny wheels to be placed on their pitches and many resemble, and are treated as, permanent homes. Other commercial sites place a greater reliance on touring campers, offering superior facilities, better security and on-site attractions such as a pub or restaurant and even entertainment. And some holiday parks have a section for tourers. These sites are often at seaside locations and have a variety of entertainments, includ-ing cafés, restaurants, sports facilities, children's play areas and perhaps even small funfairs. Premier parks are at the top of the range, usually with such attrac-tions as swimming pools, saunas and top-class restaurants.

There are family-friendly sites, adults-only sites, sites that happily accept pets and sites that abhor them. Given the wide range available, not finding one to suit your needs would be quite a challenge.

One European answer to the American motorhome; the German-built Concorde Liner
1090M is nearly 11 metres long and has all mod cons

There are any number of guides that list campsites available, from the clubs, motoring organizations, tourist boards, independent authors and the Internet. There are campsites that remain open all year round but far more offer pitches 'in season'. The contacts list at the end of this book will get you started. You will see how the clubs offer far more than merely campsites, including loan packages, insurance offers and continental and ferry travel deals. But if you are a first timer, with little experience of driving a motorhome and no campsite experience, it is wise to choose one near to home for your first visit.

Choosing Supplies

The first aspect to consider when deciding what to take with you is the length of time you will be staying on site, because the longer your stay, the more supplies you will need. But there are items you will need regardless of the length of your stay so let us begin with them.

First, you will need items that enable you to use the basic on-site facilities. One of the most important items is a filler hose for the fresh-water system. Campsites have fresh-water taps so you need a hose to carry the water to your motorhome's water filler. It should be a food-grade hose, colour-coded blue. However, campsite hose fittings are generally standard, ¾ in BSP screw fittings so you can use the garden hose variety. Many of the filler hoses in motorhome accessory shops come with these fittings or you can buy food-grade hose by length and add the fittings yourself. Generally, a hose 5 metres long will be more than adequate and not too bulky to store. Some motorhomers also take a food-grade 'run flat' cassette hose, which is much longer and can be reeled back into its cassette after use. Standard 'plug in' hose fittings, consisting of a straight connector and a ¾ in BSP tap connector will generally work, although the occasional campsite has plain, unthreaded taps. For these, you can take the type of connector that has a rubber collar with a hose clip.

Making use of an on-site mains electrical supply also involves a special piece of equipment. Ordinary 13-amp mains plugs and wiring obviously cannot be used out of doors so a site cable is used to make the connection – the hook-up – between the campsite pitch's mains supply point and the motorhome. Incidentally, the term 'hook-up' is also used for the supply point itself. Site cables are usually made with a tough, orange-coloured flexible cable with blue, Institution of Electrical Engineers (IEE)-approved plugs. The usual type of cable is 25 metres long, although one about half this length is often all you will need. The cable can cope easily with frequent unreeling and is happy in most weather conditions. There are special blue, low-temperature cables, for use in literally freezing conditions.

Site cables need no maintenance other than frequent checks to ensure that they have sustained no damage either to the cable itself or to the plug and socket. Replace any cable that shows even the slightest evidence of damage or wear. Another kind of cable is required for motorhomes that carry a TV set. Campsite pitches often have a TV aerial point, connected to a central aerial. To connect to this, you need a co-axial cable whose 'far' end has a standard aerial plug. As with the mains cable, 25 metres is a suitable length. If you forget to take one, most campsites will sell you one, as well as offering rock pegs to secure your awning. Do not forget to take a mallet, though!

As you will be carrying your own gas supply, there are only two LPG-related items you will need. You can buy a replacement LPG cylinder at most campsites but you will not be able to fit it without the right spanner. Such spanners come in two guises: a hefty, cast metal kind and a thin sort, stamped out of flat steel sheet. The former is better. The other necessity lives inside the motorhome. You may have spark igniters for the LPG-burning appliances but if you do not, a piezo crystal or battery-powered gas lighter is better than a box of matches.

Other, more vehicle-orientated equipment is worth having. A towrope is arguably essential. Where you are using a grass pitch, there is a risk of becoming bogged down. When wheel spin occurs on a front-wheel drive vehicle, the chances are that the only way your vehicle will move is straight down. Most campsites have access to a 4x4 vehicle and even a lawn tractor will pull a motorhome on to firm ground.

Many motorhomers loathe not being on the level, so they take levelling wedges along. You can drive your vehicle onto these tough, moulded plastic ramps, sometimes called chocks, placing them under the front wheels or under both wheels on one side as necessary. Dogmatic motorhomers also take a small spirit level along. And it is sensible to get a pitch marker. These little signs are used to indicate that a campsite pitch is yours. Motorhome accessory shops sell them, as do campsite reception offices. Some people use their site cable as a marker, which is a bad idea for two reasons: if left plugged in, it could give someone a shock, and if left unattended, it is likely to be stolen.

Less specialized equipment deserves a permanent home in your motorhome. You may not always use these items but if you do need them, you will be glad to have them. A basic toolkit is a must, for use both on and in your motorhome. Screwdrivers of varying sizes in flat-blade and crosshead varieties come in useful, as does a modest set of spanners, combination ones (ring one end, ordinary the other end) being the most versatile. A simple adjustable spanner also helps and a water pump spanner (which looks like a big, angled pair of pliers) will cope with tight fresh-water tap fittings. Conventional and narrow-nosed pliers are also useful, as is a self-grip wrench. All these will fit in a standard canvas tool roll, which takes up very little room. Add a good, preferably digital, tyre pressure gauge and you will be ready for most eventualities. A good, reliable torch is also worth having – avoid the cheap kind, it will probably let you down.

Domestic Supplies

Motorhomes sometimes come complete with crockery and cutlery; others you have to equip yourself. But the items are much the same. The cutlery on offer is usually simple and tough equipment. Ensure that you have as many sets as you have people to feed. Motorhome crockery may be ceramic but many motorhomers use the unbreakable melamine kind, which is light and easy to use. You will find dedicated storage for this dinnerware in the vast majority of vehicles.

Motorhome kitchenware is a bit special too. Pans tend to be smaller than their domestic equivalents and you will need a kettle to use on your gas hob; the kind that whistles when boiling is best. Just how many and what kind of pans you need depends on your culinary ambitions, but generally a frying pan and two or three saucepans with lids will suffice. Again, you will find storage locations for these items in most motorhomes.

'Watering up', i.e. filling a motorhome's fresh-water tank, entails using a blue-coded, food-grade hose. Here, the yellow connector is ¾ inch BSP, the standard UK size

As regards ablutions, you equip a motorhome washroom in much the same way as you would a domestic bathroom but on a smaller scale. Soap, towels, shampoo, shaving cream, toothpaste and deodorants can all be bought in smaller sizes and it is sensible to have a toilet bag apiece for when you use the on-site ablutions facilities. The one item you will need that is not required at home is a supply of WC chemicals. These come in two kinds: flush and waste. Not all motorhomes need the former but nearly all need the latter. Flush chemicals are invariably in liquid form and are added to the flush water, except where the motorhome's fresh-water system automatically replenishes it. Waste chemicals are available in liquid form as well as in water-soluble bags, which are more convenient to store and use.

Sleeping in a motorhome requires something to sleep in and something to sleep under. As regards bedclothes, motorhomers subscribe to one of two schools of thought. Many swear by sleeping bags and these are available in various forms – single, zip-together double or the 'mummy' kind with a hood. Others find that a pair of duvets, one to lie on, and one to snuggle under, work well in larger motorhomes – only the covers need be washed. And you will need pillows.

First-timers tend to take far too many clothes. Although most motorhomes have more than enough storage space, there are limits. It is better to take the essentials, such as underwear, socks and so on, and top them off with multi-function clothing. For example, a fleece can be leisurewear, outerwear and sleepwear. Sandals can double as slippers although the reverse does not apply. Similarly, a towelling dressing gown is unisex by definition and can be used turn and turn about for visits to the ablutions block. It is unlikely that you will need more than one 'smart' outfit apiece and do not forget that most campsites offer laundry facilities.

A small toolkit is more than merely worth having. A canvas tool roll like this takes up very little room

When it comes to food, as in other areas, economy of scale applies. You might be able to get giant, family-sized packages of consumables in the supermarket but there is limited space in a motorhome. One way around this is to transfer the contents of such packages into smaller containers, always assuming the rest will keep at home. But in most instances, the basic rule is 'keep it small and simple'.

Getting Settled

Arrangements about arrival times vary among commercial sites but most club sites have standard schedules. For example, at Camping and Caravanning Club sites, you can usually arrange to arrive at any time up to 11 p.m., which is when the barriers are locked for the night. At Caravan Club sites, the deadline is 8 p.m. Many sites cater for traffic delays by having a late-arrivals area where you can pitch for the night with the use of mains electricity. You will probably be allowed to use the site's WCs and showers but it is highly unlikely that you will have access to fresh water near the late arrivals pitches. So travelling with a few litres of water on-board is a wise move. Note that if you are late, ringing the reception office's doorbell to summon a campsite warden is very much frowned upon – after hours, the bell is strictly for emergencies. And when planning your

Wait for it … negotiating a campsite barrier presents no problem, provided you let it open fully

journey, bear in mind that many campsites are tucked away in attractive rural locations. This is delightful but the roads to the site may be tight for larger motorhomes. It makes sense to arrive in daylight if possible.

On arrival you first need to go into the campsite's reception office, to book yourself in and pay for your stay. Unless a pitch has been allocated to you, you will be invited to go into the site and choose one. When you know your pitch number, you can walk back later to the reception office, where you will be given a barrier key, card or access code.

Barriers are put at the entrance and exit of a site for security reasons, to keep unwanted visitors out and to prevent unauthorized people bringing a vehicle on site. Most in the UK are electrically operated car-park-style barriers with a pole that rises to let your vehicle pass. A few sites have the ramp kind that rises out of the ground. But whatever the type, it will respond either to an electronic 'key', a swipe/proximity card or an entry code you punch into a keypad.

The trick with barriers is to be patient. Drive close to the pole that bears the key/card slot or keypad and actuate the barrier. It will open, but wait for it to open fully. If you drive through a pole-type barrier too quickly, you may clip the upper corner of your motorhome on the pole. But once you have started driving through, the barrier will remain open.

The warden on duty will show you on a site plan the pitches that are available to you and may have recommended certain ones as suitable for the size of

Popular pitches on a typical campsite. These are hardstanding pitches at a site only yards from the shore of Loch Lomond

motorhome you have. In choosing a pitch, a hardstanding one is better than grass. Many campsites, at home and abroad, have pitches equipped with a tough, ground-level hexagonal mesh to prevent vehicles' wheels spinning or sinking into the ground. So if you see a grass pitch that is classed as hardstanding, it is a pitch with mesh.

Many commercial campsites offer 'super pitches'. They usually have fresh-water taps, grey-water drain points, TV aerial points and perhaps waste bins. You obviously pay a premium for one of these.

A pitch near an ablutions block may be convenient but these facilities are generally heavily used, so if you want a quiet time, choose one further away. Of course the special pitches set aside for disabled customers are invariably near the on-site facilities. A children's play area will be popular, as will a dog-walking area, so bear these factors in mind if you are seeking peace and solitude. Among other considerations are trees and pitch markers. Taking someone else's marked pitch is definitely out of order, even if it is only marked with a camping chair or a site cable – if in doubt, check with the reception office whether it is actually taken. And trees can offer shade in summer, which is pleasant. They will also attract birds, which is also pleasant but can give you a cleaning-up task to do. And when it rains, water dropping from trees can make life in a motorhome noisy.

Having selected your pitch, drive or reverse your motorhome onto it. Positioning your vehicle centrally looks neat and it will be obvious how far to

'Corner steadies' stop motorhomes moving on their springs on site. They aren't jacks

Plentiful storage is typical of motorhomes. Note the gas isolation valves which the top drawer's fascia normally conceals

park from the roadway. However, you must be careful not to drive on the grassed areas surrounding a hardstanding pitch – site wardens frown upon this. If you are using chocks, this is when you will drive your vehicle up on to them; the angle your vehicle adopts without wedges will show where they should go and you can easily fine-tune their positioning. Some motorhomes also have 'corner steadies', which are good for motorhomers who dislike the feeling of their motorhome's body moving on its springs as they walk around inside. You simply lower these to ground level, adding wood blocks beneath them if the ground is soft. Just remember that they are steadies, not jacks – do not try to lift the motorhome significantly with them.

The technique for connecting to the mains electricity hook-up – the pole that has the socket to accept your site cable – varies. Start by ensuring that the mains circuit breaker in your motorhome is switched off. Then open the mains connection plug's cover on your motorhome, lift the sprung blue socket cover on your cable's connector and push the connector onto your motorhome's recessed plug. Then, lead the cable to the site's hook-up, lift its socket cover and plug in your cable. At many sites, this makes the connection and the site's socket cover, under spring pressure, engages with your cable's plug to hold it secure. However, if the site's socket has a red button by it, you have to twist your cable's plug clockwise. When you hear and feel a click, the connection is made and the plug is secure. You press the red button to release it. Finally, go back and switch on your motorhome's circuit breaker. You should then have power. If you do not, the site hook-up's own breaker may have been tripped by the pitch's previous occupant. Some hook-ups' breakers are accessible and can simply be switched back on but some are concealed and must be reset by a warden.

Amenities

Most campsites have similar on-site facilities and there are accepted ways of using them. Starting with outdoor ones, one or more motorhome service points are provided. The most basic of these has a fresh-water tap and a special drain for grey water. Many have a further tap, sometimes with a hose to be used for rinsing down the area after you have drained your grey water. This additional tap does not necessarily provide drinking water.

Refilling and draining water involves taking your motorhome to a service point and you have to ensure that you do not block the adjacent roadway. When draining grey water, position your motorhome so that its drainage point is over the special drain; some motorhomes have a drain hose, which makes positioning your vehicle easier. Above all, remember to shut off your grey-water drain tap before driving away. Should you not have a grey-water tank, remember to use a bucket or wheeled water container to collect your grey water for disposal. Wardens do not appreciate their pitches being made soggy, nor do they like a motorhome's dribbling out grey water all the way from the pitch to beyond the barriers.

Black water, the contents of your WC cassette, has to be drained into a special WC chemical disposal point. At some sites, these are at or near a motorhome service point. At others, they are housed in special locations, next to or let into the outside wall of an ablutions block. Whether your black-water tank is a cassette or the lower half of a smaller chemical WC, it will be sealed when you remove it from its normal location. Equip yourself with the WC chemical you need and carry (or wheel) the tank to the disposal point. There, you will find a plastic or stainless steel hopper, or a WC-like ceramic moulding. Swinging out your waste tank's drain spout if necessary, remove the cap and start to pour the contents into the receptacle provided. On most waste tanks, you also hold in a sprung button which lets air into the tank, making pouring easier and preventing splashing.

When the tank is empty, you have to rinse it. Using the nearby tap, which may have a short hose, fill the tank $1/3$ full, replace the cap and shake the tank. The aim is to swill the water around sufficiently to clean the inside of the tank. Remove the cap, pour out the water and repeat the rinsing until the water runs clean. Then add about a litre of water to the tank. Depending on the sort of waste tank and chemical you are using, you can simply add a water-soluble WC chemical sachet, or use the tank cap to measure out the required amount of liquid chemical (be careful, it stains!). Finally, replace the cap and shake the tank a little to mix the chemical and water. When the waste tank/cassette is replaced in your motorhome, it is ready to be used again.

If you have a WC that needs its flush water replenished, you may want to add flush chemical. Some WC systems have a flush-water filler just inside the WC cassette locker door. A filling point with a water level sight glass is provided. Simply add the required amount of flush chemical and refill the flush reservoir. In WCs that separate into upper and lower sections, the flush reservoir is in the upper section, surrounding the WC bowl. Remove the filler cap, add flush chemical and fill the reservoir with clean water.

Among the outdoor amenities at campsites, you will find fire extinguishers and probably fire-alarm bells. There are usually washing-up sinks and vegetable-preparation areas, and most sites have a public telephone and a building or area with brochures, leaflets and posters giving information on everything from local supermarkets through to attractions and local medical contacts.

Going down in the world: once wheelspin happens on grass, front-wheel drive motorhomes tend to get nowhere. This is why you should carry a towrope!

Indoor facilities vary from site to site, but there are once again some that you can expect almost anywhere. Campsites have showers, WCs and hand basins; sometimes the basins are in privacy cubicles. Sites generally have at least one set of ablutions facilities adapted for disabled campers and a number of sites offer a bath. Where the use of any item is chargeable, it is normally coin- or token-operated – tokens or change can be obtained from the reception office. The amenities also tend to include hair dryers, shaver sockets, soap dispensers and hand dryers. Ablutions blocks are usually heated and there are mops and buckets so that you can clean the cubicle floor after you have had a shower. Some sites also have parent/child or family bathrooms and/or baby changing equipment. And some campsites, premier parks especially, set great store by the quality of their facilities. Apart from such upmarket additions as underfloor heating or sunbeds, some have saunas and heated indoor swimming pools.

More prosaic facilities can also be found in amenities blocks. Particularly where tent campers are accommodated, there may be a kitchen, with a food preparation area, sinks, a freezer, a cooker and a microwave oven. Most sites offer a laundry, with washing machines, tumble dryers, irons and ironing boards – coin- or token-operated. It is rare for a site of any size not to have a shop and most campsite shops are very well stocked. In addition to the basics – bread, milk, vegetables and the like – there is often food in freezers as well as books, toys and, of course, essentials for campers, like WC chemicals, soap and shampoo. Some site shops offer DVD hire and most have an arrangement for the delivery of certain items including newspapers, baked goods and so on.

When it comes to more entertaining activities, some campsites go well beyond the norm. Many have an on-site pub or restaurant and a games room with pool, video games and other such pursuits. Often, the same location offers entertainment, featuring local bands, comedy acts and the like. And holiday-park-style sites have such things as water slides, funfair rides and pony trekking.

Campsites' children's play areas tend to include swings, slides and seesaws, usually with soft surrounding flooring. Some go further, with such things as a mock fort, climbing frames and adventure trails. Where they are accepted, dogs are well catered for, with dog walks in open or wooded areas set well away from roads. Campsite reception offices or shops usually sell poop scoops.

Let Live Living

Campsites obviously have rules, most of which are perfectly sensible. For example, there is usually a rule against cyclists riding around the ablutions blocks. Similarly, you will see signs saying something like 'Everyone loves your dog – on a lead.' Most campers secure their dog with a long lead attached to a screw-in

Plugging your site cable into a hook-up like this requires a clockwise twist – the red button unlocks the plug. The white cable is a connection to the site's TV aerial

ground anchor. And you are asked, for safety's sake, to pitch no closer than 6 metres (20ft) from neighbouring motorhomes or caravans in case there is a fire.

Of course campsites differ. Some are quieter than others, some have higher levels of foot traffic, and some have more pets, more bicycles or more walkers. Most of the time everybody gets on just fine but there are a few conventions that may not be written down or signposted but that nevertheless apply. One concerns noise. In mid-afternoon, it is generally fine to play your music or watch your TV with the volume set at a reasonable level, but not late at night. Similarly when you are talking outside your motorhome, remember that sound travels at night, so do not talk too loudly. Another source of noise that is unacceptable is an engine-powered generator. On a small certificated site, you may get away with a session running a generator for battery charging but on a well-populated site, you will probably have complaints if you leave a generator running during the day and certainly if you run one at night.

Many motorhomers like to do a little local touring during the day. You can often go on and off site more or less whenever you like, but some sites lock the

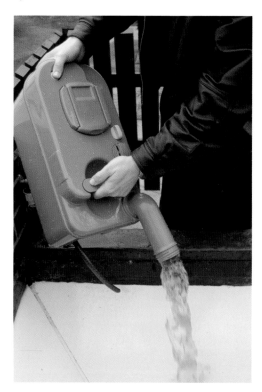

Emptying a Thetford WC cassette. Pressing the yellow button lets air enter the cassette, to prevent splashing when pouring

gates or disable the barriers between certain times overnight. And if you are setting off very early or returning late, remember to drive and pitch quietly, with as little manoeuvring as possible and minimal use of your doors. A good tip to remember is that, when reconnecting your mains hook-up, you can walk on grass in silence, but not on gravel.

Sooner or later, you are likely to come across a difficult warden. The vast majority are reasonable, cheerful people. They are welcoming, helpful and accommodating, and they do their jobs efficiently. But occasionally you find some who are quite the reverse. If a staff member becomes obstructive or abusive, remember that you are the customer. Faced with such treatment, you are quite within your rights to refuse to honour your booking and leave. If you are not satisfied with any aspect of the campsite or the way you are being treated, it is inevitably because someone is not doing their job properly, and you should have no qualms about reporting them to a higher authority. This could be the head office of the club involved or the owner of the campsite concerned. Make a note of names, events, dates, times and locations and complain in writing.

Wild Life

Some motorhomers love wild camping, others abhor it. Wild camping means staying overnight at a spot that is not a genuine campsite. Wild camping conjures up romantic ideas about the freedom of the road, but it is as well to know the reality. It is frowned upon in the UK and if you do not follow the rules, which are strict, you could end up with less freedom than you anticipated. Wild camping on a main road is illegal. On minor roads local byelaws or landowners' rules may apply. You cannot wild camp on anyone's land without permission. Some motorhomes do so and get away with it, but you could be moved on.

In Scotland, some confusion might arise, as the Land Reform Act of 2003 allows wild camping. However, here the term refers to tents, not motorhomes. Motorized camping is not included. So the laws are the same in the whole of the UK.

In recent years, there have been moves to set up 'stopovers' – one-night halts after the French model. There are websites revealing the whereabouts of such locations in the UK. The same websites usually offer an appraisal of the facilities, conditions and costs. However, at the time of writing, their establishment is still under development.

It may be refreshing to be able to park up and settle down more or less

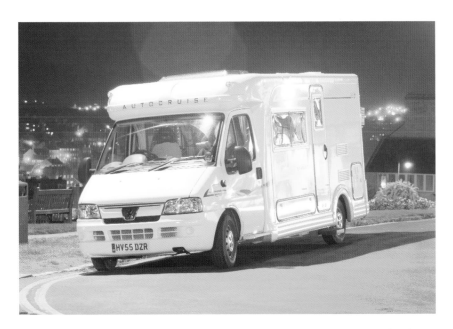

Ghost hunting on Halloween near Whitby Abbey. Motorhomes give you the freedom to exercise your imagination

anywhere *en route*, and motorhomes can be independent to an extent as regards water, electricity and waste. Moreover, the costs, if any, are minimal. On the other hand, you are on your own as regards security – there are no site barriers and no policing. The two major UK clubs oppose wild camping for this reason.

6 Accessories

Chapter 3 was designed to help you find your perfect motorhome. But if there were really such a thing as the perfect motorhome, motorhome accessory shops would not be viable. The fact that they thrive proves that there is always some extra item that people will want to fit to their motorhome. And as technology develops, new items are invented and existing ones refined and developed. So as long as there is something new or something better, there will be buyers willing to invest in it.

Your motorhome may well already have some of the accessories described here. Manufacturers of motorhomes keep their finger firmly on the pulse of the market and extras seen as being in demand tend to win their way into the motorhomes' options lists, if not into the manufacturers' standard specifications. In many instances, a set of them is included, at a knockdown price, as a special package of some sort.

Top-Up Option

As we saw in Chapter 4, motorhomes rely on LPG gas, which is held either in a fixed tank or in cylinders that can be exchanged. For many, the latter system works well enough but it has its disadvantages. Most motorhomers cope well enough with changing a gas cylinder but it can be hard work, especially with larger cylinders. Anyone who has had to carry a 13-kg cylinder for any distance will know that at around 32 kg – over 70 lb – gross weight, it takes some strength. Also, motorhome gas lockers are mounted low down, in order to keep the vehicle's centre of gravity low. Some motorhomes have slide-out LPG cylinder trays but many do not and exchanging cylinders can be tough on the back.

The other disadvantage, as we have seen, is that LPG containers are not standardized across Europe. You have to use the only generally available cylinders if you want to buy more LPG outside the UK and these are too small to be

Motorhome shows are great places to get hands-on experience of new vehicles – and choose accessories

economic in larger motorhomes. Both in the UK and elsewhere, however, you can refill fixed gas tanks at any filling station that has Autogas, the fuel that LPG-powered vehicles use. Autogas is propane so a low ambient temperature does not affect it and refilling with LPG is significantly cheaper than buying it in cylinders. This is fine for those with a fixed LPG tank, and you can have a fixed tank fitted, but there is a simpler, less expensive alternative – refillable cylinders. These remain permanently in your gas locker and can be refilled at any filling station with an Autogas pump.

Monopoly

The company with the UK monopoly on refillable LPG cylinders is Gaslow International, of Loughborough, Leicestershire. This company is unique in offering a fixed system whose LPG cylinders are sized to be direct replacements for exchangeable ones. It has European Pi-approved gas cylinders, in 6- or 11-kg sizes with 80 per cent overfill protection (see below) and a fifteen-year warranty. A fixed filler point is fitted to the motorhome and a rubber-free, stainless steel braided filler hose leads from it to the refillable cylinder. In a dual-cylinder installation, a similar hose connects the two cylinders and a high-pressure LPG hose leads from each cylinder to the motorhome's LPG regulator.

A manual or automatic changeover valve can be fitted to the existing regulator or you can specify an automatic or manual changeover valve with an integral regulator. Several different European filler adaptors are available for use with the fixed filler point. Special brackets, in three different sizes, enable you to fit the filler point inside your gas locker. Where an underfloor fitting is preferable, as in many panel-van conversions, this range of brackets is also suitable.

Using the Gaslow refillable system is as simple as using a standard LPG system with exchangeable cylinders. And as the installation lies upstream of the regulator, you can fit it without the need for certification. However, as we saw in Chapter 4, it is unwise to work with LPG unless you are confident that you know exactly what you are doing. The company has a list of motorhome and accessory dealerships where a system can be fitted for you. There are also two mobile fitting concerns which can equip your motorhome with a refillable system by appointment, at one of the numerous motorhome shows or at your home.

Two Yellow Bottles

The following is a description of the fitting of a typical Gaslow installation to a standard motorhome LPG locker. Professional fitters carried out this work in a little over an hour, although there was a delay because of the need to photograph the procedure.

The installation began with the fitting of the filler point. Unless it is mounted underneath the motorhome, this must be fitted into the LPG locker's outside wall. Mounting it in the locker door is out of the question, as the repeated opening and closing of the door could cause problems with the filler hose, and it is preferable for the filler hose to not pass through the motorhome's living area. Ensuring that there was clearance for the filler hose to be attached to the back of the filler and led to the LPG cylinder, the fitter used a hole saw to cut through the motorhome's sandwich construction wall. After attaching the filler hose to it, he coated the filler point's inner face with silicone sealant, also coating the cut area of the wall panel to prevent water ingress. Finally, he mounted the filler point to the wall with long, self-tapping screws.

Two 6-kg refillable cylinders were then fitted into the gas locker's cylinder retainers. They were strapped home in exactly the same way as their exchangeable predecessors but with the cutaways in their collars facing one another, to make access to their main valves easy. As the motorhome did not have room for an automatic changeover valve, a manually operated valve was fitted to the inlet of the existing regulator. The installation work was completed with the addition of a T-connector to the rearmost cylinder's central filler port. This accepted the filler hose leading from the side-wall-mounted filler point and a similar hose was led to the other cylinder's filler port. Two high-pressure hoses

Strapping in the Gaslow refillable LPG cylinders during an installation procedure. These stay put permanently and you can refill them anywhere you find an Autogas station

were then fitted, one from each cylinder's outlet valve to the changeover valve's two inlet ports.

The first fill-up of the installation was an easy task. Unscrewing the filler point's cover, the fitter attached the Autogas pump's bayonet-action nozzle. By pressing a button on the pump, he took the LPG delivery display to 22 litres before starting the filling (two 6-kg cylinders can hold 23 litres of LPG). When the filling was finished, he detached the pump nozzle, causing a brief, sharp hiss of escaping gas as the pressure of the LPG in the pump's filler pipe was released. The final task was to use an LPG gas-detecting probe to check that none of the connections was leaking.

Refillable cylinders cannot be overfilled. The overfill protection system lets LPG bleed out of the cylinders when they are 80 per cent full, at which point the Autogas pump will stop delivering gas. And unlike exchangeable cylinders, refillable ones can be topped up whenever you like.

Refillable LPG cylinders let you take your motorhome to the LPG rather than vice versa. They let you fill up the cylinders, with a significant saving, whenever you like and wherever there is a supply – and not just in the UK. They also save you having to carry heavy LPG cylinders and to release and make high-pressure gas connections at each exchange. Arguably the most important advantage is that there are adaptor nozzles for use with LPG pumps in Europe and elsewhere. If you use a significant amount of LPG in your motorhome, a refillable system is likely to pay for itself in a surprisingly short time.

Screen Play

You may have seen motorhomes with silver, padded covers over their windscreens and cab windows. These are insulating screens that keep the interior of a motorhome warm during cold conditions and cool in bright sunlight. They also offer privacy.

Many motorhomers call these items 'silver screens', but in fact Silver Screens is a trade name. The following description is of a set of genuine Silver Screens fitted to a standard Peugeot motorhome cab.

The screens have three layers, the exterior and interior ones being waterproof, aluminium pigmented PU Nylon. The centre layer is 'high-loft' polyester wadding. They work through a combination of insulation and reflection. The inner layer sits tightly against the cab glass and reflects heat back into the motorhome's interior, while the outer layer reflects the sun's heat on bright days. The centre layer is an insulating barrier, which, in retaining the motorhome's internal warmth, prevents condensation from appearing inside the cab glass and frost forming on the outside. The screens fit tightly to the outside of the cab, so the side windows can be opened for ventilation without fear of rainwater entering.

Silver Screens can be stored in a travelling bag and, although they come as a three-piece set, broad Velcro strips joining their windscreen and side sections mean that, after they have been adjusted to fit snugly, they can be treated as a one-piece screen. A further refinement, the 'Priva-See' panel, is a mesh section that fits between the centre section and the windscreen. This means that the windscreen section can be folded partially down or up, or removed altogether, letting light into the cab during the day, but the mesh section prevents people from seeing into the motorhome.

Fitting a set of Silver Screens is easy. An optional 'bib' section can be fitted first, to stop cold draughts entering your motorhome's cab via the base vehicle's air inlet at the foot of its windscreen. This involves opening your bonnet and tucking the bib under the windscreen wiper arms. With the bonnet closed, lift the wiper arms and open a cab door. Pockets on the screen's cab door sections slip over the doorframe; it is unimportant which door you open first. Having fitted the side section of the screen over the first door, close it and unroll the Silver Screen across the motorhome's windscreen, taking the second side section

Silver Screens can keep heat in – or out! They're quite easy to fit

round to lie against the opposite cab door. Open this, slip the second pocket over the doorframe and close the cab door. This tensions the screens to fit tightly around the cab glass, although you will need to make adjustments to the Velcro strips the first time you fit the screens. Finally, the Velcro-equipped tabs fitted to the screens are fastened around the cab mirrors' stems. Should the weather warrant their use, storm ties are also fitted, to tie the lower trailing corners of the screens firmly to the cab door handles.

In an informal test, the set of Silver Screens pictured here was fitted when the outside temperature was –5°C. Within half an hour and with no adjustment to the motorhome's blown air heating, the internal temperature rose by 3.6°C to a comfortable 20.2°C. There was no condensation at all and no need to close the motorhome's cab curtains – the cab glass was tightly covered and therefore total privacy was ensured.

Silver Screens can also be fitted inside the cab glass if desired. There are rival insulating screens, some of which are external and some to be fitted internally using rubber suckers. The latter kind is sometimes used in preference to cab curtains by some motorhome manufacturers, especially those offering smaller panel-van conversions.

Looking Back

Most motorhomes, especially larger ones, have less than ideal rear vision for the driver. Even in a panel-van conversion, the rear windows are a long way from the driver's seat. Travel seats, the washroom, wardrobe and bulkhead panels can intrude and some motorhomes have no rear window at all! In panel-van conversions, it is often possible to use a stick-on fresnel lens, which gives a wide-angle view of what is behind. However, the lens will still be a long way from the driver and can also be of little use when it is dark, especially as not all motorhomes have particularly bright reversing lamps. In a coach-built or A-Class motorhome, although having a passenger count down the distance remaining to an obstacle usually works well, errors can occur. Moreover, they have to go to the rear of the motorhome to keep watch and if there is not a rear window, opening a side window or the side entry door is the only possibility. Even when such a motorhome has a rear window, it may be small, offset or too high to offer a view of anything lower than a van. And motorhomes, which are usually built with weight in mind, are not very tough – they do not take kindly to contact with anything. The answer lies in a reversing camera system. Modern reversing camera systems are miniature CCTV installations, with a camera mounted on the motorhome's tail and a monitor in the cab. They come in simple, black-and-white varieties and colour versions, some with enhancements making them able to 'see', to an extent, in the dark. The monitor can be mounted on top of the dash or in the cab roof, fixed or folding down to occupy the place where a rear view mirror would normally be fitted. Some systems employ a rear view mirror with an inset reverse view monitor section.

Although a reversing camera system can be activated manually, it is better if it is operated by the motorhome's reversing lamp switch. Arranged in this way, the monitor shows the view to the rear when you select reverse gear.

Seeing the Light

The system has a 12-volt-powered closed-circuit TV camera, whose picture is sent, via a cable, to a tiny, cab-mounted TV screen. It is digital, and since you will be expecting to see an image that is reversed, as it would be in a mirror, the picture is itself reversed electronically. The view is from a wide-angle lens mounted high on the tail of the motorhome; it is usual to aim the camera so that the vehicle's tail panel is visible at the foot of the monitor's screen. And a recent development has two rearward views from two separate lenses. One is wide angle, the second gives a less distorted, distant view, similar to that in a conventional rear-view mirror.

Southport after sunset in the Marquis Starlet II

Although the wide-angle image is necessarily distorted by the 120-degree view, it is still possible to use it to reverse accurately. After some practice, you can use a reversing camera to help you align a motorhome's towbar with the towing hitch of a trailer – reversing to within ½ in or less of the 'target'. And in the dark, reversing camera systems with night vision easily outperform conventional rear-view mirrors. A bank of LEDs on each side of the lens and infrared enhancement means that an image is available in near blackness. The motorhome's own reversing lamps illuminate the scene anyway, but when reverse gear is not selected and the lights are extinguished, it is still possible to discern detail in very low ambient light.

A simple installation of this sort is more than adequate for the majority of motorhomers. However, it is possible for the cab monitor to receive more than one signal. Some owners of big American motorhomes have several cameras and can switch views, to see what is happening not only at the rear but also on the driver's blind side and even at bumper level at the front. It is also possible for the monitor to display other inputs, such as from a DVD player or a TV tuner. Naturally, entertainment content of this kind has to be disabled when the motorhome is driven.

Many reversing camera systems' cameras have a built-in microphone, so that as well as being your 'eyes', the system becomes your 'ears'. Consequently, you

Tail end tell tale: the view from a reversing camera. The image is reversed because it replaces what you'd see in a rear-view mirror

can hear car engines, pedestrians' footsteps and so on. A good reversing camera will also have an automatic iris to adapt to the available lighting, a waterproof housing and electric heating to prevent condensation or frost from obscuring the view. One-touch screen dimming and audio muting are also common.

It is possible to fit such a system yourself, the trickiest parts being leading the signal cable from the camera to the cab (although there are wireless systems), and rigging a 12-volt power feed to be switched on by selecting reverse gear.

An alternative to a reversing camera system is increasingly appearing on new cars. Reverse beepers use proximity sensors, usually mounted low on the rear of the motorhome. They detect the presence of obstacles and activate a beeper mounted in the cab. The speed of the beeping increases as the obstacle is approached, usually changing to a continuous tone when it is very close. Beeper systems work fairly well, but the limitation with some is that they cannot always differentiate between benign items such as long grass and more damaging obstacles.

What Comes Naturally

The majority of motorhomes have a chemical WC where chemicals need to be replenished whenever the waste tank needs emptying. This arrangement works perfectly well but it has its disadvantages. The chemicals are not cheap and when they are in liquid form, spills can cause stains. Although the chemicals have been tested and confirmed as biodegradable, their cumulative effect on the environment cannot be too good. Moreover, they are another consumable item to carry. There is an alternative which fits common, standard WCs with a separate waste cassette. After buying the kit and perhaps having it fitted, the only further cost is the consumption of a miserly amount of 12-volt electric current when the WC is in use.

The German-made SOG system is a very simple, practically 'fit and forget' item. It consists of a low-powered electric extractor unit, basically a tiny fan in a moulded plastic housing, which is usually fitted to the inner face of the WC's service locker door. A moulded vent, with an integral charcoal filter, fits on the outside of the locker door. Inside the locker, a flexible pipe leads from the extractor unit to a special fitting that replaces the waste cassette's original pressure relief valve. A microswitch, fitted to the mechanism that allows the cassette's sealing blade to be opened and closed, switches the extractor on whenever the blade is opened.

The system works by creating a weak vacuum at all points inboard of the extractor unit. When the fan is running, the waste cassette and WC bowl are subject to this vacuum. Consequently, odours are drawn out of the WC and its

This is all that's externally visible in a SOG WC extraction system. The housing contains a charcoal filter

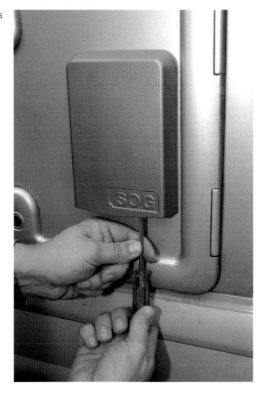

cassette and vented, via the charcoal filter, to the outside air. Being drawn out and not confined, they never achieve enough of a concentration to cause offence.

So, how does the waste material degrade? Normally, the WC chemicals slow this process, also perfuming the waste/flush water/chemical mixture. The SOG system draws oxygen through the waste cassette, across the surface of its contents. This actively promotes decomposition of the waste material. According to SOG, adding chemicals will hinder this process. There is no need to add anything and ordinary, soft toilet tissue can be used.

The SOG system is practically unnoticeable in use. The extractor fan is switched on automatically, and though it can be heard running, is very quiet. It consumes a paltry 0.43 watts. The only other difference between a standard chemical WC and its SOG-equipped alternative comes when the cassette needs emptying. When removing the cassette from the motorhome, you simply detach the extractor's flexible pipe from the waste cassette and close off the connector with the stopper that SOG supply. The cassette is then emptied in the normal way. As WC chemical disposal points are either outdoors or let into the side of a building, the lack of the chemicals' odour-control effect is not a significant problem.

Anyone with average DIY skills can fit a SOG system and it is available for both bench-type and swivel-bowl Thetford WCs. It is recommended that the charcoal filter element is changed yearly and that the flexible pipe and its connecting elbow are periodically sprayed with a silicone lubricant. Otherwise, the system is maintenance-free.

Alarming News

A motorhome can easily be stolen, or 'rung' – given a false identity and new paint and graphics, and sold. A motorhome with a TV, DVD player, CD/radio, clothing, a camera, laptop computer, jewellery and other personal goods on-board can be gutted in a very short time. The pickings are rich and, what with plastic windows and simple door locks, the way in can be child's play.

There are two ways of providing security. One is to fit security items that are 'passive', ranging from simply running a luggage strap across both the cab doors' pull handles to adding tough security locks to the locker doors and entry doors. One or more floor-mounted steel anti-theft posts can be set up, behind which you can park your motorhome in your drive, and there are pedal locks, steering wheel locks and the like. The main point about passive security is that it should be very, very tough and highly visible. Apart from arrangements that identify the vehicle, such as huge numbers on the roof for police helicopters to spot or the registration number etched into the glass, passive security buys time or deters a thief. If a motorhome is made difficult to break into, to drive away or preferably both, a thief is encouraged to look elsewhere. The aim is to force a thief into spending more time getting into the motorhome, preferably also adding the need to make some noise into the bargain. And where the arrangement is not so highly visible, adding stickers to the vehicle that tell people that the arrangement is there also helps.

In many instances, however, passive security simply is not enough, and an active system is needed. Like passive arrangements, active security can start simple. DIY stores sell free-standing, battery-operated passive infrared (PIR) alarms, which can be placed to detect an intruder's presence. These can be used to guard a locker or the interior of the vehicle. The snag is that just one alarm can easily be muffled or smashed by a thief. But the remote control key fob switch that accompanies such an alarm can be programmed to activate more than one unit. And to protect your motorhome adequately, a set of at least four alarms is necessary. Should an unwelcome visitor appear, a total of around 392 decibels of siren sound, starting 10 seconds after the thief's presence is detected, is often enough. Apart from being painful to the ears, this output will make the thief disappear in short order. After a while, the alarms will reset themselves.

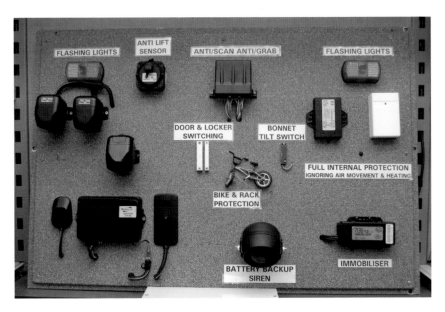

Alarming equipment! This 3D schematic shows some of the elements of the Strikeback T alarm from Van Bitz

This kind of alarm represents the 'entry level' and there are sophisticated alarm systems that do far more than merely make a noise. The Strikeback T is a respected system. Exclusive to Taunton company Van Bitz, it can be tailored to suit virtually any motorhome and the typical installation described here will give you a clear picture of what it can do.

Like passive security items, active security systems benefit their owners by being visible. The Strikeback T system is rendered highly visible by bright LED indicators, on the dash top and mounted externally both front and rear. When the system is armed, these flash to let everyone know the system is present and working.

Thieves can quickly find and muffle a siren that is working, but the Strikeback T system gets around this by having three sirens, each with its own, internal NiCad battery. If a thief manages to disconnect the motorhome's battery, the alarms will sound. If he cuts or tears out the wires leading to the sirens, they will sound and, having their own power source, will keep on sounding.

Strikeback T also has an external loop cable that can be fed through valuable items outside the motorhome, such as a motorcycle, a towed car, bicycles, camping furniture and so on. Cutting or unplugging this cable triggers the alarm. Other triggers include a tilt switch that protects the motorhome's bonnet. This switch triggers the system when the bonnet is opened and is more reliable than the more common, corrosion-prone pin-type switch. Contact switches protect the motorhome's exterior entrances, including its locker doors.

Movement inside the motorhome could be detected by the type of PIR sensors in the freestanding, battery-powered alarms mentioned above. Some rival systems also rely on PIR detection but it has its drawbacks. It can be prone to false alarms. The Strikeback T alarm system protects the inside of the vehicle with radio sensing, which is known to be highly reliable and not given to 'crying wolf' – the last thing you want, particularly at a campsite. And if you are in your motorhome you can arm the system without activating the radio motion detector so that you have 'perimeter protection'. If a thief tries to enter via the motorhome's doors or manages to break open a locker door, the alarm will sound, but your own movements will not trigger the system.

A hi-tech thief might have a scanner or code grabber to find out your remote transmitter's internal code, but in the Strikeback T system, the unit that receives the arming signals has random encryption to guard against this. Each time a code is used, it is one of 72 million billion combinations. And if you lose your key fob transmitter, Van Bitz has special computer equipment that allows the lost transmitter's unique code to be replaced with a new, unique one.

Apart from telling thieves that the system is working, the LED indicator lamps can tell you what is happening – or has happened in your absence. If you leave a door or locker open by mistake, the LEDs' 'Morse' code will tell you about it. When the system is armed, it self-monitors the integrity of the protected elements thousands of times per second. And when you disarm the system, the LED will flash out codes denoting whether the alarm has been triggered and by what.

When leaving your motorhome parked, either *en route* or on site, arming of the Strikeback T system is confirmed only by the LED indicators and the motorhome's own exterior lights – there are no beeps to disturb others. If the alarm is triggered, the sirens run for twenty-five seconds, leaving no one in the vicinity in any doubt that something's amiss. When the triggering event is over, (i.e. the thief has run away), the system will perform a self-test and rearm itself.

The system also has a sub-system called Strikeback Concept, which uses GSM (Global System for Mobile Communication) technology to send a text to your mobile phone to tell you that the alarm's been triggered. It also provides your motorhome's latitude and longitude and the time of the GPS fix that established them. You can then call the police and let them know that there has been a break-in. And if your motorhome has been stolen, you can text the system and tell it to immobilize the engine. The engine cannot be cut instantly for safety reasons but when it is stopped, it will not restart. The immobilization command can be reversed with another text message from your mobile phone. The text messaging facility works using Vodaphone's pay-as-you-go messaging service. It can also send you a monthly update of the vehicle's position and status as well as on-demand information about the battery voltage and internal temperature – useful when the motorhome is stored for the winter.

Unsurprisingly, the Strikeback T alarm system has Thatcham approval, Thatcham being a governing body responsible, among other things, for setting vehicle security standards. Importantly, this is the right kind of approval, being in the Light Commercial Vehicle listing. Van Bitz fits Strikeback T at its Taunton address, where there is a campsite whose facilities are offered to customers. The receiving vehicle can be taken along for a while-you-wait fitting, or left with the company. Van Bitz also has five independent fitting agents, located at: Banbridge, County Down; Newstead, Nottinghamshire; Warrington, Cheshire; Allesley near Coventry; and Seaford, East Sussex.

Meta Systems, the European maker of Strikeback T, manufactures OEM (Original Equipment Manufacturer) and aftermarket electronic equipment for, among others, Maserati, Ferrari, BMW, Saab, Mazda, Alfa Romeo, Renault, VW, Audi, Fiat and Peugeot. The Strikeback T system is exclusive to Van Bitz and its appointed fitting agents. The system's electronic control unit (ECU) has a lifetime warranty for the original customer and all parts and labour are fully guaranteed for a minimum of twenty-four months from the date of installation. Purchasing a maintenance contract for a third year will extend this.

Obvious – as befits a passive security device. This locking staple keeps your motorhome's entry door closed and your belongings safe inside. It can double as a helping handle but it should really complement an alarm

As this description clearly illustrates, Van Bitz has thought of every possible eventuality to fight the motorhome thief, even down to a panic button inside the host motorhome, for use in the event of a 'live' intrusion. But the system described, though typical, is not complete – there are still more options, including an additional immobilizer, virtually any number of trigger switches to protect any item that can be opened, and much more. And do not let us forget the optional 172-decibel Devil's Wail interior siren, which has the power to deter – not to mention deafen – any intruder.

The Strikeback 2 alarm system's cost is significant. Then again, so are the costs of having your motorhome or its contents stolen, having to arrange alternative transport and replacement goods, and having to sort out the associated insurance claims. Since the system can be tailored to suit any motorhome, from the most modest camper van up to a top-of-the-range A-Class model, its versatility explains its popularity, in part at least. More significantly, the peace of mind offered could be considered worth much more than just the financial outlay.

Retaining your Rubber

Most of the components of a motorhome are important but some are more important than others. For example, the engine keeps you mobile, the heating keeps you warm, the cooker keeps you fed and the electrical system lets you see what you are doing after dark. But you cannot manage without tyres. With a motorhome, a puncture on the road can be particularly trying, if not downright dangerous. At best you will have to stop, in a place where you can change a wheel or use the newer tyre sealant and electric air compressor combination provided by some base vehicle manufacturers. This assumes that you can change a wheel or reinflate a tyre, which is not always easy, particularly if the tools you need are buried in a locker and if the wheel nuts are tight. At worst, you could lose a tyre, probably also losing most of your control over your motorhome.

There is a solution which is used by the armed forces, the ambulance service, the fire service and the police. In public displays, this solution has been shown to work remarkably well. In the motorhome demonstration, the front tyre of a coachbuilt model is deliberately deflated by a small, shaped charge on its sidewall being detonated. The relevant corner of the motorhome drops as the tyre goes flat, but the vehicle continues at an undiminished speed, the tyre stays on the wheel and the driver is clearly quite at ease.

The reason is Tyron and, as in all good solutions, the idea is quite simple. When a tyre is fitted to a wheel, its beads – the parts that ultimately occupy the flanges of the wheel rim – have to be forced over the rim by a tyre-fitter's

Invisible yet still in action. Inside this deflated tyre, a Tyron band is
keeping the motorhome rolling

machine. An arc of each bead has to sit in the well of the wheel rim while the
opposite arc is levered over the rim itself. Once the tyre beads are seated
correctly and the tyre is inflated, the beads seal tightly against the wheel rim's
flanges. In the event of a blowout, the beads can slip down into the wheel well
and the tyre fitting process can be suddenly and uncontrollably reversed. The
tyre can be 'skinned' off the rim completely, or it can be shredded between the
rim flanges and the road surface. Neither is a good recipe for grip or control.

Tyron bands comprise two semicircular arcs of flat steel, with plastic spacing
bobbins on the inner face. When fitted together with special, high-tensile bolts
and nuts, the bands form a circle that sits tightly, on its spacing bobbins, in the
wheel well. So, if a blowout occurs, the tyre beads cannot be forced into the
wheel well. Instead, they run on the tough, flat surface offered by the Tyron
bands. This means that, though flat, the tyre can still be used and the driver can
head for a place where a repair can be carried out in safety. Just how far the vehicle can be driven depends on the type of tyre involved and on the load it must
carry. But the fact remains that the tyre is still usable and the need to stop virtually immediately is removed.

Tyron can be fitted at many tyre bays, or a member of the Kwikfit mobile
team can fit them at your home or at a suitable location. Only the outer bead
of the tyre need be disturbed; once this has been detached from the rim, the tyre
is compressed with a special tool and the Tyron band is assembled in the wheel

well. Once the band is in place, the tyre is reseated and inflated as normal. And when replacement tyres are needed, 'Tyron fitted' stickers on the wheels and the special, long Allen key the fitter passes on to the customer, mean the bands can be refitted inside the new tyres.

Live Location

You will not get far in the world of motorhomes and motorhoming without encountering satnav, a piece of verbal shorthand for 'satellite navigation'. Many people call the unit that helps you navigate, with the aid of satellites, a satnav, but this unit is more properly called a portable navigation assistant (PNA). This unit can tell you all sorts of things, including where you are, how fast you are going, how to get to where you are headed and how long it will take.

This depends on the Global Positioning System (GPS), a group of satellites initiated by the USA in 1973, and completed by 1978. Originally for military use, the network was ultimately made public. The PNA, provided it can 'see' at least three GPS satellites, uses information they transmit to locate you anywhere on earth. Civilian PNAs are typically accurate to around 10 metres (32 ft).

PNAs also have internal 'maps', software that knows where roads, round-abouts and even, on occasion, speed cameras are located. Using a combination

No, Fiona isn't overtaking! Piloting by PNA (satnav) on a pleasant afternoon in France

A PNA (Portable Navigation Assistant), also known as a satnav, can make finding your way around far easier

of this internal knowledge and the information the satellites provide, a PNA can give you information on how to get to where you want to be.

Using a PNA is easy enough. Giving the unit a clear view of the sky is simple, being usually just a matter of fitting it in its windscreen mount so that it can 'see' upwards. Most PNAs have touch-screen input so you can 'type' your destination in with the screen's 'keys'. Most also have a word completion function, so if you input 'G – L – O', for example, you will get 'Gloucester'. The destination accuracy varies. Some accept part of a postcode, others accept all seven characters of one, and all know road and street names, many letting you put in a house number too. Once you have asked the unit to navigate and assuming it has a 'fix', it will start giving you instructions. It is usual for a PNA to offer both visual and audible instructions. The former are shown on the screen, with options of a bird's-eye view or a 3D view, which change as you progress. In every case, your position is shown as a reference point, usually an arrow-shaped icon, and you can select additional displays which can take the form of simple schematics of roundabouts and junctions. You can also choose to be shown such information as your compass heading, speed, height above sea level, estimated time of arrival and so on. The audible part is spoken instructions, in a voice you choose, male or female. Some PNAs also tell you about speed cameras, displaying the applicable speed limit and giving a chime or intoning 'beware' if you exceed it. PNAs also feature re-routing and some use a system called Traffic Message Channel (TMC), which is an FM radio system that tells your PNA about traffic problems, inducing it to reroute you accordingly.

The versatility of PNAs puts you in control of the information presented. You can select the fastest or the shortest route and decide whether or not to use or avoid toll roads, minor roads and motorways. You can seek out points of interest (POIs), from restaurants to amusement parks, and be taken to the ones you choose. The same elements are available abroad. You can update the internal maps and some units can even play music files or display digital picture files. Moreover, there is no subscription fee for the use of the satellite constellation; it is there twenty-four hours a day, 365 days a year.

In a motorhome, a PNA can be worth a great deal. It can make paper maps obsolete, although some motorhomers still take one along. It can save you time and frustration and keep you updated on your location, speed and progress. However, there are elements to remember about GPS navigation that put its usefulness into perspective.

The first thing to be aware of is that a PNA is your guide, not your master. PNAs cannot tell lies but certain situations can make them seem able to. So if your PNA advises you to make a U-turn in the middle of the M25 it probably means its signal has become compromised! Similarly, the accuracy of a PNA's navigation depends on the accuracy of its mapping. Some are better than others and if the PNA suggests that a road does not exist, it may not be correct. In some locations, the satellites' signals can become delayed or distorted so the PNA may ask you to turn off some yards after you have driven past the turning; in this case, just wait, it will find the next turning for you.

At the time of writing, PNAs can be programmed to give you routing for categories like 'fast car', 'normal car' or 'caravan', and some even say 'lorry'. Do not be misled; a PNA knows nothing about the size of the vehicle you are using, these options merely relate to average speeds. So when you find yourself travelling along a narrow farm track, with foliage touching both sides of your motorhome and its roof, do not blame the PNA.

In fact, there are reports of PNA producers being about to offer a solution to the problem of their products not catering for larger vehicles. More than one big lorry has become irretrievably wedged down a tiny country lane. Perhaps in the near future, an option of routes specifically for bigger vehicles will be a universal PNA feature. For now, the trick is to use your eyes as well as your satnav. And never forget that where you drive is ultimately up to you, it is not the PNA's decision.

Cruise Director

Some motorhomers like to embark on extended tours. As this involves spending long hours at the wheel, anything that makes driving easier is welcomed. To some, having cruise control smacks of laziness. To many, the 'electric foot' that operates the accelerator for them represents a labour-saving device with the added benefit of reduced fuel consumption. For those who do a great deal of motorway driving, cruise control is a boon and it now appears as standard equipment on numerous new vehicles.

Whether it is factory-fitted or an aftermarket addition, cruise control functions in much the same way. Usually, once you have reached your desired speed, you activate the system with a press of a button. The cruise control then keeps the vehicle at that speed, or very near to it. In most systems, you can preset several speeds, selecting the most appropriate at will. When an incline, a headwind or both intervene, the accelerator pedal will descend unaided, until the set speed is re-established. And when the speed increases, courtesy of a downhill stretch and/or a tailwind, the control cuts the throttle, again achieving the required road speed.

Some drivers worry that cruise control can take over, or stick, but the system can be overridden quickly and easily. When cruising, it is possible to accelerate and decelerate using two buttons, mounted either on or by the steering wheel.

Being a fairly compact A-Class, the Marquis Mirage 6000U New Life fits easily on a small Spanish campsite pitch

Such changes remain in the system's memory so they allow you to tailor your road speed precisely to traffic conditions. And it does not matter if you forget that the cruise control is working and change gear. The moment you start to depress the clutch pedal, the cruise control is switched off. As this also happens when you touch the brake pedal, you need not worry about the vehicle running out of control – using either the press buttons or the brake or clutch pedal puts you back in command, instantly. And with some cruise controls, if you try to ascend a hill in too high a gear, putting the engine and transmission under strain, the system will simply shut itself off, cutting the throttle for you. Moreover, regardless of how the system has been switched out, the desired speed can be resumed at the touch of a button.

Cruise control works by detecting the speed at which you are travelling and using a microprocessor to activate a unit that operates the accelerator. The speed detection method varies. In modern vehicles, the speedometer uses a signal transmitted by an electronic speed sensor. The cruise control's micro-processor is hard-wired into the vehicle to use this signal. In older vehicles without such sophistication, a speed signal can be given by attaching a magnet to a rotating component, such as a drive shaft or propeller shaft, and mounting a fixed sensor nearby so that an electronic pulse is produced at each rotation. The microprocessor uses the speed signal's information to control the position of the throttle, via a servo unit mounted on the engine. This may be a 12-volt electric-powered item or it may be powered by the engine's induction vacuum. In either event, the servo operates the throttle with precision.

If you want cruise control, a general rule applies concerning the fitment of a vehicle manufacturer's system. For all but the simplest items, retrofitting factory equipment, be it cruise control, cab air conditioning or front fog lamps, can be very costly. Fortunately, there are aftermarket cruise controls, which can be fitted to most vehicles, even older ones. It is possible to fit cruise control your-self and, in general, the younger the host vehicle, the easier fitment becomes. In older motorhomes, matters tend to be complicated by the need for a speed signal to be provided. Once fitted, the cruise control system needs to be set up in a one-off exercise. There is also the option of having a system fitted. Most motorhome dealers' service departments will do this for you.

Visionary Ideas

When looking at new or recent motorhomes, you will probably have noticed that virtually all of them have a provision for a television. Some motorhomes offer little more than a convenient shelf with adjacent power and aerial sock-ets, while others go the whole hog with one or more dedicated TV cabinets, complete with a special, multi-position mounting arm or turntable for a flatscreen TV, or for a conventional tubed one.

Let us start with the basics. The standard domestic TV has a glass tube, which makes it heavy and therefore not ideal for use in a motorhome, particularly in a TV cabinet. In the case of a collision, inertia could tear it loose from any mounting and propel it into the driver or passenger.

This leaves two options. If you do use a tubed TV, stow it low down in a locker when travelling, preferably in a spot close to the base of a cab seat. At the very least, ensure that it is stored behind something relatively impenetrable, such as a refrigerator. The other option is a flatscreen TV, which has a liquid crystal display, also known as an LCD screen. They are light and come in mains or 12-volt-powered varieties.

There are two kinds of television aerials for motorhomes. The first is a device that looks like a miniature version of a house's aerial. These are often folded for travelling and some have a moulded plastic body and extendable antennae. These are directional aerials, and they are sometimes hidden away, to appear on a separate mast on site. Still other versions are internal and are never seen outside the motorhome. The other kind might look a little like a flying saucer; it is the omnidirectional aerial.

An LCD flatscreen TV is light and compact. This one is showing a Sky programme via a self-aligning satellite dish

A directional aerial must be aimed towards a TV transmitter mast. There are tricks to help you do this successfully. If you look around at houses in the area, you will see that their aerials all tend to point the same way. Aim your aerial in the same direction and you should receive a signal and can fine tune the angle of your aerial, often from inside your motorhome, to get the best reception. If you are unsuccessful, it may be that the signal frequency in the area differs from the last one you used. Campsite staff can help and they usually know in which direction the TV mast lies.

Omnidirectional aerials can receive a television signal that is coming from any direction – in theory. In practice, they can do this if the signal is consistently strong, but at many campsites, the signal can be weak or variable. There are, however, ways around this problem. One is carried on board. Sometimes installations have a signal amplifier fitted between the aerial itself and the TV aerial socket, regardless of the kind of aerial involved. This amplifier uses a dedicated 12-volt power source. One point where new motorhomers make an error is that they do not realize that the amplifier has to be switched on!

The other option is an aerial connection provided by the campsite. It is usually fitted to the mains hook-up post and uses a standard coaxial aerial cable and plugs – the campsite reception office will stock aerial cables if you do not have one.

There are other sources of signals that can be shown on your motorhome's TV. Assuming the relevant cables are available, anything that can play a DVD disc can be plumbed into the TV set. The same goes for a domestic-style VCR, for as long as videotapes remain available. But there are still more advanced means of receiving a suitable signal.

In houses, satellite TV has been available for quite some time. There are now also pieces of bespoke hardware specifically for mobile use, and many motorhomers take their own digital receiver along on holiday. Starting with the simplest, there are tripod-mounted satellite dishes. The snag is that TV transmission satellites orbit the earth at an altitude of 23,000 miles, nearly twice that of GPS satellites. Even though their orbits are geostationary – the satellites stay put in relation to the earth's surface – finding one can be tricky. Let us look at how you might track down the satellite Astra 2 (actually a number of satellites orbiting the earth close together), which serves the UK.

Set up your satellite dish and ensure that it is level. You now have to determine the dish's angle of elevation. This angle varies, depending on how far north you are. Fortunately, receiving equipment manufacturers provide charts giving the required angle for given latitude. For Aberdeen, it is 19.73°, for Plymouth, 24.72°. All you need is a map to go with the chart, so that you can find a spot on your latitude. The final parameter is the angle of azimuth, which is the compass point at which the dish must be aimed. For Astra 2, the bearing is 28.2° east of south. In theory, armed with a spirit level, an elevation chart, a compass and a satellite dish on a good tripod, you can aim the dish with precision. If all this sounds like a bit of a performance, that is because it is one! Happily, technology comes to the rescue, in the shape of the satellite finder. This has either a gauge or a rank of LED indicator lights, and a tone generator. Plugged into the dish's signal connection with a cable and switched on, it indicates the strength of incoming satellite signals. With the dish roughly set up, you tune the finder until its lights or gauge just cease to register. Turning the dish slowly makes the lights come on, or the gauge needle read, and the tone generator gives a rising note. Tweaking the angles of elevation and azimuth until the tone or reading peaks means your dish is pointing directly at whichever satellite you are seeking.

There are other technological enhancements on offer. One is the Camos Dome. Inside the dome is a satellite dish, on a rotating, 12-volt-powered mounting. The Teleco Magicsat Easy is more easily recognizable as a satellite dish. This also has a rotating mount, but while it travels set neatly just above a motorhome's roof, it is raised and rotated by its motors to find satellites. Both

The Teleco Magicsat Easy will play 'hunt the satellite' for you. Just switch on your TV, press a button and wait to be entertained

Motorhomes have a dedicated TV cabinet like this, with 12-volt and mains power and an aerial socket. Tubed TVs like this one should always be stowed low down for travelling

these units seek out satellites automatically, using signal-strength sensing. So, you just select the satellite you are after, press a button and let the dish or dome do all the work – simple, if costly!

When correctly aimed, a satellite dish can give very clear, top-quality pictures and sound. But it cannot 'see' through trees, buildings, vehicles and people. And while rain and snow can compromise the quality of signal reception, satellite channels generally remain at least watchable.

There is one further piece of equipment you need before you can watch anything emanating from a satellite: the receiver or 'digibox'. These generally use mains electric power, although there are 12-volt-powered alternatives and the usual connections involve F-connector-equipped aerial leads and a SCART lead to run to the TV.

The UK is currently in the throes of switching to digital broadcasting. 'Terrestrial' sources will remain available digitally and the means of receiving their output will vary. Here, then, is an outline of the available equipment and the means of using it in a motorhome. As the accessible channels and their contents change, keep tabs on them via the press, TV and the Internet. Check particularly the website at RoadPro (see the contacts list at the end of this book).

This TV drops down into the work surface below when not being used.
It stays there during travelling

This TV descends from the head-level locker. It is ready for immediate use

A set-top or separate receiver uses satellite signals; 12-volt versions are available. A digital receiver, of the kind associated with the switchover, works with a house's aerial. It is known that a Freeview receiver works with a high-mounted directional aerial so in theory, a 'domestic' digital receiver should also work.

A 'digibox' works via a satellite dish. Currently, providers include Free To Air, Freesat and Sky. For the latter, you need a Sky installation at home, including a live phone-line connection. This has to be operative for 12 months before you are free to take Sky on the road, in the UK and Ireland. Should you go further, study your contract's terms and conditions but remember that the Sky viewing card has no idea where it is being used.

These facilities will beam in as many different programmes as you could want, some 'encrypted' so you'll need your subscription to decode and watch them. As the output is liable to continue expanding, there's no excuse for boredom on a wet afternoon with onboard digital reception of TV and radio programmes.

Pulling Power

Being based on commercial vehicles, motorhomes can not only carry large loads; they can tow substantial amounts as well. But before towing anything, you obviously need the necessary hardware.

Towbars for motorhomes are made of square-section steel, around 4 mm thick, perhaps with 'cheek pieces' up to 10 mm thick. Motorhome towbars are generally custom-built. Some motorhomes have a lengthy tail overhang – the distance from the centres of the rear wheels to the rear panel – which means that the downward weight applied to the towing point by a trailer is effectively magnified. The longitudinal members of the towbar act as levers.

Before bolting a towbar on the tail of a motorhome, you have to factor in its weight. As the motorhome carries the bar, its weight has to be deducted from the motorhome's payload figure. It is not too unusual to find one weighing 34 kg (nearly 75 lb).

The towbar manufacturer will also tell you the towing limit – maximum weight of the laden trailer you may tow – and the maximum download on the tow ball. For towed trailers, this is usually around 75–100 kg.

The motorhome's manufacturer will specify the maximum towing weight, which is the heaviest weight you may tow with your motorhome. This might be the same as the towbar maker's towing limit or it may be more or less. You should use the lower value in your calculations. Finally, there is the gross train weight (GTW). This is the permitted maximum weight of the loaded motorhome plus that of the loaded trailer. We will look at loading and weights in more detail later.

Provided the towed load, including the trailer, is within the weight limits, you can tow whatever you like. You will see motorhomes towing all manner of things. Some people add luggage room by towing an open or enclosed box trailer. Others tow a motorcycle or a small car, still others a racing car, a glider or a boat. Moreover, some motorhomers extend the principle of carrying a bicycle or two on a tail rack to carrying a motorcycle. Here, a special motorbike rack is used. Such racks are carried on the towbar's towing hitch and most of them have a loading mechanism. Ranging from a simple, tilting motorcycle channel to a hydraulic, scissor-action mechanism that lifts the bike into place, they make loading easy. Some even do the lifting with the aid of an electric motor. Naturally, the weight of the towbar plus rack plus motorcycle must be subtracted from the motorhome's payload and the permitted download on the tow ball must not be exceeded. It is also important to note that the weight of the motorcycle and rack should sit directly over the tow ball. Adding any rearward extension to the combination adds leverage, effectively increasing the load on the tow bar.

Towing a small car can be useful with large motorhomes. For the most part, the larger motorhomes rarely leave a campsite; having a small car can make life extremely convenient.

Assuming the combination is light enough, even a medium-sized motorhome can tow a small car on a trailer. The Auto-Trail Cheyenne 632 scarcely noticed its faithful follower – a Microcar MC1

The words 'small car' are by no means misleading. The French Microcar, the Smart car and some of the smaller offerings from the big name manufacturers can be seen behind motorhomes. In many respects, substituting 'light' for 'small' will make the reason for choosing such cars crystal clear.

For towing a car, there are two pieces of hardware from which to choose. One, the A-frame, is seen by many as the more convenient but it has its drawbacks. An A-frame is exactly what its name implies, an A-shaped structure with a towing hitch at one end and a strong point at the end of each of the 'legs' of the A. Fitting one to a car involves modifying it, so that the frame's strong points have something just as strong to which they can be attached. After you unhitch the A-frame from the tow ball, you must remove it from the car before you can drive it.

There are three snags with A-frames. The first is that reversing more than a very short distance in a completely straight line is impossible. The A-frame is hitched so that it can pivot horizontally around the tow ball. However, the points where the frame and car are joined together cannot pivot, so when travelling forward, the car cannot wander from side to side, but when reversing the car will try to steer itself to one side or the other, putting immense strain on its strong points, as well as on the bodyshell, the A-frame, the towbar and the motorhome's chassis. This happens because the car's suspension geometry can let the steering turn to follow the motorhome when the two are travelling forwards. Going backwards, the geometry will make the steering turn fully to one side or the other very quickly. This means that if you need to reverse, you have no choice other than to unhitch the car.

The second snag is that before it can accept an A-frame, the car to be towed has to be equipped with strong points. Once fitted, these could represent a modification that the insurance company needs to know about. The result, assuming the insurance company will permit it at all, is likely to be an increased premium. Also, since strong points are by definition strong, fitting them could affect the way the vehicle's deformable front bodywork behaves in a crash. They could also have a deleterious effect on the triggering of the vehicle's airbags.

The third snag concerns legality. In the UK, you can tow an unbraked trailer with a gross weight of 750 kg. This does not refer to the car's kerb weight, but to its maximum gross vehicle weight, its maximum authorized mass. This is usually 300–400 kg more than the car's kerb weight.

There are A-frames that are offered with a system that mechanically applies the car's own brakes. In law, this A-frame/car combination is considered to be a braked trailer. Unfortunately, the types of A-frame with braking do not conform to European Directives in the Construction and Use Regulations, nor do they in any way conform to the European Directive for Braking 71/320/EEC and amendments regarding braking requirements. Moreover, A-frames are not

If the towbar – and the motorhome's user payload – can cope with the weight, using a motorcycle rack saves towing a trailer. This rack is hydraulic and can be pumped up easily to its running height

necessarily legal everywhere in Europe. At the moment, the Department of Transport feels that 'The use of "A" frames to tow cars behind other vehicles is legal provided the braking and lighting requirements are met'. Its spokesman goes on to say, 'However, while this is our understanding of the meaning of the regulations, it is only the courts which can reach a definitive interpretation of the law.' This seems to be very much a grey area but there are reports of the use of A-frames being considered as illegal as using a suspended towing rig or a dolly to move a car that has not actually broken down. At present, A-frames seem to be allowed in Germany and the Netherlands but not in France or Spain. However, the situation in each country seems to change practically overnight so you should always keep an eye on developments. If in any doubt, get in touch with the UK clubs or check the Internet for news of the latest regulations.

The alternative way to tow a small car is on a trailer. A two-wheeled trailer is usually perfectly adequate and the trailer can have its own braking system. Modern car trailers of this kind are well developed for their allotted task. They have integral loading ramps, lights, a jockey wheel for manoeuvring when unhitched and plenty of locations for ratchet tie-down straps.

UK law concerning trailers is perfectly clear. A towed combination of up to 3,500 kg gross weight can be anything up to 7 metres long, not including the towing hitch and drawbar. The maximum permitted width is 2.3 metres. Trailers have a manufacturer's payload and one with a gross weight allowance of more than 750 kg must have brakes.

Whether braked or not, trailers must have a 50 mm ball coupling that meets both BSI and ISO standards. Unbraked trailers must by law have a secondary coupling that will retain some measure of steering control, should the hitch become uncoupled, and prevent the towing hitch's hitting the ground, perhaps causing the trailer to cartwheel. All the wheels on braked trailers must have brakes and the towing hitch coupling must be hydraulically damped and have an auto-reverse braking facility. This gives braking during overrun but stops the brakes being applied during reversing. The trailer brakes' efficiency must meet EEC Directive 71/320. Braked trailers must also have a parking brake that operates on at least two of the road wheels, on the same axle. The final point about brakes is that there must be an emergency breakaway cable fitted to the parking brake's linkage and able to be fixed to a strong point on the towing vehicle. In the event of the trailer becoming detached, this cable applies the trailer brakes automatically. Not using the breakaway cable is an offence.

Who may tow a trailer? This is best explained by driving licence category: Category B: a vehicle up to 3,500 kg with a trailer up to 750 kg, where the trailer's maximum authorised mass (MAM) doesn't exceed the vehicle's unladen mass and the combination's MAM doesn't exceed 3,500 kg. Category B+E: as above with a trailer over 750 kg; you must pass a theory test to add + E

This French-built Microcar can be driven aboard the Brian James trailer. The whole ensemble is light in weight and the motorhome hardly notices it on the road

to your licence. Category C1: a vehicle between 3500 kg and 7,500 kg with a trailer up to 750 kg. Category C1+E: such a vehicle towing a trailer over 750 kg provided the trailer's MAM doesn't exceed the vehicle's unladen mass. 'Grandfather rights' on a pre-1997 licence give you this entitlement up to a combined MAM of 8,250 kg. Adding it after this date takes the figure to 12,000 kg. See page 22 for the licence categories for heavier vehicles and trailers.

The only place you cannot legally tow a trailer is in the outside lane of a motorway with three or more lanes. In the first two lanes, you can travel at up to 60 mph, and the same speed limit applies on dual carriageways. On any other road, the limit is 50 mph; any lesser speed limit posted naturally applies. And whatever you carry on a trailer must be securely fastened and present no danger to other road users.

The main advantage of any conventional trailer, including box and motorcycle trailers, is that it can be reversed. Reversing a trailer takes some skill and the shorter the trailer, the trickier the task, but it is not too difficult. This is a definite reason to budget for a reversing camera system. Whether you have a motorcycle or scooter on a towbar-mounted rack or a conventional, wheeled trailer, being able to keep an eye on what is happening behind facilitates hitching, driving and reversing.

When travelling forwards, you will find that your motorhome, with its torque-laden turbo diesel engine, commercial vehicle chassis and hefty brakes, will scarcely notice that it is towing, unless your trailer is huge or very heavily laden. Just do not forget to allow for the arc the trailer's inside wheels will describe through a bend.

The Frankia coachbuilt is a garage model. Note the length of its tail overhang

Power Games

We have discussed the use of 230-volt electricity in motorhomes. However, there are those who prefer not to be dependent on a mains connection. While the motorhome's leisure battery is charged both when there is mains power and by the vehicle's engine alternator, its level of charge is as much a consumable as LPG and water, but there is an alternative way of charging the leisure battery in the field as it were, as well as ways of providing 230 volts without a mains connection.

The current for the former can come from one or more solar panels, properly termed photo voltaic (PV) panels. PV panels were developed in the 1960s, to provide a renewable power source for orbiting satellites. They are now available to houses, boats and motorhomes. They rely not on heat but light. This makes the 'solar' term something of a misnomer; PV panels give a better output in the clear light of northern latitudes than they do in a hazy equatorial suntrap. Equally, they can work on overcast days; provided there is light. The amount of heat received by a PV panel is irrelevant – in fact, a high ambient temperature reduces their output.

Although PV panels have become more efficient over the years, their contribution in terms of current is modest. If you divide the PV panel's wattage rating by 14.3, you will get a fair idea of the amperage it can deliver. So a 100-watt panel provides a little under 6 amps, if conditions are ideal. This means the panel should be aimed directly towards the strongest light source all day long. Panels with an automatic tracking system are available – at a cost. Apart from being expensive, tracking panels have a further cost in that they consume electric power in their search to maintain the best input. Assuming a fixed, roof-mounted panel is working as efficiently as it can when the sun is high, its most efficient period is limited, and obviously the latitude makes a difference. Always assuming that there is light to be converted into power, shadows or grime on the panel will reduce its efficiency. And the balance within the power production/consumption equation shifts when the days become shorter in winter.

A PV panel cannot run a motorhome's onboard 12-volt electrical items directly, for two reasons. On the one hand, light of sufficient intensity is not permanently available. On the other hand, even if enough light was consistently available, the demands of the motorhome's 12-volt system would easily outstrip the current even numerous panels could provide. For this reason, such panels are invariably wired to trickle charge the leisure battery.

The ideal situation is when the PV panel charges the leisure battery sufficiently during daylight to run the motorhome's 12-volt items throughout the hours of darkness. While this is theoretically possible, in practice a PV panel will only extend the time for which the leisure battery has enough charge to run the items without needing recharging. And working out how efficiently a PV system will do this is near-impossible, as you cannot forecast the amount of light that will be available on any one day.

Fitting and wiring a PV panel is not too difficult for someone with average DIY skills and there is a variety of types and sizes on offer. However, you will need to include a device called a charge controller, sometimes called a solar regulator. This is necessary because a PV panel can provide power at a higher voltage than the battery can handle; without a charge controller in circuit, the battery could be severely damaged. And in darkness, the reverse can apply – the battery will try to power the PV panel. Charge controllers have a blocking diode – an electrical 'one-way valve' to prevent current flowing from the battery to the panel.

In the final analysis, PV panel power is worth having provided it is not seen as a replacement for more powerful battery-charging equipment. But, remember that the cost of the panel, its wiring and charge controller, perhaps the cost of having it fitted, and the direct weight and aerodynamic loads it imposes on the host vehicle must all be borne in mind.

Inverters and Generators

There are two ways that you can power items requiring 230 volts while having no mains connection. However, as with PV panels, there are limitations. One way is to use an inverter. This is a device that accepts a 12- or 24-volt input and gives a 230-volt output. The alternating current in a mains power supply has a smooth sine wave pattern. There are two types of inverter. Pure sine wave inverters mimic the characteristics of the mains supply's current; they tend to be more reliable and last longer.

Modified or quasi-sine wave inverters fall into two schools. The better units boast internal circuitry that can filter out the interference caused by producing a modified sine wave. While such inverters can provide mains power for many different items, they are not suitable for current-sensitive power consumers such as computers and TVs. Any appliance with a motor will work better with real mains electricity, or with the output from a pure sine wave inverter, and some appliances can be damaged if they are used for any length of time with a modified sine wave inverter. The second kind of modified sine wave inverter will run a microwave oven, hairdryer and table lamp, but it will not do motor-equipped items any good. Inverters also consume your precious low-voltage DC power. Broadly speaking, inverters are only 80–90 per cent efficient, so if you have an item, say a mobile phone with both a mains charger and a 12-volt 'cigar lighter' charger, it will cost you 10–20 per cent less in terms of power consumption to use its 12-volt charger.

To work out how big an inverter you need, all you need to do is total up the wattage of the mains items you intend to use. If you want to use a 30-watt TV, plus a 1,000-watt hairdryer and a 650-watt microwave oven, you will need a 1,680-watt inverter. But although power consumers are rated at a given wattage their demand at the instant they are switched on could be ten times that. For this reason, you need to know about all the inverter's power ratings – the at-rest or quiescent rating, the intermittent-output rating and the peak-power rating.

It is essential to be aware of the limitations of the inverter's incoming connection. Claims that inverters with up to 300 watts output can be run directly from a cigar lighter socket should be viewed with suspicion.

Generally speaking, an inverter of 200 or more watts should be directly connected to the battery. Of course, leaving the inverter permanently connected will flatten the battery so a switch is needed to turn it off or isolate it – better models have a remote controlled switch. To avoid too great a voltage drop, place the inverter as close to the battery as you can and ensure the wiring is of a sufficiently heavy gauge.

Given these limitations, an inverter can be useful. It makes sense to buy the right one – expensive and over-specified can be as undesirable as cheap and under-rated. So, do your research and do not accept manufacturers' claims as irrefutable.

The second means of acquiring a wireless mains supply is to use a generator. Many American motorhomes carry a fixed onboard generator that can usually be started remotely from inside the motorhome and could even be used when travelling. There are similar units for European motorhomes but a portable generator is often preferable. Such items come in a variety of sizes and there are two- or four-stroke petrol models and some diesel-powered alternatives.

Calculating the size of generator that will meet your needs is similar to determining the required output of an inverter. Generators are usually rated in kilowatts, although often you will also be given kilovolt amperes (KVA). This refers to apparent power as opposed to real power. Some appliances' needs can vary – and not just when they are first switched on. Varying conditions make a difference between some items' demands for current; they can require more current than their wattage suggests. Volt amperes are a measure of *load*. Subtracting 25 per cent from the KVA output usually gives the rating in kilowatts.

While power output is an obvious parameter, there is the nature of the power output to consider. Domestic mains supplies fluctuate above and below the 230-volt level by 10 per cent and most generators can match this. However, the frequency of domestic mains supplies varies from the standard 50 Hz only by 0.1 per cent, whereas a generator's frequency can vary from 53 Hz at no load to 49 Hz at the full load marked on its data plate. For this reason, sensitive devices such as computers and televisions can suffer when supplied by a generator. Some manufacturers, notably Honda, use inverter technology to smooth their products' power delivery but this comes at a cost.

Bigger motorhomes and most American motorhomes have an on-board generator.
Starting is usually achieved using a press button inside the vehicle

Apart from these aspects, you need to consider which fuel best suits your needs. There is little to choose between two- and four-stroke petrol generators, although the latter generally run more smoothly. Diesel-powered generators are tempting as they run on the same fuel most motorhomes use. However, they are generally more expensive, heavier and noisier than their petrol-powered rivals.

Running time is another factor you should think about. Manufacturers and retailers quote fuel consumption in litres per hour, usually at a given load, but some also quote a running time in hours. In any case, if you know both the fuel consumption and the size of the fuel tank, you can calculate for how long the machine will run on a full tank of fuel.

Of all the variables among generator specifications, two are important for motorhome use. Weight is a significant factor for two reasons. Whether the generator is fixed or free-standing, your motorhome still has to be able to carry it. And if you have to extract a freestanding generator from the locker in which it is stowed and then set it up, you will have to cope with its weight yourself. Then there is the noise level. Some generators make little noise, but what does not sound intrusive in an A-road lay-by may not be tolerated at the dead of night on a campsite. For those who wild camp away from civilization, a generator can be a splendid power source, but for those who use campsites, running a generator at night or even for any length of time during the day will attract complaints – or invite ejection.

Keeping in Touch

Courtesy of mobile phone networks, you can remain in touch with others even when you are on holiday. But today you can do even better. Modern technology means you can use a number of services, and the technology is surprisingly easy to use.

Let us begin with the mobile phone, which offers two simple methods of communication: speech and text messaging. They have come a long way, and can now be used to access the Internet and e-mail and take photographs.

To understand how to use wireless digital technology, you only need a rough idea of how it works. Some prefer to have every last acronym and piece of jargon at their fingertips but here it is only necessary to have some understanding of the systems involved. And the easiest way of understanding them is to think in terms of their range.

Let us start by considering a standard home telephone. A wire connects this instrument's handset to it so its range – the distance over which it can work – is the length of that wire. Now think about a cordless phone. This still has a base unit connected to the telephone socket on the wall but its handset has no wire. The range is the distance at which the base unit and handset can exchange signals. This can vary depending on the hardware and on the phone's immediate environment; walls and so forth reduce the range, sometimes

Motorhome entertainment: with the right hardware and if in range of a Wi-Fi hotspot or a 3G mobile phone signal, you can enjoy the Internet and keep up with your e-mail

dramatically. This is analogous to most digital communication, be it radio, TV, Internet or whatever. The point is that digital data streams all have a range that can be affected by various parameters.

Many mobile phones offer a communication system that is similar, in terms of range, to a cordless phone. Bluetooth is a short-range wireless radio system that allows mobile phones to communicate digitally with one another. Over a distance of about 32 ft or 10 metres, Bluetooth-equipped phones can transmit and receive data, including message, sound and picture files. This happens at a fairly modest speed but it is usable for all practical purposes. Your use of Bluetooth may not be limited to such exchanges but its relevance comes later.

Next up in the range table is a system that has its own set of standards and exists under a brand name. Wireless Fidelity, better known as Wi-Fi, is a technology whose name was coined by the Wi-Fi Alliance. This body is a consortium of separate, independent companies that agree on a set of common, interrelated technologies based on standards set by the Institute of Electrical and Electronics Engineers, IEEE for short. The salient point is that Wi-Fi is a medium-range wireless technology, whose signals can be accessed over a range of about 95 metres which is just over 300 ft.

Finally, we come to the long-range end of the scale. The distance from your mobile phone to the mast it is using can vary and the range across which signals can be exchanged between your phone and a mast can also vary. The signal is divided in terms of time as well as space and it is this division that affects the range. This means that the maximum range for voice and text messages is 35 kilometres, or nearly 22 miles. However, this is the figure for conditions that are 100 per cent ideal. For all practical purposes, depending on the terrain and the amount of development around the mast, the range is 1 to 3 kilometres; the maximum is a little under 2 miles.

As with other digital signals, that which stands in the way affects reception, which is the reason why mobile phone conversations – and Satnav guidance – go awry in tunnels. From here on, things literally become clearer. As has been mentioned, satellite navigation signals come from 12,000 miles above us. Satellite TV signals are relayed from about 23,000 miles up but the point remains: digital signals can be transmitted wirelessly. And we use them every day. Call your auntie in Australia and you can be sure of one thing – there is not a wire running from Melbourne to Milton Keynes … your chat is going via satellite.

We already know how some of these services can be used in and around your motorhome but to take full advantage of them, we can examine the equipment that uses them. Let us once again start simple, with the mobile phone.

Modern mobiles quickly pass beyond the basic speech and text facilities. Many come with Bluetooth and can consequently 'speak' to other Bluetooth-equipped mobile phones. When you see someone walking along the street or driving past apparently speaking to himself, look closer. Chances are he'll have a Bluetooth earpiece. Using it, he'll be in touch with whoever is calling – and able to drive legally or walk along with neither hand encumbered by a phone.

Some mobile phones, and most of their bigger brothers, PDAs (Personal Digital Assistants), come with both Bluetooth and Wi-Fi. While many phones and PDAs can receive e-mails using a system called GPRS, those equipped with Wi-Fi can access e-mail more quickly as well as being able to go online to use the Internet. If the Wi-Fi signal is good, Internet and e-mail can be used at fairly high speeds, i.e. far more quickly than on a computer with only the old dial-up type of connection.

The PDA forms the mobile 'bridge' between phones and computers. Most laptop computers come equipped with Wi-Fi these days and can therefore use the Internet and exchange e-mail wirelessly. Even an older laptop can be made to receive Bluetooth and Wi-Fi with the aid of a plug-in transmitter/receiver, commonly called a 'dongle' – you need one for each system. Where the 'bridge' part comes in is that both mobile phones and laptop computers can be used with Bluetooth, Wi-Fi and the 3G system. A Wi-Fi-equipped mobile phone or PDA can take advantage of the technology and access the Internet. Such a phone can also become a mobile modem for a laptop computer by using a 3G connection. Just as it used to be with a dial-up connection, a phone can be used to transmit and receive information for the computer. The difference is that 3G is fast and, moreover, the phone or PDA need not necessarily be connected to the computer … the data can be exchanged using Bluetooth. And if your mobile phone does not do 3G, you can buy a modem card that does and set up an account with a mobile phone service provider to access 3G. Plug the card into your laptop, install the necessary software and you are Internet ready.

Nuts and Bolts

The practical aspects of using these remarkable technologies are both easy to understand and easy to use, with certain limitations. Now we know what is available, all we need to know is on which hardware it is to be found.

We know for a start that devices with Bluetooth can communicate with one another. Making them do so is not difficult and, once functional, Bluetooth works more or less automatically. Generally, the system tells you what is happening and asks your permission if it is in any doubt. So if your phone lights up and asks you to allow something to come in via Bluetooth, just be sure you know what it is. Why? Because your phone will pick up any Bluetooth signal that is in range, so the data you want to transfer could be joined by a teenager's flirtatious message to her Bluetoothing paramour!

Now for Wi-Fi. This has moved ever-onwards since it began in 1997. Many offices use it as a means of powering a Wireless Local Area Network – also known as a WLAN. However, 'public' Wi-Fi is available via providers who have some 250,000 'hotspots' between them. A hotspot has a device called a router and these are dotted around the country, in cafés, restaurants, hotels, shopping centres, railway stations and airports.

Turning on your computer or phone's Wi-Fi facility will let you access any hotspot that is in range. The usual outcome appears in your Internet browser. When you open this, a page will appear, inviting you to use the Internet via the provider, on a pay-as-you-go basis. So, you can use your debit or credit card to buy time on the Internet. Should you wish to use the facility more extensively, there are two options. Some providers, such as that used by many McDonalds restaurants and those at some continental campsites, offer free access. Alternatively, you can open an account with one or more providers. The relative costs are usually explained on the page that comes up, or at a linked page. With an account, you need to generate a user name and password and you can usually monitor how much time you have used and how much is left in a given period. Wi-Fi services are slowly being introduced to campsites in the UK though, at the time of writing, this is in its infancy.

There are just two words of warning concerning Wi-Fi. The first involves security. The security within most Wi-Fi systems is pretty good but it is not foolproof – be very careful if you want to undertake online banking, or any other security-sensitive exercise. Often, public providers offer information concerning security. Second, routers and WLANs exist in many offices and private houses. Sensible owners protect their network with a user name/password combination but some either forget to do this, or simply do not know how. Sometimes, you can find yourself parked in or near a town and receiving Wi-Fi without the need to pay or log in. Both later Microsoft Windows and Macintosh operating systems will find Wi-Fi signals and connect you to one automatically. If you use a private system – even unintentionally – you are 'piggybacking' and you could be arrested for stealing the service … you have been warned.

The 3G system that has such promise is also subject to some restrictions, though these stem more from the technology than from abuse. 3G is a relatively new service and, as such, it is still developing. When a 3G signal is strong and consistent, the results are excellent. However, the coverage has its boundaries. Should you be parked or camping at a location with no signal, there will be no Internet access. Should the signal be weak or patchy, the speed of the access can vary and the traffic – the amount of use the system is experiencing – can make a difference. 3G is a shared resource and as the number of users in a particular area increases, the throughput for each user reduces. In other words, the system slows down.

With a little knowledge, the right hardware and the appropriate accounts, you can use the same Internet and e-mail facilities you might have at home, and they can be tremendously useful on the road. You can go to the web to find

The 8.49-metre, tag-axle Bavaria 183 is a four-berth A-Class
motorhome, ideal for families

out about campsites, and refer to vehicle manufacturers and the various vehicle and campsite clubs. You can check the websites of local attractions and events, look up the history of an area you are visiting and even book tickets online. You can also see national and international news reports, weather forecasts and even live webcam pictures showing local conditions.

A laptop computer also makes a splendid travelling companion. Using Microsoft AutoRoute, you can plan your journey down to the last detail; this and other programs let you add GPS satellite positioning. There is also a website from which you can download sets of 'pushpins', denoting the locations of campsites, for use with Microsoft AutoRoute's maps (see the contact list for details). And if you have the relevant equipment, you can add digital pictures to a log of your travels. Bear in mind that all the appropriate hardware will interrelate and will generally run, or be able to be recharged, from your motorhome's on-board power sources.

Weight a Minute

What accessories you take in your motorhome will depend to some extent on their weight. You need to understand weights in relation to motorhomes. Like a commercial vehicle driver, you can be stopped for a roadside weight check and if your vehicle is overloaded, you could be prevented from travelling on and even fined. Overloading your motorhome can also put parts of it under undue stress, particularly the rear axle and tyres, and you could experience a suspension failure or a rear tyre blowout at speed.

In considering this question we need to understand what is meant by two terms: mass and weight. Weight denotes what an object weighs – the figure scales display; mass is the amount of matter it possesses. There is a scientific distinction, but for our purposes they are the same.

There are two sets of weights to deal with. The first can be considered vehicle weights, and they are:

1. **Gross vehicle weight (GVW)**. This is the vehicle's maximum laden weight, the most it can legally weigh with everyone and everything on board. The more legalistic maximum authorized mass is the same value.
2. **Gross train weight (GTW)**. This is the maximum permitted weight of both the vehicle and what it is towing. Obviously, this is only relevant when something is being towed.
3. **Permitted front-axle loading**. This is the maximum weight that can legally be carried by the vehicle's front axle. This is marked '1' on the vehicle's chassis plate (VIN plate).
4. **Permitted rear-axle loading**. This is the maximum weight that can legally be borne by the vehicle's rear axle. This is marked '2' on the vehicle's VIN plate.

The second set refers to what we can call 'motorhome' weights, the ones the motorhome manufacturer provides. They are:

1. **Mass in running order (MIRO)**. This is the weight of the vehicle as it leaves the factory. It usually has an allowance for the driver and a 90 per cent fuel load.
2. **Maximum technically permitted laden mass (MTPLM)**. This is the motorhome's weight when it is fully laden and ready to go.
3. **User payload**. This is the figure that most concerns us. It represents the motorhome's capacity to carry all your belongings – you, books, pitching gear and anything you want to take. It is the MIRO subtracted from the MTPLM and it matters because exceeding it means overloading.

Leverage

It may seem that you could pack in equipment up to the user payload and drive off, but in practice it is not quite so simple. If your motorhome has a 600 kg payload and you only load 400 kg of gear in it, you may still not be legal and safe. You may, for example, have exceeded the permitted rear-axle loading. If, of course, you put this gear *between* the axles you would be within your limits.

The point here is weight distribution. All motorhomes have a rear overhang and the further behind the back axle the weight lies, the greater the load on this axle. This factor becomes still more important when towing and tail loads are involved. Some people carry a motorbike on a rack that sits on a towbar attached to the motorhome. In that case the weight of the rack and the towbar must be added to the equation. Similarly, towing a trailer involves more than the gross train weight. The noseweight of the loaded trailer ultimately exerts a load on the rear axle too.

You should therefore check your vehicle's weight at one of the many public weighbridges around the UK. If you do not know where your nearest is, check Yellow Pages. For a reasonable fee, the weighbridge operator will give you accurate figures for both your motorhome's axles and its total weight. All you do is drive onto the weighbridge so that one axle is being weighed. When that figure is noted, you have the whole vehicle weighed. A simple sum then gives the loading on the axle that wasn't weighed.

There is another piece of advice when loading a motorhome. Keeping heavy items low down will help maintain a low centre of gravity. Loading heavy equipment high up can have a marked effect on the motorhome's on-road characteristics, and heavy items can fall.

A weighbridge operator at work, preparing a printout of the full and individual axle weights of a motorhome

7 Going Overseas

Taking a motorhome to Europe is not as daunting as it may seem, but there is quite a lot to think about, in terms of paperwork, special hardware and consumable items. And there are any number of travel guides and organizations to help you.

Paperwork

Bureaucracy works slowly, so it makes sense to get hold of the papers you need in the early stages of your planning. The items that take longest to acquire are passports for any pets you intend to take with you. The organization to contact about this is the PETS Travel Scheme. In fact, getting pet passports is easy but it can take up to eight months, much of which time is taken up by veterinary vaccinations and blood tests. Your pet can be microchipped by a vet in minutes but the necessary anti-rabies shot must be administered between twenty-eight and thirty days before blood is taken for testing. Assuming that the blood test gives a satisfactory result, a further six months must elapse before a final blood test. If that test is satisfactory, your pet can go abroad because it will be at liberty to re-enter the UK unhindered. The costs of these various tests and treatments also vary and you should also be aware of the rules concerning pets at the camp-sites you plan to use.

Of course, everyone in your party will need a valid passport. You can get the relevant forms at any post office or you apply online (see the contacts list at the end of this book for the web address). You will need passport photographs. The whole process takes some time, and while you can get an express application through quickly, it costs.

Currently, you can get a new passport, a renewal passport or an amended one for £51.00, or if the applicant is a child under fifteen, for £34. The process should take three weeks but it is sensible to add a week to be sure. If you do not have four weeks, a fast-track application will secure your passport in one week,

This UK-registered Mobilvetta Kimu is quite at home by the impressive entrance to a German *schloss*

at a cost of £77.50, but you have to visit a passport office. There is also the one-day Premium service, which also requires a visit to a passport office. A child's passport under this service will cost £83.00 while for an adult passport the cost is £96.50.

For most European countries, a UK licence is fine. However, if you do not have the new 'credit card' style licence, you will need an International Driving Permit (IDP) in some European countries. You can get one from one of the motoring organizations. Do not forget that everyone who will drive your motorhome needs the relevant papers.

The next essential is a European Health Insurance Card (EHIC). A European Union-wide agreement means you can get medical treatment anywhere in the EU, with an EHIC. As with passports, the appropriate forms can be obtained from a post office. The card is free and should be presented at any medical facility you might need to use. It will cover all the costs of emergency medical treatment and 60 per cent of non-urgent treatment. As with passports, every traveller needs his or her own EHIC. If you apply at a post office, each application carries a fee of £2.00 and you will receive the card within twenty-one days. If you apply online or by phone, it is free and you can expect to receive the card in seven to ten days.

But remember that an EHIC is not a substitute for valid travel insurance.

The rest of the paperwork is not official, but it is still essential. Some campsites will want you to leave your passport or some other document at the reception office for the duration of your stay. Parting with your passport is unwise, so leaving something else would be preferable. Most EU campsites recognize the Camping Card International (CCI), and at some sites it will attract a discount. The CCI also provides insurance against third-party claims arising from an accident at a campsite. Often, a CCI comes as part of the travel packages offered by both the UK camping and caravanning clubs. Alternatively, you can obtain one from the Motor Caravanners Club; see the contact list for details. Insurance is another necessity. Extending your existing policy to cover your possessions when abroad is simple and not necessarily prohibitively expensive. Insurance for using your motorhome abroad can be extended too. In all cases, you will need to check exactly what you'll get for your money. Will you be protected against all possible eventualities? Will the European breakdown organization know about motorhomes? Will the recovery truck cope with a big motorhome? Get the answers before you go and if the quotes are frightening, shop around. You must carry documentation proving that you have valid motor insurance cover on your motorhome.

Like vehicle and breakdown cover, personal health, travel, goods and pet insurance can come in packages. Again, you need to know what you are buying and look out for loopholes. Medical care not covered by an EHIC must be paid for abroad so you need to know that the payment or reimbursement of such charges is included. And if you are planning any 'risky' pursuits such as hang gliding or potholing, make sure you are insured for them.

As far as your possessions are concerned, watertight insurance cover abroad is a must. Some items may be included in personal insurance policies, or as part of your home contents policy. Where individual items are worth more than a certain value, they often have to be named so check what constitutes the water-

One co-author's EHIC. A European Health Insurance Card is a necessity on the Continent – it *could* prove vital

shed value figure and how the naming procedure works. And ensure that your policies include repatriation of you, your vehicle and your pets if necessary.

Book Early

You will need to book pitches on campsites and a place on the ferry. Moreover, unless you live very close to a ferry terminal, you will need to book campsite pitches in the UK.

You can make your bookings of both pitches and ferry places online, in which case you will receive e-tickets that you can print out. Or you can do it by telephone. In both instances, you would use a debit or credit card to pay and often you will need nothing more than a note of the appropriate times and places and your booking reference numbers. It is a good idea to book early, especially for the ferry. As time goes on and the vessel's available vehicle spaces are taken, the cost rises. So if you book as early as you can, you could get a significant reduction in the cost of your ferry travel.

Both the major UK clubs for campers, caravanners and motorhomers can help with your arrangements. The Camping and Caravanning Club has a travel division, the Carefree Travel Service. It deals with 168 carefully selected campsites in no fewer than eighteen countries, although with one exception none is owned or run by the club itself. It will provide details of sites, including seasonal restrictions, information on entertainment and activities, and information for disabled people.

In addition to campsites, the Carefree Travel Service can offer special rates with major ferry companies, including P&O Ferries, Brittany Ferries, Stena Line, DFDS Seaways and Condor Ferries. Dogs Away, a partner organization, offers information services for taking pets with you, including all you need to know about the pet passports scheme.

Carefree has a thirty-year association with the breakdown company Europ Assistance, so it can offer breakdown cover and insurance packages, including personal travel insurance and emergency medical insurance. Should your vehicle break down and be irreparable within eight hours, a hire car or alternative accommodation will be arranged. There is a 24-hour emergency line that will link you to a multilingual team of coordinators including doctors, nurses, legal advisors and travel consultants.

The Caravan Club is the largest organization of its kind in the UK. Like the Camping and Caravanning Club, it has a travel division, the Travel Service in Europe. This offers ferry and Eurotunnel crossings to members at preferential rates. Campsite bookings can be made and combination crossing and campsite packages are available. The Club co-operates with the French Camping Cheque organization, which in 2005 included 500 sites in Europe. This system, aimed at those wishing to take off-peak holidays and tour with a degree of flexibility, can be quite a money-saver. The cheques are part of a package, which must include a ferry crossing and at least seven camping cheques. Each cheque is valid for one night's stay, including electricity, for up to two people plus a car and caravan or trailer tent, or a motorhome. Any number of cheques can be purchased but there are no refunds for unused ones. Note also that local tourist tax and other service costs are not included.

The Caravan Club also offers inclusive holidays, which cover site fees plus a range of visits, activities and excursions. Optional excursions, payable locally, are often available. There are also Connoisseur boating holidays in France, Italy and Ireland.

The club's insurance facility is called Red Pennant. Offering specially designed holiday insurance for motorhomers, caravanners and trailer tenters, it is a flexible system with a 24-hour free helpline. Cover can be extended to include roadside breakdown assistance, vehicle and passenger repatriation, continuation of holiday travel or accommodation, cancellation cover, medical cover and ski cover. And the club's best-selling *Caravan Europe* site guides are worth having. Between them, the two volumes give information about over 7,400 sites in twenty-two countries, including advice on everything from essential equipment to driving abroad.

Preparing your Motorhome

Planning for a trip abroad is mostly common sense. First, will your tyres cope with extended use? According to the Royal Society for the Prevention of Accidents, the signs of a pensionable tyre include cracking and crazing on the sidewalls caused by flexing in use, tread distortion and deformation of the tyre's carcass. Normally, tyres that are in regular use should be replaced every ten years. However, when the use is irregular, as with motorhome tyres, premature

The flagship Concorde Liner 1090M has home-from-home proportions for en route comfort

ageing can occur. This can be exacerbated by ultra-violet light and the increased salt content in the air at the coast. Also, some cleaning products can affect the chemical composition of the tyres' carcasses. For these reasons, it is wise to inspect your tyres carefully before any lengthy trip. In this instance, the fitness of the tyres is about more than just the amount of tread remaining.

Ensure that your spare wheel is good and can be accessed and removed. An underslung spare wheel, always assuming its tyre is not flat, rotten or both, might be immovable. Have any thin or cracked tyres replaced and lubricate anything that needs it – this includes ensuring that you can loosen the wheels' fastenings with the van's own tools. Adding a dab of copper grease to each wheel nut or bolt is effective, preventative maintenance. You should also know how the vehicle jack works.

Having your motorhome serviced before your trip is a good idea. This will ensure that the engine, tyres, brakes, steering, etc. are in prime order. You could also have a full or partial habitation service, so that you know your LPG system, charging equipment, water and waste systems will stay the course. Of course remedial work can be done abroad, but it is simpler and quicker to have it done at home.

There are items you need to acquire, not only to be legal and safe abroad but also to keep you on the road. In most continental countries, it is a legal require-ment to carry a spare set of vehicle bulbs. The 'Good Samaritan' law requires every driver to stop and provide assistance when encountering an accident or incident, providing it is safe to do so, so a first-aid kit and a fire extinguisher are invaluable. You should also carry a warning triangle – or two, if you are heading for Spain. These should be 50–150 metres behind and (in Spain) in front of your vehicle if it breaks down. Being seen equals being safe, which is why it is a good idea to carry a reflective jacket or waistcoat for all the occupants of your motorhome. Some countries insist that these are kept in the vehicle's cab. Use them not just after dark but in any poor visibility.

Most UK vehicles come with 'Euro' number plates, with your home country's indicating letter and a circle of yellow stars on a blue ground. At the time of writing, two EU countries also require that you have a GB sticker or plate as well, and it makes sense to add a GB plate anyway, even if your motorhome has Euro number plates, so that people are fully aware that someone sitting on the 'wrong' side is driving the vehicle.

You need a means of altering the way your headlights dip. UK headlights dip to the left, which will dazzle oncoming drivers in countries where everyone drives on the right. You need not go to the expense of fitting a set of right-dipping headlights. You can usually use 'beam benders' which are more accurately described as 'beam blockers' or 'headlamp beam deflectors'. These soft plastic 'lenses' are self-adhesive and, when attached to your headlights' lenses, modify the beam pattern to prevent dazzle. They are sold as universal

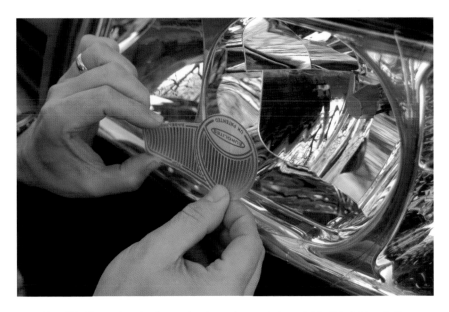

Headlight 'beam benders' are a legal requirement abroad. On this light unit, the deflector is *supposed* to be upside down!

items that are trimmed to suit their host vehicle, and fitting them is a five-minute job. Full instructions are included so all you need is a good pair of scissors. Most motor accessory shops have them and even if you forget to buy some, they are also sold in the onboard shop in ferries.

The tiny Hella headlamp units found on many A-Class motorhomes and on some coachbuilt models are different. Converting them to right-hand dipping is a simple matter of rotating them in their mountings.

The remaining items you will need relate more to your motorhome than to its base vehicle. Unless you have a fixed LPG tank or a Gaslow refillable installation with continental adaptors, or are certain your UK cylinders will last, you will need a Camping Gaz adaptor (see the contacts list). Acquiring your own Camping Gaz cylinders in the UK is also advisable.

For longer trips abroad, you could buy cylinders locally. Look around at filling stations and the like and when you see the same advertisements for LPG supplies again and again, you will have found a provider who has numerous outlets. There will naturally be a difference between your cylinder connection and that on whichever cylinder you choose. But as newer French motorhomes are fitted with a Euro regulator, there may be the appropriately equipped 'tail' to connect a French LPG cylinder to your motorhome's regulator.

The electrical fittings on some continental campsites are identical to those in the UK but many have a local arrangement – a waterproof, two-pin socket for which you obviously need the appropriate plug. Short adaptor cables, with a UK socket on one end and a two-pin plug on the other, are available from motorhome and caravan accessory shops. These cannot solve the bugbear of the reverse polarity mentioned in Chapter 4, but accessory shops sell reverse polarity adaptors and, unless your motorhome has a reverse polarity indicator on its transformer charger, you will need a polarity detector. This is a plug-in item with indicator lights and will display the status of your electrical system. Reverse polarity is not particularly dangerous but some mains-powered items cannot cope with it.

There is also fresh water to consider. Many continental campsites have the same ¼ in BSP fittings as British ones, but not all do, so you may have to deal with a variety of taps. The simplest solution is to carry a universal tap adaptor, which has a soft plastic collar and a clip with a thumb butterfly. There are few taps that this will not fit.

A travelling tool kit is useful for all manner of tasks, on base vehicles, on motorhome fittings and on-site. It need only be a simple affair, with a set of metric spanners, some flat-blade and crosshead screwdrivers and some pliers. Water pump pliers help when you have to unscrew a fresh-water tap's spout and it is worthwhile taking both a self-grip wrench and an adjustable spanner. A Leatherman tool, also known as a multi-tool, is an invaluable companion, offering speedy access to pliers, screwdriver bits, a saw, a file and so on. A Swiss Army knife – the more complicated the better – will get you out of many a scrape. A good torch is also essential.

Pack Drill

Strange as it may seem, packing a motorhome for a European trip is not the same as packing it for the UK. The differences are small but significant. Most of the consumable goods you will find in the UK are also available abroad, but there are some that are not, and that you will have to take along. You must also pack the dedicated chargers for your rechargeable hardware, such as digital cameras, mobile phones, laptop computers and electric toothbrushes. You are also advised to make sure you have enough of any prescription medicines you use to last throughout your trip, plus some in reserve; as regards non-prescription medication, anything you need will be available across the Channel. And for your crossing, if you suffer from seasickness, you will need something for that malady. Your pharmacist will advise you but Sea-Legs or Stugeron are both effective.

Credit and debit cards work abroad, but it is wise to take some euros. Not many businesses accept travellers' cheques, but if you lose them you can reclaim their value.

An *étranger* on Jersey, the Ace Capri copes with the island's narrower lanes

Virtual Tour

Below is an idea of what to expect on a trip to Europe. It refers to France, but going to other countries is very similar.

If you are going via Eurotunnel, you just check in and park in a marked lane. You have to display a pass, which you simply hang on your rear-view mirror. Then, you drive onto the railcar, taking care not to park across the join with the next one; the staff will help you park correctly. You must turn off your LPG system and open a roof vent. Then, you just sit back and relax; it is a good idea to take something to read because after a few miles the train's windows black out until forty minutes or so later you see the French sky.

A ferry departure is a little more eventful. Having driven to the port of departure and checked in, you will be asked to drive to a given lane, displaying your windscreen pass as at Eurotunnel. You will be asked for your passport. It is also possible that UK Customs will want to give you and your vehicle the once over but this is nothing to worry about. The customs officials will only ask you some simple questions and might want to look in a locker or two. On board you will be shown where to park. Then you just apply your handbrake, turn off any motion-sensing alarm, lock up your vehicle and go exploring. No one is allowed on the car deck when a ferry is at sea, so no one will interfere with your motorhome. And if a lively crossing is expected, the deck crew will see to chocks.

The parking is tight on a ferry's car deck but don't worry, the staff will guide you

If you are taking a pet along, there will be a kennels where it will be housed; depending on the vessel, they will be on either the car deck or on an upper deck. Visits can be arranged but animals are not permitted to mingle with the passengers.

There is a lot to see and do aboard a ferry. All have a range of food outlets, from a simple burger bar to a classy restaurant. There are children's play areas and often an entertainer. Longer-haul crossings, such as those to the Netherlands, tend to have a cinema as well as live entertainment. There will also be shops, which will open when the vessel has departed. While not strictly duty-free, one shop will offer normally heavily taxed goods at favourable rates and you can buy magazines, sweets and souvenirs. There will also be a bureau de change, should the need for more euros arise.

To the seasoned traveller, the ferry may be no more than a waterborne bus but even the short Dover–Calais hop is exhilarating. The whole trip only takes about 90 minutes, but you are traversing one of the busiest seaways in the world, so there is always something to see, even after dark.

During your crossing, your mobile phone will behave a little oddly. This is because it is 'roaming' and the French network it picks up will send you texts to show it is working.

As you approach land, the call will come for you to return to your vehicle. You can do this in a relaxed manner, provided that you are ready to start up and drive off when asked. But do not start your motor before this – some drivers do and the atmosphere on the car deck can become a touch too thick for comfort. Do not forget to have your passports to hand.

Once on *terra firma*, the first thing you will notice is that everyone drives on the right. This is more of a culture shock than a practical one and it soon becomes second nature. On the practical side, your passenger has to make himself or herself useful – ticket machines, road toll booths and the like will be on the passenger side. It is also likely that you will need a little help when pulling out at junctions, as your passenger's over-the-shoulder view will be more informative. You will also be overtaking on your 'blind' side. Initially at least, restrict your overtaking to dual carriageways.

You will soon become accustomed to other French road oddities. The traffic lights, for example, have no amber, just red and green. They also have eye-level repeater lights on the traffic lights' stanchions. French roundabouts are also strange at first, as they have a very marked camber. If your motorhome seems to be rolling more than usual, it is just the camber. And at this point, your motorhome is no longer a motorhome – in the local parlance, it is a *camping-car*.

Understanding French road signs is easy enough. The familiar circular and triangular shapes signify the same as they do in the UK. A *carrefour* is a cross-roads and *rappel* means 'reminder'. The speed limits and distances obviously are in kilometres and on *autoroutes* (motorways) the speed limit varies from 110 kph if wet to 130 kph in dry conditions. The sign to watch out for is a yellow, diamond-shaped one with a black bar across it on a white background. This is a *priorité à droite* sign, meaning you must give way to traffic joining from your right. This is rare nowadays but you must beware if there is such a sign, because what can feel to you like a main road is effectively secondary.

There are different classifications of road. Those prefixed with 'C' are *routes communales* and those prefixed with 'V' are *routes vicinales*; both are minor roads. Routes with a 'D' prefix are *routes départmentales* – B-road equivalents. An 'N' prefix means a *route nationale*, the equivalent of a UK A road. *Autoroutes* are toll roads, and as a result are smooth, quiet, fast roads. Lorries are forbidden at weekends and, in any case, commercial traffic is light away from big towns. There are service areas at 20-km intervals, ranging from simple grassy rest areas to stops with all the trimmings.

On the whole, French roads are quite good, but there are speed cameras and the police can impose an on-the-spot fine (always insist on a receipt). French roads do not have cats' eyes or roadside white lines, which can make night driving a touch tricky.

The method of paying on autoroutes is simple. When you join you pass through an automatic barrier, which will dispense a ticket. When the district changes or when you leave the autoroute, there will be a *péage* or toll booth. You present your ticket and pay, in cash or with a credit card. The vast majority of *péages* will not accept travellers' cheques or UK Switch cards.

Money Talks

Major credit cards, however, are accepted virtually everywhere, and filling stations generally accept debit cards. There are automatic, all-night filling stations but be aware that they do not accept UK cards, only special, French fuel cards. In France, diesel fuel is *gazole*, while unleaded petrol is *sans plombe*, and the colour coding at the pumps is identical to that in the UK.

UK debit cards work in cash machines but most banks add a surcharge for using your card abroad. So it is more economical to draw plenty of euros and use them, rather than put numerous small purchases on your debit card.

Supermarkets in France are not merely big – they are gigantic. There are independent shops in the same complexes, so they are really small shopping malls. They usually have large car parks, so parking your motorhome is not a problem. Inside the building you can find just about anything, including engine oil to fuses, and you will find more varieties of cheese, bread and wine than you thought existed. When buying from the fruit and vegetables aisles, you have to weigh your own purchases but the buttons on the scales have pictures, so the language barrier is not an obstacle. There are small cafés in the complexes, which do fresh, tasty meals at very reasonable prices. But the one thing supermarkets of any size lack is free carrier bags, so take along bags of your own when shopping.

The high-street-type shops are characterful. These are *boucheries* (butchers) and *boulangeries* (bakers) independent of the supermarkets, and there are large numbers of shops selling souvenirs, postcards, etc., and some even have English newspapers. There are plenty of street cafés and bars. A good cup of tea is a rarity; it comes in small cups and you usually have to choose from a variety of tea bags and also ask for milk, hot or cold, according to your personal preference. Wines and beers are always on offer and virtually everything costs less than its equivalent in Britain, given a favourable exchange rate.

In general, France is noticeably motorhome-friendly. For example, they have jetwashes with gantries so that you can wash your motorhome's roof, unlike in the UK. Parking is not generally a problem and you can get exchange Camping Gaz cylinders quite easily.

Sites-seeing

On French campsites, the pitches may be smaller than on UK sites and many are grass. That said, pitches with ground-level mesh surfaces are available and are the more desirable in wet conditions. If you have booked a pitch with electricity, you will receive a 230-volt supply but a 16-amp current is unlikely. If you have the right connection hardware and can do a polarity check, you only need to remember that the electric supply point will trip out more easily. This means running heavy demand appliances singly.

French campsite users place greater emphasis on communal washing-up and ablutions facilities than the British. Hot water, showers and sometimes baths are on offer, although some, like the laundry facilities, may need tokens, bought from the reception office. The facilities are usually plentiful, and many sites have an outdoor shower for dogs. Off-season, some facilities may be limited and showers may be available only on a unisex basis.

French WCs are a little unusual. Some are in cubicles with short doors, which can make matters draughty. It is also common to find not a pedestal WC but a 'squatter'. French washrooms are similar to British ones, but a basin plug is very rare, so take along your own universal plug. Exterior facilities generally include a central fresh-water tap, unless you have a fully serviced pitch. And sometimes the chemical WC emptying point is hard to find or non-existent. It may be that waste must be disposed of in a conventional toilet. Where there is a dedicated emptying point, it may be set relatively high up. If this is the case, it is better to empty your waste cassette more frequently to keep its weight manageable.

A-Class act: The Bürstner Aviano i684 is among the lower-priced A-Class models

There are alternatives to conventional campsites in France and using them can save you a significant amount of money. They are the *aires*. There are different kinds. An *aire* is simply an open space, while an *aire de service* is an open space with services, such as electricity, water and drainage facilities. They are not to be confused with *aires de repos*, which are overnight stopping places at autoroute services.

Bornes are service points for motorhomes, at which you can get about 100 litres of fresh water for a couple of euros. An hour's electricity may be on offer too and you will find disposal points for grey and black water nearby, which can usually be used free of charge. Some *bornes* are anonymous, but if you see signs for Euro-relais, Sanistation or Flot Bleu, you will have found a *borne*. They can be found at filling stations, service areas and lay-bys and in some small towns. So the presence of a *borne* does not necessarily indicate that there is somewhere you can pitch. Payment may be simply coin-in-the-slot, but sometimes you need tokens which can be purchased at the filling station's cash kiosk or perhaps at a small shop or *tabac* nearby.

Many *aires* are established by towns or villages seeking a little passing trade, and their location and quality varies greatly in consequence. As you do not need to book, you will be taking a chance on there being a place and on whether the location is rural or urban. But remember that *aires de service* are not campsites – they are really meant simply for overnight halts. In fact, some have a three-

A *borne* offers fresh water, electricity and drainage facilities, usually for a small fee

night limit and there will be a sign to tell you what is and is not permitted. Costs can vary but they are usually reasonable. A *borne* associated with a campsite will be more expensive while those at some *communale* or *privée aires* are free.

Roadside signing for *aires* can be patchy but there are special guides, including the *Guides des Aires de Service* and the *Guide officiel étapes touristiques camping-car*, available from the Camping and Caravanning Club or via the French version of the Amazon website. See the contacts list at the end of this book to find out where else to acquire these guides.

The France Passion scheme is another alternative to conventional campsites. Its Invitations Formula is a free option offered to motorhome owners by 840 wine-growers and farmers from almost all the regions in France. This means that overnight stays are available at over 4,000 free stopover parking spaces in the most beautiful vineyards and domains in France. After joining the scheme as a guest by filling in an online form and sending payment by cheque, bank transfer or credit card, you will receive a personal invitation card (*carnet des invitations*), a windscreen sticker, and an invitations booklet for the current year. Details are in the contacts list.

The final option is to use *aires de repos*, the overnight areas at autoroute services. Here you will have shops, filling stations, public WCs and good parking. However, they are thieves' favourite hunting ground. They know that a motorhome with a British plate is a holidaymaker's vehicle, with cameras, clothing, credit cards, travellers' cheques and cash on board. They also have the perfect high-speed getaway route. The best advice is to avoid *aires de repos*.

Should you have the misfortune to be robbed, go and tell the police immediately – you will find *gendarmeries* at regular intervals on the autoroutes. *Voleurs* is the French for thieves and you will need a *deposition* from the police to prove a robbery has occurred, otherwise you will not be able to make an insurance claim.

There are three other practices to guard against. One is the simple, snatching theft carried out in slow traffic. In the time it takes you to realize what is happening, a thief can whip open a cab door, take a handbag or purse and be gone, perhaps on a moped or scooter. Locking your cab doors stops this. The second involves a mock 'damsel in distress' or even a mock police officer. If you find yourself being flagged down in the middle of nowhere, for no apparent reason, drive on. If the police officer is genuine, he or she will have a police car.

The third practice is a so-called 'gas attack', in which the thief sprays a narcotic gas into your motorhome to knock the occupants out before breaking in and stealing goods at his leisure. Reports of such attacks being on the increase have been appearing in the media but the facts tell a different tale. According to Dr Gilbert Park, a leading consultant in anaesthesia, the most common narcotic gas that criminals can acquire is that sold in aerosol sprays and used to induce engines to start. These contain diethyl ether – an effective anaesthetic but with drawbacks. First, it is a powerful vapour that can start people coughing and irritate their airways. Second, it takes some minutes to send someone to sleep, even when administered directly via a mask, and during that time it can cause restlessness and possibly a period of excitement. Dr Park finds it hard to believe that a concentration of this gas powerful enough to put someone to sleep could be introduced into a vehicle. It would bring on drowsiness with a lower concentration of ether, particularly if the motorhome's occupants were tired after travelling or had enjoyed a glass or two of the local wine.

Interestingly, the unmissable, pungent smell of ether is not mentioned in most reports of a gas attack. Dr Park's advice is that, if you suspect you have been gassed, behave as though you had had sedation in hospital, leaving twenty-four hours for any effects to wear off before trying to continue driving. In his opinion, the main reason for fitting a gas-detecting alarm to a motorhome is the risk presented by the flammability of ether and other gases. Even if a gullible criminal believed he could knock out a motorhome's occupants with a gas, triggering such an alarm would most likely frighten him off.

One school of thought suggests that thieves only target vehicles whose occupants they can reasonably assume to be tired after a long drive, secure in the knowledge that the gas they spray into the motorhome will further deepen the sleep of the exhausted. Just how the thieves figure out the occupants' level of tiredness is not explained. There are no records of gas attacks on users of established campsites.

The French Connection and Beyond

It is naturally difficult to give the flavour of a whole country in a single chapter. In fact, longer books than this have been filled with descriptions of France and still failed to explore every aspect. Experience of the country has revealed much of France's character as well as giving an insight into the characters of some of its inhabitants. It is true to say that for the most part, the French are neither Anglophiles nor Anglophobes. They seem almost universally helpful – to motorcaravanners, that is – and are willing to go the extra mile, or kilometre, to ensure your holiday remains enjoyable. In France, the highways are mostly in good shape and there is clearly a degree of civic pride involved. The district and attraction signs bear explanatory images, churches and other archetypal buildings are floodlit at night, and many town centres are cosmopolitan and lively.

A universal picture: the upper plug is a Continental 2-pin in an adaptor, the lower one is a standard IEE plug as used in the UK. The blue water hose in the background denotes this is a fully serviced pitch

Another overarching factor is that the country is big. This makes for a variety of vistas and rural France feels far less crowded than the UK does. There are also individual characteristics to enjoy in different areas. Northern France makes no secret of the way both world wars have affected it and there are elements that are sobering to the thinking traveller. You do not, for example, need much imagination to picture how the broad expanses of the Normandy Beaches once looked. The South of France has its expensive, exclusive areas but it also has charm, and the feel of the country ranges from languid to vibrant. Let us just say, miss it and you miss out.

The Continent does not stop at the French border and nor need you. The beauty of the EC's universality lies in the way it has opened Europe up to motorhomers and, for that matter, to anyone willing to travel.

In many respects, once you have used a motorhome in France, you have effectively 'cracked' the Continent. This is not quite the blanket statement it seems. There are many individual differences between countries, both in terms of driving in them and culturally speaking. However, many of the rules, regulations and practices are similar if not identical. Thanks largely to the global influence of the United States, it is rare to find people, at least away from more rural areas, who do not have at least a smattering of the English language. Similarly, most motorhomers who go touring equip themselves with guidebooks and phrase books and are willing to try their luck with the EC countries' mother tongues. For those wishing to get more from *la belle* France and for those wishing to go further afield, there is information in plenty. The UK clubs, the motorhome magazines, the ferry companies, the motorhome manufacturers, motorhome accessory makers and just about every service business involved have recognized that European travel is popular. There is no paradox in these organizations having made such travel far easier than it used to be.

Epilogue

So there we have it, *Motorhomes: The Complete Guide*. Using motorhomes, whether you consider it as a hobby or as a lifestyle choice, is no more static than are the motorhomes themselves. Technology marches on, laws alter, new legislation is introduced and tastes change. Motorhome manufacturers and the associated accessory makers and service providers keep up with trends; sometimes they are responsible for starting them. In the end analysis, you can get more out of motorhoming than you thought possible and this is not necessarily down to what you put into it.

We hope you have enjoyed learning about motorhomes and motorhoming and that you have found our tutelage helpful in the course of your motorhoming life. Where we go next is as much down to what the motorhome world wants of us as it is our choice. Wherever that may be will become clear but that is another story ... and quite possibly another book!

David and Fiona Batten-Hill

List of Contacts

Official Contacts

DVLA
Drivers Customer Services (DCS)
Correspondence Team
DVLA
Swansea
SA6 7JL
E-mail: drivers.dvla@gtnet.gov.uk
Web: www.dvla.gov.uk

DirectGov
Web: www.direct.gov.uk

Web links that can tell you all you need to know about driving law and licences in the UK and abroad. Some content of the websites is linked but each also covers specific topics.

UK Passport Office
Tel: 24-hour Passport Adviceline 0870 521 0410
E-mail: online forms
Web: www.ips.gov.uk/passport/

There will shortly be seventy-six passport offices in the UK. Those at Belfast, Glasgow, Liverpool, London, Newport and Peterborough have both regional and interview offices.

European Health Insurance Card
Tel: EHIC Information Service 0871 050 0509
Web: www.ehicard.org

Can be used to cover any necessary medical treatment due to either an accident or illness within the European Economic Area (EEA). The card entitles the holder to state-provided medical treatment within the country they are visiting and the service provided will be the same as received by a person covered by the country's medical scheme.

Gateway to the European Union
Web: www.europa.eu

The portal to new websites with a vast amount of information on European matters. Check 'travel' particularly.

Loan Comparison Websites

www.moneysupermarket.com
www.unravelit.com
www.moneywise.co.uk
www.money.easy-quote.co.uk
www.moneyextra.com
www.moneyexpert.com
www.moneyfacts.co.uk
www.moneynet.co.uk

Gas

Calor Gas Limited
Athena House
Athena Drive
Tachbrook Park
Warwick
CV34 6RL
Tel: 0800 626626
E-mail: telemarketing@calor.co.uk
Web: www.caravanning-online.co.uk

Information on LPG cylinders, associated products and accessories, including a Calor/Camping Gaz adaptor. At the Caravanning Online website, Calor Gas has taken the hard work out of searching for caravan-related information and put it all into one readily accessible website.

Gaslow Refillable LPG System Fitting

CMR Group
Fareham House
Fareham Drive
Yateley
GU46 7RE
Tel: 0845 260 2666
Mobile: 07836 689900/752009

Gaslow Refillable LPG System

Gaslow International Ltd
Unit 1, Weldon Road
Loughborough
Leicestershire
LE11 5RA
Tel: 0845 4000 600
Fax: 0845 4000 700
E-mail: sales@gaslow.co.uk.
Web: www.gaslow.co.uk

The Gaslow range incorporates refillable cylinders and associated installation systems. In addition, the company's patented butane and propane gauges are among a unique Gaslow series of adaptors, regulators and changeover systems for all models of motorhomes, boats and caravans, both old and new!

BP LPG UK

1 Cambuslang Way
Glasgow
G32 8ND
Tel: 0845 300 0038
Fax: 0141 307 4869
E-mail: lpguk@bp.com
Web: www.bpgaslight.co.uk

BP Gaslight cylinders are lightweight, translucent plastic LPG cylinders in 5- and 10-kg sizes. Roughly half the weight of similarly sized steel cylinders, their construction allows users to view the level of the remaining LPG.

Propex Heatsource

Unit 5
Second Avenue Business Park
Southampton

SO15 0LP
Tel: 023 8052 8555
Fax: 023 8052 8800
E-mail: info@propexheatsource.co.uk
Web: www.propexheatsource.co.uk

Manufactures some of the most advanced gas heaters available today for a variety
of applications. It supplies products across the world through a network of distrib-
utors and dealers.

Silver Screens

Silver Screens
PO Box 9
Cleckheaton
West Yorkshire
BD19 5YR
Tel: 01274 872151
Fax: 01274 862963
Web: www.silverscreens.co.uk

Manufacturer and stockist of the well-known Silver Screens, J & M Designs offers
a range of products designed to help motorhomers cope with extremes of heat and
cold both entering and leaving via a motorhome's cab glass.

SOG

SOG System
Symonspeed Ltd
1 Cleveland Road
Torquay
TQ2 5BD
Tel: 01803 214620
Fax: 01803 215628
Mobile: 07836 779700

Stockists of the German SOG system, Symonspeed also supply and fit Airride
pneumatic suspension. For more on this, see: www.airide.co.uk.

Alarms

Strikeback T Alarm System
Van Bitz
Cornish Farm
Shoreditch
Taunton
Somerset
TA3 7BS
Tel: 01823 321992/01823 353235
Fax: 01823 354946
E-mail: info@vanbitz.com
Web: www.vanbitz.com

Van Bitz is the official sole UK distributor of the market-leading Strikeback motorhome security system. It and its trained agents have been appointed the official Trackstar motorhome installers and customers may enjoy a stay in Van Bitz's award-winning, fifty-pitch touring park. The company also has five independent fitting agents, located at Banbridge, County Down; Newstead, Nottinghamshire; Warrington, Cheshire; Allesley near Coventry; and Seaford, East Sussex.

Tyre Safety

Tyron
Gaslow International Ltd
Unit 1
Weldon Road
Loughborough
Leicestershire
LE11 5RA
Tel: 0845 4000 600
Fax: 0845 4000 700
E-mail: sales@gaslow.co.uk
Web: www.gaslow.co.uk

Tyron is a patented lightweight wheel well-filling band that converts a standard steel or alloy wheel into a safety wheel. When fitted, it will improve significantly the performance and safety of any wheel and tyre in the event of deflation.

Camping Card

Camping Card International
Web: www.campingcardinternational.com

A respected proof of identity that has the same value as a passport for campsite owners. The CCI also offers some measure of insurance to campers using one.

Electronics

Conrad Anderson
57–59 Sladefield Road
Ward End
Birmingham
B8 3PF
Tel: 021 247 0619
Fax: 021 247 0974
Technical Freephone: 0800 279 6939
E-mail: steve@conrad-anderson.co.uk
Web: www.conrad-anderson.co.uk

Conrad Anderson is a supplier and installer of vehicle electronics. Offering a comprehensive range of products from air-conditioning units to in-vehicle audio, the company provides a free electric hook-up and water to customers wishing to stay overnight prior to having equipment fitted to their vehicle.

Trailers

Armitage Trailers
Unit 11,
A1 Ferrybridge Business Park
Fishergate
Ferrybridge
West Yorks
WF11 9NA
Tel: 01977 607155
Fax/Tel: 01977 607157
E-mail: enquiries@armitagetrailers.com
Web: www.armitagetrailers.com

Almost twenty years' experience designing and fabricating towbars for virtually every kind of motorhome on the road. The company also sells and manufactures a wide range of trailers with so many variations that it can fulfil most buyers' needs 'off the shelf'.

Brian James Trailers Ltd
Sopwith Way
Drayton Fields Industrial Estate
Daventry
Northants
NN11 8PB
Tel: 01327 308833
Fax: 01327 308822
E-mail: post@brianjames.co.uk
Web: www.brianjames.co.uk

Offers specialist car transporter trailers for the full range of vehicles from Smart cars to Rolls-Royces.

High-Tech Accessories

RoadPro Ltd
Stephenson Close
Drayton Fields Industrial Estate
Daventry
Northants
NN11 8RF
Tel: 01327 312233
Fax: 01327 301198
E-mail: sales@roadpro.co.uk
Web: www.roadpro.co.uk

For twenty-seven years RoadPro has been supplying 'practical products on the move'. With their own motorhome as a test-bed, they are one of the leading suppliers of satellite and Freeview TV systems, 12-volt TVs, inverters, solar panels, battery chargers, rear-view cameras and other high-tech products designed especially for use in vehicles.

Clubs

Motor Caravanners Club
22 Evelyn Close
Twickenham
Middlesex
TW2 7BN
Tel: 020 8893 3883
Fax: 020 8893 8324
E-mail info@motorcaravanners.eu
Web: www.motorcaravanners.org.uk

This organization, formed in 1960, offers a wide range of information and member services, especially via its comprehensive website.

The Camping and Caravanning Club
Greenfields House
Westwood Way
Coventry
CV48JH
Tel: 02476 475448
Web: www.campingandcaravanningclub.co.uk

At over 106 years of age, the Camping and Caravanning Club is the largest and longest established organization of its kind in the world. As a not-for-profit organization, it is run by members for members; profit is invested in club campsites and services.

The Caravan Club
East Grinstead House
East Grinstead
West Sussex
RH19 1UA
Tel (Membership Enquiries): 01342 318813
Web: www.caravanclub.co.uk

Provide services and activities for 1 million caravan, motor caravan and trailer tent owners, as well as offering a superb choice of quality caravan parks and caravan sites throughout the UK and Ireland. The club also has the largest caravan insurance scheme in the UK.

Motorhome Builders and Distributors

Danbury Motorcaravans
Great Western Business Park
Armstrong Way
Yate
Bristol
BS37 5NG
Tel: 01454 310000
Web: www.danburymotorcaravans.com

Build brand-new VW Type 2, VW T5, Fiat Doblo and Renault Master-based motorhomes. There is a choice of short- or long-wheel base models, low or high roof.

IH Motor Campers
Great North Road
Knottingley
West Yorkshire
WF11 0BS
Tel: 01977 677118
Fax: 01977 677117
E-mail: reception@ihcampers.co.uk
Web: www.ihmotorhomes.com

A luxury motorhome builder.

Auto-Trail VR Limited
Trigano House
Genesis Way
Europarc
Grimsby
North East Lincolnshire
DN37 9TU
Tel: 01472 571000
Fax: 01472 571001
E-mail: sales@auto-trail.co.uk
Web: www.auto-trail.co.uk

Auto-Trail's motorhomes provide both luxury and comfort.

Microcar UK
Stratford-upon-Avon
Warwickshire
CV37 0HD
Tel: 01789 730094
Fax: 01789 730069
E-mail: enquiry@micro-car.co.uk
Web: www.micro-car.co.uk

Microcar, part of the Bénéteau Group, is the manufacturer of the Microcar and its sole British distributor supplies 60 dealerships in the UK, while there are 800 Microcar agents throughout Europe. The Microcar is a lightweight vehicle with automatic transmission driven from a fuel-injected 505 cc, vertical twin-petrol engine.

Oakwell Motorhomes Ltd
Tom Molyneux and Paula Mitchell
65/67 Pontefract Road
Barnsley
S71 1HA
Tel: 01226 293300
E-mail: sales@oakwellmotorhomes.com
Web: www.oakwellmotorhomes.com

A family-run company that supplies new and used American RVs with fully
backed warranty from its supplying motorhome manufacturer Gulfstream Coach
Inc.

General Accessories and Guides

Outdoor Bits
Fuzion Concepts Limited
483 Green Lanes
London
N13 4BS
Tel: 0845 8698940
Web: www.outdoorbits.com

In addition to a wide range of accessories and consumables, offers four guides to
aires de service in France.

Littoral Manche-Atlantique Trailer Park Guide Book
Details 228 *aires de services* around the northern and western coastlines of France.

Montagne Trailer Park Guide Book
Details 179 *aires de services* in the following mountain areas of France: Massif
Central, Pyrénées, Alpes du Sud, Alpes du Nord, Jura, Vosges and Alsace.

Bretagne Trailer Park Guide Book
Details 200 *aires de services* in the following areas of France: Le Finistère, Les Côtes
d'Armor, l'Ile et Vilaine, La Loire Atlantique and Le Morbihan.
Details 254 *aires de services* in the following areas of France: Châteaux de la Loire,
Auvergne, Périgord, Tarn, Lot, Midi-Pyrénées and Vallée du Rhône.

Le Guide Officiel Etapes Touristiques Camping-car
Published annually, is available from French supermarkets early in the season and
from www.amazon.fr. If you have an account with Amazon.co.uk, you can use your
existing login information at this website.

France Passion
BP 57
F – 84 202 Carpentras
Cedex
France
Web: www.france-passion.com

The France Passion scheme's Invitations Formula is a free alternative to the use of campsites in France. It is offered to motorhome owners by 840 wine-growers and farmers from almost all the regions in France. This allows you to stay free of charge on their property. The scheme provides over 4,000 free stopover parking spaces in the most beautiful vineyards and domains. The only cost involved is for an Invitation Handbook.

Motorcaravanning.co.uk
Tel: 01789 778462
E-mail: enquiries@motorcaravanning.co.uk
Web: www.motorcaravanning.co.uk

A web-based venture that uses e-mail as its preferred means of communication. Goods or services are normally provided via direct delivery, while the website offers a huge range of information about motorhoming both at home and abroad. The telephones are not manned continuously but there is a voicemail service on which you can leave your e-mail address.

Eberspächer UK
Headlands Business Park
Salisbury Road
Ringwood
Hants
BH24 3PB
Tel: 01425 480151
Fax: 01425 480152
E-mail: enquiries@eberspacher.com
Web: www.eberspacher.com

A major supplier to many car and commercial vehicle manufacturers which has developed new markets, including motorhomes.

Truma UK Ltd
Park Lane
Dove Valley Park
South Derbyshire
DE65 5BG
Tel: 01283 586050
Fax: 01283 586051
E-mail: sales@trumauk.com
Web: www.trumauk.com

Renowned for its energy-efficient blown air heating systems, high-performance gas and electric water heaters and combination boilers. The company also stocks BP Gaslight LPG cylinders and connection hardware.

Webasto Product UK Ltd
Webasto House
White Rose Way
Doncaster Carr
South Yorkshire
DN4 5JH
Tel: 01302 322232
Fax: 01302 322231
E-mail: info@webastouk.com
Web: www.webasto.co.uk

One of the leading manufacturers of innovative products to the automotive and transportation industries.

Pet Services

Dogs Away
Dartford
DA2 7NW
Tel: 08450 171073
E-mail: contact@dogsaway.co.uk
Web: www.dogsaway.co.uk

Ensures that your dog's welfare during a trip abroad is paramount. Dogs Away has years of experience in the travel industry.

Pet Travel Scheme (PETS)
Department for Environment, Food & Rural Affairs
Customer Contact Unit
Eastbury House
30–34 Albert Embankment
London
SE1 7TL
Tel: Defra Helpline 08459 33 55 77
E-mail: helpline@defra.gsi.gov.uk
Web: www.defra.gov.uk/animalh/quarantine/index.htm

This Defra website explains what you have to do to bring your pet into the UK through the Pet Travel Scheme without putting it into quarantine.

Road Safety

RoSPA
RoSPA House
Edgbaston Park
353 Bristol Road
Edgbaston
Birmingham
B5 7ST
General Information: 0121 248 2000
Sales Information: 0870 777 2227
Training Information: 0870 777 2227
Consultancy Information: 0870 777 2034
Fax: 0121 248 2001
E-mail: help@rospa.com
Web: www.rospa.com

A registered charity that campaigns for change, influences opinion, contributes to debate, educates and informs.

Train and Ferry Services

Eurotunnel Group
Ashford Road
Folkestone
Kent
CT18 8XX
Tel: 08705 353535
Web: www.eurotunnel.com

The fastest cross-Channel operator can take you to the Continent in only thirty-five minutes. Its new fares structure also offers you good value, giving you cheaper fares and more flexible options. Rough seas or high winds never delay Eurotunnel and crossings are frequent – up to 3 departures an hour at peak times.

P&O Ferries
Channel House
Channel View Road
Dover
CT17 9TJ
Tel: 08716 645645
E-mail: customer.services@poferries.com
Web: www.poferries.com

Boasts the largest fleet of ships offering a wide range of services and facilities, the most comprehensive route network and the most frequent passenger and freight services to the Continent.

Stena Line Limited
Stena House
Station Approach
Holyhead
Anglesey
LL65 1DQ
E-mail: info.uk@stenaline.com
Web: www.stenaline.co.uk

Offers low fares and a speedier ferry travel service to Ireland and Holland.

SeaFrance Limited
Whitfield Court
Honeywood Road
Whitfield
Kent
CT16 3PX
Tel: 0871 663 2546
E-mail: enquiries@seafrance.fr
Web: www.seafrance.com

SeaFrance is the only French-owned cross-Channel ferry service on the Dover to Calais route and currently offers 15 daily return crossings using its four-strong passenger fleet. Ten of these crossings are operated by the company's two superferries, the award-winning SeaFrance *Rodin* and her sister ship, the SeaFrance *Berlioz*.

Condor Ferries
The Quay
Weymouth
Dorset
DT4 8DX
Tel: Reservations 0870 243 5140
Ferry Services Hotlines: UK 01202 207216; Jersey 01534 872240; St Malo (0) 825
165 463; Cherbourg +33 2 33 88 44 88
E-mail reservations@condorferries.co.uk
Web: www.condorferries.co.uk

Services to the Channel Islands and Brittany.

Norfolk Line Ferries
Export Freight Plaza
Eastern Dock
Dover
CT16 1JA
Tel: 01304 218400
E-mail: doverpax@norfolkline.com
Web: www.norfolkline-ferries.co.uk

Operates on the Dover–Dunkerque route.

Brittany Ferries
Millbay
Plymouth
Devon
PL1 3EW
Tel: 08709 076103
E-mail: see website
Web: www.brittany-ferries.co.uk

Services from Portsmouth, Poole and Plymouth to Cherbourg, Caen, Roscoff, St
Malo in France and to Santander in northern Spain.

DFDS Seaways
Scandinavia House
Parkeston
Harwich
Essex
CO12 4QG

or

International Ferry Terminal
Royal Quays
North Shields
Tyne & Wear
NE29 6EE
Tel: Customer Services: 0871 522 9955
E-mail: FAQ@dfds.co.uk
Web: www.dfds.co.uk

Caledonian MacBrayne
The Ferry Terminal
Gourock
PA19 1QP
Tel: 8000 66 5000
Fax: 01475 635235
E-mail: reservations@calmac.co.uk
Web: www.calmac.co.uk

Sail to twenty-four destinations on Scotland's west coast.

Irish Ferries
Ferryport
Alexandra Road
Dublin 1
Tel: 08705 171717
E-mail: holidaysinireland@irishferries.co.uk
Web: www.irishferries.com

Carries passengers and freight between Ireland, Great Britain and continental Europe.

Storage

Caravan Storage Site Owners' Association
Market Square House
St James Street
Nottingham
NG1 6FG
Tel: 01159 349 826
Fax: 01159 419 359
E-mail: see website
Web: www.cassoa.co.uk

A nationally recognized body providing an official register of safe and secure storage sites. It helps site owners improve their security and services, to prevent caravan crime and to provide a strong lobbying voice to influence the views of people who make a difference in caravanning.

Vehicle Inspections

AIM Vehicle Inspections
23–29 Albion Place
Maidstone
Kent
ME14 5DY
Tel: 0870 0428520
E-mail: info@aim-vi.co.uk
Web: www.aim-vi.co.uk

The AIM Assured Motorhome Plus inspection service will provide a qualified engineer who will carry out a comprehensive 156-point visual inspection on vehicles up to 3.5 tonnes.

Breakdown Services

Automobile Association
Tel: Breakdown cover (sales) 0800 085 2721
European breakdown cover 0800 072 3279
E-mail: online form
Web: www.theaa.com

RAC
RAC Motoring Services
Great Park Road
Bradley Stoke
Bristol
BS32 4QN
Tel: 08705 722722
E-mail: online form
Web: www.rac.co.uk

Motorhome Hire

Elite Motorhomes
Thorpe Road
Middleton Cheney
Banbury
OX17 2QY
Tel: 0845 3900111
E-mail: bookings@elite-motorhomes.co.uk
www.elitemotorhomes.co.uk

Provides motorhome hire.

MotorHolme
Golders Farm
Fox Road
Bourn
Cambridgeshire
CB3 7TX
Tel: 08707 666 007
Fax: 08701 303 908
E-mail: hire@MotorHolme.co.uk
Web: www.motorholme.co.uk

A specialist motorhome sales and hire company, with the largest motorhome hire fleet available in the UK. It has vehicles nationwide including in Wales and Scotland.

The Motorhome Group
The Paddock
Norwell Woodhouse
Newark
Nottinghamshire
NG23 6NG
Tel: 0845 095 6610
Fax: 0845 280 6392
E-mail: sales@motorhomegroup.com
Web: www.motorhomegroup.com

Arranges and oversees the hiring of privately owned vehicles. It ensures its members conform to the UK Hire National Standards of Quality of Service and seeks to attract only discerning hirers.

Midland Motorhomes
Blaby Road
South Wigston
Leicestershire
LE18 4SG
Tel: 08701 601401
E-mail: info@american-motorhome-hire.com
Web: www.american-motorhome-hire.com

Provides American motorhome hire with delivery and collection.

Generators

Just Generators
Britons Lane
Sheringham
Norfolk
NR26 8TS
Tel: 01263 820202
Fax: 01263 826190
E-mail: enquiries@justgenerators.co.uk
Web: www.justgenerators.co.uk

Offers the highest-quality generators available in the UK. Brand names include Honda, Subaru, Yamaha, SMDO, Pramac, Stephill and Briggs & Stratton.

Training

Tockwith Training Services
The Training Centre
Sherbutt Lane
Hessay
York
YO26 8JT
Tel: 01904 737049
Fax: 01904 737058
E-mail: bookings@tockwithtraining.co.uk
Web: www.tockwithtraining.co.uk

Offers training in driving vans, coaches, buses and trucks to DVLA standards.

Computer Software

Microsoft AutoRoute Pushpins
E-mail: john.harrison@jollyinteresting.co.uk
Web: www.jollyinteresting.co.uk

Among a wealth of other information and links, John Harrison's website carries a very useful tool for planning camping trips around the country and abroad. The locations of all Caravan Club and Camping and Caravanning Club sites plus their respective Certificated Locations and Certificated Sites, and Civil Service Motoring Association sites, are now available for download in several Microsoft AutoRoute pushpin formats. This page now includes French campsites.

Glossary

20-foot, 6-metre rule The minimum distance required between pitched motorhomes or caravans for fire safety on a campsite.

3G Third-generation mobile telephony system. It can be used to access the Internet and e-mail by using a mobile phone as a modem for a computer.

Ablutions block A building containing showers, WCs and wash hand basins at a campsite.

ABS Anti-lock braking.

A-Class motorhome A motorhome based on a chassis cowl, on which the body-work is made entirely by the motorhome manufacturer.

AES Automatic energy selection. A feature of some three-way refrigerators that allows them to use the available power source(s) automatically.

A-frame A rigid A-shaped metal structure used to tow a car.

Aire de repos An overnight stopping place located at a French *autoroute* service area.

Aire de service An area that offers an overnight stopping place in France.

Aire An official motorhome parking area or service point in France.

Al-Ko A German company's chassis conversion that replaces the base vehicle's rear chassis.

Autoroute A French toll motorway.

Base vehicle The light or medium-weight commercial vehicle that is modified and/or added to by the motorhome manufacturer.

B-Class motorhome The American term for the equivalent of a UK and European camper van.

Beam benders Properly headlamp beam deflectors; self-adhesive plastic 'lenses' used to modify headlamps' dipped beam pattern so as not to dazzle oncoming drivers on the Continent.

Berths Sleeping locations in a motorhome.

Black water Chemically treated or raw effluent from a motorhome's WC cassette or holding tank.

Blown-air heating A heating system in which the warm air output of a single source of heat is distributed through ducting to adjustable outlets by low-voltage fans.

Bluetooth A short-range digital communication system used between mobile phones, personal digital assistants and laptop computers.

Borne A motorhome service point in France, usually offering fresh water and a timed output of electricity. Usually placed at *aires de service* but may be found at filling stations and in lay-bys.

Bubble window A popular term for a motorhome's double-glazed acrylic window.

Butane A colourless, odourless, heavier-than-air liquefied petroleum gas which is given a characteristic smell to warn of leakage. Sold in blue-painted cylinders, it does not flow well at a low ambient temperature.

Calor Gas The largest distributor of LPG (q.v.) in the UK.

Camper, camper van A motorhome that is recognizable as a conversion of a light commercial panel van.

Camping Gaz A trade name for butane gas, widely available in the UK and on the Continent.

Cassette A removable black-water holding tank.

Cassette blind An internally mounted roller or pleated blind in a rigid, plastic housing, which may also contain a flyscreen.

CCI Camping Card International. A credit card-style item accepted in lieu of a passport by participating campsites in Europe. Also confers a measure of insurance cover.

C-Class motorhome The American term for the equivalent of a UK and European coachbuilt motorhome.

Certificated location The Caravan Club's term for a small, five-van campsite that is usually available only to club members.

Certificated Site The Camping and Caravanning Club's term for a small, five-van campsite that is usually available only to club members.

Chassis cab A commercial vehicle cab unit with bare chassis rails extending from behind the cab. It is the basis for most coachbuilt motorhomes.

Chassis cowl A functional engine and chassis with no exterior bodywork, the basis for an A-Class motorhome.

Chemical toilet A WC, usually equipped with a holding section or separate waste cassette in which special chemicals are used to treat effluent.

Chocks Moulded plastic ramps used to level a motorhome when on a campsite pitch. Also known as levelling ramps.

Clipsal plug A low-voltage plug with two flat pins that is accepted by a Clipsal socket. Largely superseded by a conventional cigar-lighter plug.

Coachbuilt motorhome The commonest type of motorhome, consisting of a bodyshell fitted to a chassis cab, where the bodyshell has an extension that sits on top of the cab roof.

Compressor refrigerator A refrigerator that runs on 12-volt power and operates in a similar way to a domestic refrigerator.

Conversion heater A warm-air heater that works in the same way as a conventional vehicle heater. Usually placed to warm the area behind the cab in a coachbuilt motorhome.

Convertor Generic term for the individual or concern that builds motorhomes on light commercial vehicles.

Corner steadies Screw-operated or electrically powered legs used on site to prevent a motorhome's body from moving on its springs as the occupants move around inside.

Demountable, dismountable Known in the USA as a 'slide-in', a motorhome bodyshell mounted on a pick-up truck. The bodyshell can be raised on legs to allow the truck to be driven away and used normally.

Dinette A dining area consisting of two transversely mounted facing seats or sofas flanking a table. Also termed a 'Pullman-style dinette'.

Docking lights Side-mounted, rearward facing lights fitted to the side skirts of some motorhomes. Used when pitching in darkness.

Downlight A downward-facing lamp with a 12-volt incandescent bulb, usually of the halogen type. May have a clear or frosted glass and be switchable.

Drop-down bed A bed that can be lowered from the cab roof in an A-Class motorhome. The cab seats fold down to accommodate the bed.

ELCB Earth leakage circuit breaker. A device that cuts the current in the circuit it protects when it detects any contact with earth.

EN 1646 A standard of inspection validated by the National Caravan Council and supported by the Society of Motor Manufacturers and Traders. Motorhomes that meet this standard carry a badge to verify the fact.

Euro regulator The kind of LPG regulator that is common to all European motorhomes after 2003. It delivers butane or propane at a pressure of 30 millibars.

Fifth-wheeler A combination of a pick-up truck and a caravan-style body. The 'fifth wheel' is the attachment point of the trailer and it sits in the pick-up truck's load bed.

Fixed-roof camper A motorhome based on a panel van with a standard low roofline.

Flame-failure device A safety device that, unless maintained at a specific high temperature by burning LPG, stops the flow of gas to the burner it protects.

Flyscreen A fixed, folding or retractable mesh panel that covers the inside of an open door, window or roof vent to prevent insects from entering a motorhome.

Free-standing table A table that can be used inside or outside a motorhome.

French bed A fixed bed that has a cut corner to permit access to an adjacent washroom or wardrobe.

FSH A full service history. Usually pertaining to the base vehicle of a motorhome offered for sale.

Garage A large, usually tail-mounted locker in a coachbuilt or A-Class motorhome, normally used to carry equipment, bicycles or a small scooter.

Gazole French for diesel.

Generator A liquid fuel-powered, engine-driven unit that provides 230-volt electrical power. Many American motorhomes have an on-board generator.

GPS Global positioning system. A network of satellites that provides precise information on an object's position.

Graphics The usually self-adhesive, decorative accoutrements used to enhance the exterior of motorhomes.

Grey water Water that has been used for washing up, showering or personal ablutions.

GRP Glass-reinforced plastic. A construction or cladding material consisting of a resin reinforced with strands of glass.

GTW Gross train weight. A figure provided by the motorhome manufacturer, in accordance with the dictates of the base vehicle's maker. It is the total permissible weight of the motorhome, its trailer and the load the trailer carries.

GVW Gross vehicle weight. The maximum weight of a motorhome and all it carries. This is equivalent to the maximum authorized mass (MAM).

Half-dinette A dining area that has one sofa, usually fitted behind a transverse table.

Hardstanding A campsite pitch that either has a gravel, tarmac or cement surface, or a ground-level plastic mesh that prevents sinking in and wheelspin.

High-top camper A motorhome based on a panel van with a tall roofline. The high top may be an addition but is more likely to be the original van's roof.

Hook-up The 230-volt power point at a campsite pitch or the connection between this and a motorhome.

IDP International Driving Permit. Only necessary in Europe for drivers who have not upgraded to a photo-card licence. One is necessary in many non-European countries.

Internal height The dimension from a motorhome's floor to the inside of its roof panel. May be expressed as maximum and minimum dimensions, according to the vehicle.

Inverter An electrical power converter that accepts a 12-volt input and yields a 230-volt output.

Island bed A fixed bed that can be accessed from both sides.

Isolation valve, gas isolation valve An in-line valve used to shut off the LPG supply to a single item. Often mounted in a rank.

Layout The arrangement of a motorhome's furniture.

LED Light emitting diode. A light source used singly and in multiples in motorhomes and in torches. Many vehicles have indicator, reversing and stop/tail lighting that uses LED illumination.

Leisure battery A 12-volt battery that supplies the power for the electrical systems concerned with the habitation of a motorhome.

LHD Left-hand drive.

Linear kitchen A motorhome kitchen in which the furniture is set in a straight line.

L-kitchen A motorhome kitchen in which the furniture is in an L-shape.

L-lounge A seating area that is L-shaped.

Low-profile motorhome The kind of motorhome with a shallow, overcab luton section that contains storage lockers, rather than a bed. Sometimes, the entire bodyshell is lower than that of an equivalent coachbuilt model.

LPG Liquefied petroleum gas. The most common source of power for heating, cooking and refrigeration in motorhomes. Supplied in blue (butane) or red propane cylinders. Propane can vaporize at a much lower ambient temperature than butane.

Luton An extension of a coachbuilt motorhome's bodyshell that sits on top of the cab roof. A full-sized luton usually contains a double bed.

MAM Maximum authorized mass. This is the maximum amount a vehicle weighs, in tonnes or kilograms. This term is used by the DVLA in relation to vehicle licensing laws. It is the equivalent of gross vehicle weight (GVW).

MCB Micro circuit breaker. An electrical safety device, essentially a resettable fuse, that cuts the current in the electrical circuit it protects.

Micro motorhome A small, usually coachbuilt motorhome.

MIRO Mass in running order. The weight of the motorhome in a roadworthy state, including an allowance for certain onboard elements.

Monobloc tap A tap with a single control that when lifted alters water flow, and when turned alters water temperature.

Monocoque A bodyshell that is constructed in one piece.

Motorhome service point A campsite facility where grey water can be drained and fresh water refilled.

MTPLM Maximum technically permitted laden mass. This term is used by motorhome manufacturers for the maximum weight of the motorhome.

OEM Original equipment manufacturer. A term used in reference to spare or optional parts.

OTR price On-the-road price. The amount you pay for a motorhome that is ready to use.

Overcab bed The bed in the luton of a coachbuilt motorhome. It may be fixed or hinged for storage when not in use.

PAS Power-assisted steering.

Payload Sometimes called 'user payload', the MIRO figure subtracted from the MTPLM figure. Usually expressed in kilograms, it represents the weight a motorhome can carry.

PDI Pre-delivery inspection.

Péage A toll booth on a French *autoroute*.

Pedestal table A table with a single or perhaps two legs, which fit into a floor socket.

PIR Passive infrared. A means of detecting the presence of intruders by sensing a moving source of heat.

PNA Personal navigation assistant. A device for receiving positioning information from the GPS and aiding navigation.

Porta Potti A trade name, now used generically to describe a small portable chemical toilet.

Power panel An electrical switch panel used to control the low-voltage equipment in a motorhome.

Pusher A rear-engined American motorhome with rear-wheel drive.

PV panel Photo-voltaic panel, the correct term for a solar panel.

RCCB Residual current circuit breaker. A device used for protecting electrical circuits. Equivalent to an RCD.

RCD Residual current device. A safety device that cuts the current in the electrical circuit it protects when it detects any contact between the live and neutral parts.

Revenue weight The maximum authorized mass or gross vehicle weight used to determine the taxation class for a vehicle's road fund licence. If the weight is below 3.5 tonnes, the vehicle is subject to taxation at the private light goods rate. If it weighs more than 3.5 tonnes, the private heavy goods vehicle rate applies.

Reverse beepers A distance-sensing mechanism that gives an audible warning of objects close to a motorhome's tail when it is reversing.

Reverse polarity Where the live and neutral connections are reversed in a campsite's mains hook-up. Can be detected with a reverse polarity indicator.

Reversing camera A small tail-mounted camera that gives the driver a rear view on a cab-mounted monitor.

Rising-roof camper Sometimes called an elevating roof or pop-top camper, a motorhome with a roof panel that can be raised to give additional headroom when the vehicle is at rest.

Road tax/road fund licence The taxation imposed on UK vehicles for using the road network.

Rock peg A special, large kind of tent peg, usually used for securing a motorhome's awning on site.

Roof vent A roof-mounted opening ventilator.

RV Recreational vehicle. In America, this refers to any type of motorhome but in the UK it refers to a large American model.

Sandwich construction A common constructional method used in motorhomes' walls and roof panels. The 'sandwich' consists of an aluminium exterior and a plywood interior flanking an insulating foam plastic layer. The external aluminium skin may be GRP-clad.

Sans plombe French for unleaded petrol.

Satnav A common term for a PNA.

Semi-rigid pipework Used in water systems, it is superior to convoluted piping which can trap germs and promote odours.

Silver Screens Thick, tailored insulating screens for a motorhome's cab glass. The name is universally used for all such items but it is in fact a trade name.

Site cable A water-resistant 230-volt cable with blue, IEE-approved fittings. Used to connect a motorhome's mains system to a campsite's mains hook-up.

Slide-out A feature of some American motorhomes, a section of bodywork that slides outwards to liberate extra interior space.

SOG system A low-powered forced air extraction system that is an aftermarket addition allowing a WC to be used without chemicals.

SORN Statutory off-road notice. You must complete and submit a SORN form to the DVLA when your vehicle is kept off the road and is not taxed.

Spot lamp An aimable interior light, usually with a 12-volt halogen bulb. It may have clear or frosted glass and be switchable. Some are mounted on current-conducting tracks.

Tag-axle chassis A chassis with two rear axles in tandem. Invariably used on front-wheel drive motorhomes.

Tail overhang The distance from the centres of a motorhome's rear wheels to the furthest extremity of its rear bodywork.

Tail The common term for the flexible pipe that leads from a Euro regulator to an LPG cylinder's connection.

Three-way refrigerator A refrigerator capable of running on 12-volt and mains electrical power and on LPG.

TMC Traffic Message Channel. An FM radio channel that PNAs use to reroute drivers in response to traffic problems.

Top box An external, roof-mounted storage box.

Towing weight Usually stipulated by the motorhome manufacturer, this is the maximum weight the vehicle can tow. The figure is made up of two elements, the weight of the trailer itself and that of the load the trailer carries.

Transformer charger An electrical device that distributes 12- and 230-volt electrical power in a motorhome. Modern examples incorporate fuses, circuit breakers and a reverse-polarity warning indicator. These units also deal with the charging of the engine and leisure batteries, both from the mains and from the vehicle's generator.

Travel seats Seats equipped with lap and diagonal seat belts. Also called designated travel seats.

Turbocharger A device often fitted as standard to a motorhome base vehicle's diesel engine. It uses the pressure of the exhaust gas, leaving the engine to increase the pressure of incoming air and thus increase the engine's power output.

U-lounge A lounge layout that consists of two facing longitudinal sofas flanking a rear bench section. Infills allow this arrangement to be assembled into a large double bed.

VIN Vehicle identification number. Often stamped into the metal of the motorhome base vehicle's bodywork but also displayed on a VIN plate.

Warranty The manufacturer's guarantee, which may cover the conversion work and be allied to a base vehicle warranty or may cover the entire motorhome.

Weighbridge A weighing station at which the axle and total weights of a motorhome may be measured. Public weighbridges charge a small fee for this service.

Wet locker An externally accessed locker designed to accept wet clothing, footwear and equipment.

Wheelbase The distance between the centres of the front and rear wheels of a base van, chassis cab or chassis cowl.

Wild camping Staying overnight at a location that is not a formal campsite.

Winnebago An incorrectly used generic term for an American motorhome. It is a company name.

Thanks to

This, the 'without whom' part of the book, refers to the concerns and individuals whose input made this book not only possible but also far more easily written than it might have been. Grateful thanks, in no particular order, are owed to …

David Millington at the NTTA, for his advice and guidance on the legalities of trailers.

Andrew Harris at RoadPro, for verifying the accuracy of the sections on television reception, inverters and generators.

Richard Kitchener and David Elliot at Propex, for information on space and water heaters.

Paul Stockport at Brian James Trailers, for the use of one of the company's car transporter trailers.

Andrew Kelly at Norfolkline Ferries, for information on the company's rationale.

Peter Vaughan at *Which Motorcaravan* Magazine, for his inspirational help from day one.

Rob McDonnell at The Warners Group plc, for the chance to travel to work.

Jonathan Heynes at Microcar UK, for the extended loan of an MC1 model.

Tom Molyneux and Paula Mitchell at Oakwell Motorhomes Ltd, for the opportunity to photograph an American A-Class in captivity.

Stuart Turpin, Scott Stephens and Gavin Claricoates at Auto-Trail VR Ltd, for their invaluable input to this book.

Nigel Kitchen at IH Motor Campers, for access to the factory floor and to accumulated knowledge.

Brian Rees and the staff at P&O Ferries, for providing research facilities afloat on several occasions.

The staff at Stena Line, SeaFrance, Condor Ferries and Caledonian MacBrayne, for repeatedly ferrying us about.

The dockside staff at Stranraer, Rotterdam, the Hook of Holland, Larne, Mallaig, Arran, Dover, Portsmouth, Santander, Calais, St Malo, St Helier, Fleetwood and Harwich, for invariably keeping our feet – and our tyres – dry.

Martin Coleman at Brainstormers, for producing the excellent cutaway illustrations in short order.

John Hale at Robert Hale Ltd (Publishers), for putting all this on paper.

Sarah Mounsey, formerly of Robert Bosch UK (Blaupunkt), for her electronic and practical guidance.

Ellis Butcher at Cumbria Tourism, for his inspiration and help.

Eddie & Lynda Jones, owners of Van Bitz, Taunton, for access to and information about the Strikeback T system.

Ian Hughes at Scan-Terieur Ltd, for automatically putting us in touch with several satellites.

Ruth Walmsley at the Camping and Caravanning Club, for letting us stay the course at many campsites.

Fiona Bewers at the Caravan Club, for the same service.

Several telephone helpline staff at the DVLA, for helping us plot a course through the UK driver licensing laws.

Wayne Brear at Armitage Trailers, for invaluable assistance and information on trailers and the law.

Jason Jones at Danbury Motorcaravans, for his much-appreciated help concerning VW Combis.

Mike Moore at Tockwith Training Services, for steering us through current LGV and HGV test practices.

Gary Abel at Just Generators, for taking charge of the technical accuracy of the relevant section.

Richard Bentley at Autocruise, for his continued input to a variety of projects.

Simon Collis, formerly of *Motorcaravan* Magazine, for getting us off to a flying start.

Michel Desmidt at T-Mobile, for information on 2G and 3G mobile communication systems.

And finally, thanks to the motorhome manufacturers, accessory makers, service industries, motorhome dealerships and campsite staff, for keeping us on the road for the last four years.

Index